ASSEMBLERS, COMPILERS, AND PROGRAM TRANSLATION

ASSEMBLERS, COMPILERS, AND PROGRAM TRANSLATION

PETER CALINGAERT

*University of North Carolina
at Chapel Hill*

Computer Science Press

Computer Science Press
11 Taft Court
Rockville, Maryland 20850

6 7 8 9 10 11 12 Printing   Year 89 88 87 86 85

Library of Congress Cataloging in Publication Data

Calingaert, Peter.
  Assemblers, compilers, and program translation.

  (Computer software engineering series)
  Bibliography: p. 270
  Includes index
  1.   Assembling (Electronic computers)   2.   Compilers
(Electronic computers)   3.   Translators   (Computer programs)
I.   Title.   II.   Series.
QA76.6.C337   001.6'425   78-21905
ISBN 0-914894-23-4

PREFACE

This book is concerned with computer programs which translate other computer programs. They are generally known as *translation programs* or *translators*. Construed narrowly, the term "translator" denotes a program which transforms the representation of an algorithm from one language to another. It generates an output program to correspond to an input program. The content of the input program is by and large preserved, but its encoding is changed. Often the input encoding is more oriented to human communication and less to machine communication than is the output encoding. Such translations are performed by assemblers and compilers. Macro processors and linkers, on the other hand, perform translations in which changing the encoding is secondary to other functions, text substitution by the former and resolution of symbolic references by the latter.

The narrow construction of "translators" excludes two types of programs, interpreters and loaders, but both are treated in this book. The result of interpretation is not to recast an algorithm, but rather to execute it. Yet many of the functions performed by interpreters are identical or similar to those of the translators which generate output programs. Moreover, interpretive and generative translators not uncommonly cooperate in the execution of a program. Loaders are often classified as control programs, and so they are, but there are three reasons for studying them with translators. One is that they are often combined with linkers. A second is that the requirement to perform relocation constrains the form of the output produced by other translators. The third is that in performing relocation, the loader really is acting as a translator.

Of the many students or practitioners of computer science, few will ever be called upon to build a compiler, or other complex translator. Yet some knowledge of translators is indispensable, for several reasons. All programmers, except perhaps those who code in raw decimal for a pocket computer, use translators all the time. The efficacy with which they use a computer system is enhanced by an understanding of the translators which serve as intermediaries in expressing their instructions to the system.

Moreover, two important areas of both practical and theoretical interest are more easily accessible to persons with knowledge of translators than to those without. It is obvious that the study and design of programming languages are dependent upon understanding how programs written in those languages can be translated. It is perhaps less evident that some knowledge of translators is helpful in the study of operating systems. One reason is that issues of binding time, which are often clearer in the context of translation, are important in control programs too. Another is that many of the demands upon an operating system, particularly in storage management, are direct consequences of source-language requests and translator function. A third reason is that the mechanisms of generation and interpretation are widely used in control programs.

Furthermore, many computer professionals will be concerned with the design of application systems. The user of such a system communicates his processing requirements by means of what is in effect an application language. In designing both that language and its translator, the application system designer must be able to determine which translation techniques are appropriate and must be able to use them effectively.

Finally, the increasingly widespread use of microprocessors, with their often rudimentary programming support, has expanded the need for translators. The emphasis here is usually on simple translators to run on the microprocessor itself, although the use of a more powerful computer to generate code for the microprocessor is often a suitable alternative.

Many books on translators treat only a few types, often compilers alone, or perhaps assemblers and loaders. They thus forgo the opportunity to note similarities and distinctions among different translators, to highlight important choices between translation techniques, or to show how various translators cooperate with each other. Instead, they offer depth at the cost of restricting the breadth of coverage. I believe strongly that more balanced coverage is preferable to early specialization.

Some books tackle both translators and operating systems. Those designed for a one-semester course must treat many topics superficially because of the constraint on length. Those designed for a one-year course can avoid superficiality and benefit from interleaving related matters from the two areas. But even they are forced to cope with a serious problem in exposition. It is simply this: operating systems are more difficult for most readers to understand than are translators. The normal consequence is that the operating systems topics are covered to significantly lesser depth than the translator topics. The alternative, of course, is a book whose different parts are significantly different in difficulty. Rather than impose either of these disadvantages upon the reader, I have restricted the scope to translators.

This book is designed primarily for use as a one-semester text by advanced undergraduate or beginning graduate students, but is suitable also for self-study by programmers and other computer professionals. The readers are assumed to have some experience in programming in an assembler language and in a programming language, and to be capable of reading programs in languages such as Algol, Pascal, or PL/I, although they may not be conversant with all the details of their syntax. In fact, algorithms in the book are expressed in a bastard Pascalgol, with limited adherence to any particular standard of syntax. Readers should be familiar with the representation and manipulation of arrays, queues, stacks, and trees, and with the use of linked lists. Although the readers should have studied the role of individual bits in representing both instructions and data in a machine, it is not expected that they have done so for more than one machine. In particular, readers are not assumed to be familiar with both direct-addressing and base-addressing machines, nor with both single-accumulator and multiple-accumulator architectures. Prior acquaintance with the theory of formal languages, although it cannot but help, is nowhere assumed.

The book is organized as follows. Chapter 1 presents an overview of the objectives of translation, the languages to be translated, and the types of tools and translators. It continues with a brief historical chronicle and concludes by asserting the distinction between translator function and implementation which is to permeate the rest of the book. Chapter 2 is about assembly without either macro or conditional processing. It presents the standard two-pass assembler, first in rudimentary form and then endowed with many of the commonly encountered optional features. One-pass assemblers are introduced here to accent the concept of binding time, which is used throughout the book as a theme, even when not referred to by name. Chapter 3 is a digression into several programming language matters: reusability, block structure, modes of module activation, linkage mechanisms, and parameter correspondence. The chapter is included as a concise review of issues particularly important to translation, and may be omitted by readers who have studied programming languages well. Chapter 4 is devoted to macro processing, treated generally as parametric substitution of text, but emphasizing the generation of source code for further translation. The coverage includes nested definitions and calls. In Chapter 5, the two major translation mechanisms, interpretation and generation, are described and compared. Conditional assembly, which depends on the notions of interpretation, is discussed afterwards, as is the combination of macro processing with assembly.

Chapter 6 discusses three functions important to many different types of translators, both generative and interpretive. These are lexical and syntactic analysis, and the management of symbol tables. Formal context-free grammars are introduced and two parsing methods presented. Operator precedence is the example of a bottom-up method, chosen for its efficiency in parsing expressions. Recursive descent is the example of a top-down method, chosen for its ease of implementation. The latter method is extended to lexical analysis, for which the table-driven implementation of a finite auto-maton is also described. A brief review of selected data structures, hashing functions, and overflow techniques appropriate to symbol tables is followed by a more thorough discussion of symbol tables for languages with block structure. Chapter 7 constitutes, in conjunction with Chapter 6, a miniature exposition of compiler design. It stresses data and program representations, semantic processing, and the machine-dependent steps. Code optimization and error handling are treated only briefly.

Finally, Chapter 8 is devoted chiefly to linkers and loaders, both sepa-rately and in combination. Although loaders are often studied in con-junction with assemblers, the subject appears last for three reasons. One is because compilers, too, produce programs which must be linked and loaded. A second is that deferring Chapter 8 allows more time for the interesting programming assignments which can be based upon earlier chapters. A third reason is that relocating loaders, and particularly dynamic loading and dynamic linking, provide a natural transition to the study of operating systems.

Departures from the text sequence are nevertheless quite feasible, par-ticularly if an instructor is available to smooth over any discontinuities. Linkers and loaders can indeed be combined with assemblers; Chapter 8 can follow Chapter 2. Those instructors who prefer to treat first the matters common to all translators can cover Chapters 3 and 6 immediately after Chapter 1. Chapter 7, on the other hand, depends in varying degrees on each of Chapters 3-6 and cannot readily be advanced.

The instructor who prefers a more leisurely pace, or who wishes to cover most of the material in a quarter rather than a semester, can omit one or more topics without loss of continuity. The most suitable candidates for omission are nesting in macros (4.5 and 4.6), recursive macros (5.3.3), the combination of macro processing with assembly (5.4), character recognition (6.3.3), lexical ambiguity (6.3.4), symbol tables (6.4), compiler organization (7.2.3), extensions to the basic compilation process (7.4), linkage using a transfer vector (8.2.3), dynamic loading (8.2.6), and dynamic linking (8.2.7). Although the omission of one-pass assemblers (2.4) makes rather little extra work for the instructor, I recommend against it strongly. Not to explore fully the resolution of forward references is educationally unsound.

The exercises are independent of specific real translators, although many are based on the languages and programs used for illustration. Over a hundred are included, grouped at the end of each chapter. Some permit the readers to verify their understanding of the material specifically pre-sented. Others challenge them to apply their understanding to unfamiliar situations. Most of the exercises are original and class-tested. A few particularly fine exercises have been adapted from other writers, to whom appropriate credit is given.

The original inspiration for this book was dissatisfaction with the textbooks available for a course I taught in 1973 and 1974, introducing students to both translators and operating systems in one semester. Although I intended initially to design a book covering both subjects, I decided for the previously stated reasons that separate one-semester books would be more useful. Redesign of our curriculum replaced the earlier course with a one-semester course on translators alone. That course and the present book were designed together in 1976 and a first class test of both undertaken in early 1977. Armed with strategic feedback from outside reviewers and tactical feedback from students, I undertook a thorough, albeit not extensive, revision and tested the book again in the first semester of 1978. The present text incorporates further changes made in response to student observations at that time.

Several persons assisted me, either directly or indirectly, in the preparation of this book. I became aware of many of the issues in translation through study of the thoughtful books by Frederick P. Brooks, Jr., and Kenneth E. Iverson [1969], and by Peter Wegner [1968]. My present or former colleagues David B. Benson, Howard A. Elder, and Mehdi Jazayeri taught me much about programming systems in general and translators in particular. Another colleague, Stephen F. Weiss, contributed substantially to the over-all organization of the book and of the underlying course. The students who took Computer Science 240 in 1977 and 1978 aided in the many aspects of debugging the text. In particular, Paul R. Bowman prepared a detailed written critique of the last three chapters. Ellis Horowitz, Brian W. Kernighan, Paul Oliver, and David Russell read the manuscript with great care, and offered much helpful advice. Kristine J. Brown executed with speed and good cheer the task of entering the entire book and its many revisions into our text editing system. To each of these persons I am deeply indebted.

Chapel Hill, North Carolina
5 November 1978

CONTENTS

7   Compilation

8   Preparation for Execution

Chapter 1

OVERVIEW

1.1 OBJECTIVES OF TRANSLATION

A translator permits the programmer to express an algorithm in a language other than that of the machine which is to execute the algorithm. Why should the programmer select a language other than machine language? After all, in so doing he commits himself to the costs incurred in performing translation, and these costs would be obviated by programming in machine language. Nevertheless, the machine-language programmer is rare. The reason is that machine language is very ill-designed for human communication. This is not the fault of the machine designers. The purpose of machine language is to express algorithms in a form in which the machine can interpret them efficiently. Because automatic computers utilize two-state storage and switching devices almost exclusively, sequences of binary digits provide the most natural form for expressing instructions. Sequences of binary digits prove very unnatural, however, for humans to construct or to understand. Consequently, programmers prefer to express algorithms in a different form.

But it is more than personal preference which mandates the use of more expressive languages than those whose sentences are merely strings of zeros and ones. The greater ease of expression in other languages confers important benefits. One is increased accuracy of programming. Errors are easier to avoid and to detect both when a larger symbol set than {0,1} is used, and when the program text is shorter, as is typically the case. Another benefit is increased programmer productivity: what can be written more easily can be written more rapidly. A particularly important benefit is the relaxation of the restriction that the programmer be intimately familiar with the computer to be used. If a language is available in which concepts are expressed in terms related not to the computer, but rather to the problem which the user is trying to solve, then the power of the computer can be placed at the disposal of workers who are not computer experts.

1

Moreover, if the language is independent of the computer, programs can be transported between computers which have different machine languages. This leads to further increase in programmer productivity and to the advantages of exchanging programs. The cost, for any number of programs, is limited to the construction and use of one translator for each desired machine language.

The input to a translation program is expressed in a *source* language. It may represent either a nonalgorithmic specification of what the computer is to accomplish or an algorithmic specification of the steps in that accomplishment. The result of performing the translation may be the execution of the required algorithm (whether specified explicitly or not) on a machine whose language, the *host* language, is other than the source. Alternatively, the translator may produce as output a representation of the algorithm in a *target* language. That target language is often the machine language of some computer, which is then able to execute the algorithm. Sometimes a non-machine language is chosen as target, typically a language which is itself the source language for another translator, which then yields the desired result. If the target language is machine language, the translator output is often referred to as *machine code.*

1.2   SOURCE LANGUAGES

Algorithmic source languages differ in the degree to which they reflect the structure of the target machine. Those in one group are designed to permit the programmer to control machine operation in detail. They necessarily reflect the machine structure explicitly, and are known as *assembler* languages. A given assembler language is intended for use with a single machine design. Assembler language differs from the binary machine language chiefly in that operations and their operands can be referred to symbolically, without concern for actual encodings or numeric addresses.

Representation of an algorithm in machine-independent terms is considered to be at a higher level of abstraction than is offered by assembler languages. The most common designation for languages which permit algorithms to be so expressed is *programming languages.* Sometimes they are called "user-oriented" to distinguish them from the *machine-oriented* assembler languages. Among the best known languages of this group are Fortran, COBOL, Algol, PL/I, Pascal, and APL. These programming languages are characterized by more powerful primitive operations and more powerful control structures than are available in machine language or in assembler language. An example of their operations is reading a record from a file specified only by name; another is exponentiation. Typical control structures include repetition of a group of instructions until a specified condition is satisfied. Often, but not necessarily, these languages are designed to resemble a natural language, such as English, more closely than could an assembler language.

Problem-oriented is sometimes used as a synonym for "user-oriented", but often it connotes instead a degree of specialization toward a particular problem area. The languages LISP for list processing and SNOBOL for character string manipulation could be placed here, along with COGO for civil engineering or APT for machine-tool control.

Nonalgorithmic source languages differ widely in their areas of application. Examples include specifications of reporting programs and of sorting programs. The former specifications include descriptions of data fields and report formats; the latter include descriptions of data records, keys, and desired sequences. In many operating systems, the command language provides another example of a nonalgorithmic source language.

1.3   TRANSLATION MECHANISMS

In translating an algorithm, whether into direct execution on the host machine or into a target-language program for later execution on the target machine, it is necessary for the translator both to analyze and to synthesize. It must analyze the source-language representation of the algorithm to determine what actions are ultimately to be performed. It must also synthesize those actions, either into direct performance or into a target-language representation.

Source-language analysis incorporates three stages: lexical, syntactic, and semantic. *Lexical* analysis is the determination of what symbols of the language are represented by the characters in the source-language text. For many programming languages, lexical analysis would classify "PRESSURE" as an identifier, "13" as an integer, "(" and "< =" as special symbols, "'LANGUAGE'" as a character string, and ".314159E+01" as a so-called "real" number. Examination of the text to identify and classify symbols is known as *scanning*, and lexical analyzers are therefore often called *scanners*.

Syntactic analysis is the determination of the structure of the source-language representation. If the source-language text is that of an assembler language with a fixed format for each instruction, this analysis could be trivial. In a particular assembler language the symbol in card columns 10–14 might, for example, always specify the operation code of the machine-language instruction to be performed. If the format is not so constrained, or if the source-language is more complex, syntactic analysis poses more of a challenge. Lexical analysis of the programming-language program fragment "A + B * C" would establish that it is composed of three identifiers separated by two special symbols. It would probably also determine that the special symbols represent binary operations. The major task in syntactic analysis of the fragment would be to determine whether the operation represented by "+" was to be performed before or after that represented by " * ". In making the determination, the syntactic analyzer would apply a specification of the rules for constructing symbol strings of the programming language. This set of rules is known as the *grammar* for the language. Application of a grammar to determining syntactic structure is known as *parsing*, and syntactic analyzers are therefore often called *parsers*.

Semantic analysis determines the *meaning* of the source-language program in the sense that it identifies the actions specified by the program. For the string "A + B * C" semantic analysis would determine what particular actions are specified by "+" and by " * ". Although semantic analysis is, for reasons we shall discuss later, often performed in conjunction with syntactic analysis, it is conceptually a different process.

The synthesis of action by the translation program involves one of two mechanisms. *Interpretation* is the direct performance of the actions identified in the process of analyzing the source-language program. For each possible action there exists a host-language subroutine to perform it. Interpretation requires the proper subroutine to be called at the right time with the appropriate parameters. *Generation* is the creation of target-language code to perform at a later time each action identified by analysis of the source-language program. Appropriate parameters assist in shaping the code sequence to be produced. Many persons restrict the term "generation", using it only for source languages nearer the machine-oriented end of the spectrum, and apply "compilation" to those more user-oriented.

1.4   TYPES OF TRANSLATORS

Translators which synthesize actions by interpretation are called *interpreters*. Although we have been discussing translation *programs*, it is important to observe that interpreters may be made of hardware as well as software. In fact, every computer is an interpreter of its own machine language, because it translates machine-language instructions into actions. As a result, every sequence of program translations includes a hardware interpreter at the end, even if no software interpretation precedes final execution. For reasons which will become clear when translation mechanisms are later examined carefully, interpretation is easier than generation. Consequently, interpreters are usually the easiest translators to write, but they tend also to result in much slower execution than do generative translators.

It would seem natural to designate as "generators" those programs which translate by generation. The term is indeed used, but it is customarily restricted to programs, such as report program generators (RPG) and sort generators, whose input is nonalgorithmic. Of the generative translators from algorithmic source language, the most important are assemblers, compilers, linkers, and loaders. For the simplest *assembler*, the target language is machine language and its source language has instructions in one-to-one correspondence with those of machine language, but with symbolic names for both operations and operands. The translator just converts each assembler-language instruction into the corresponding machine-language instruction, collecting those instructions into a program. Less elementary assemblers translate the program into a target-language form which permits the program to be combined with other programs before execution.

Many programs contain sequences of instructions which are repeated in either identical or nearly identical form. The repetitious writing of such sequences is obviated by the *macro processor*, which allows a sequence of source-language code to be defined once and then referred to by name each time it is to be assembled. Each reference, which may use parameters to introduce controlled variation, results in the generation of source-language text for a subsequent translation. *Conditional* macro processors provide for the conditional performance of part of the translation.

The *compiler* translates from a programming language as source to a machine-oriented language as target. Each source-language instruction is usually translated into several target-language instructions.

The *linker* (also "binder", "consolidator", or "linkage editor") takes as input independently translated programs whose original source-language representations include symbolic references to each other. Its task is to resolve these symbolic references and produce a single program. There is typically little difference between the linker's source and target languages.

The *loader* takes a program produced by assembler, compiler, or linker, and prepares that program to be executed when ultimately resident in a particular set of physical main storage locations. The loader's target language is machine language; its source language is nearly machine language.

Loading is intimately bound with the storage management function of operating systems, and is usually performed later than assembly and compilation. Some actions in linking must be deferred until load time and others may be deferred until execution. It is therefore convenient to classify linkers and loaders as control programs. This they are, but they are translators as well and interact closely with assemblers and compilers. It is instructive to study linkers and loaders in both the operating system context and the translator context.

1.5 HISTORICAL NOTES

The earliest computers, even those considered large at the time, executed single programs written in raw machine language. To keep track of storage use, the programmer customarily prepared by hand a "memory map" on which he wrote symbolic names for the variables whose values occupied the corresponding locations. Computers became larger and faster. When main storage reached a thousand words or so, the memory map became too unwieldy. Moreover, it was much easier to think of symbolic operation codes, such as "LOAD" and "ADD", rather than of the decimal or even binary numbers used to represent them in machine language. These needs led to the elementary symbolic assembler. Another early development was the *absolute* loader, a program which would take a machine-language program, whether prepared by the programmer or produced by an assembler, read it into main storage, and transfer control to it.

Within a few years, two major new features appeared. One was designed for computers whose main storage was on magnetic drum, for which the maximum random access time greatly exceeded the minimum, by a factor of perhaps 50. The *optimizing* assembler assigned to data and instructions those storage locations which would minimize execution time. Because the main storage media in current use present a uniform random access time, this feature is no longer needed. The second feature, provision of macro generation and conditional assembly, soon extended the power of assemblers. Unlike the first, this feature was not limited to a particular hardware design, and is still in widespread use.

A nearly parallel development was due to the rather limited instruction repertoires of early machines. Instructions which were desired, but not provided in the hardware, were incorporated into a language which could be used instead of machine language or the similarly circumscribed assembler language. Since the hardware was unable to interpret programs in the resulting language, interpretation was performed by programs, called *interpreters*. Among the most popular features provided by the early interpreters were three-address instruction formats and floating-point arithmetic operations.

Not only the floating-point arithmetic subroutines, but other subroutines, both arithmetic and nonarithmetic, constituted growing libraries of subroutines available to all users of a system. If the subroutines were written to be executed while occupying fixed locations in storage, then their use was highly constrained, because not more than one program can occupy a given storage location. Added to this was the problem that the user program which called the subroutines needed storage of its own. The conflicting storage requirements were resolved by producing both the system subroutines and the assembler output in a form in which addresses were specified not absolutely, but only relative to the start of the program. A *relocating loader* would read the program into whatever storage locations were available, and then insert the correct absolute addresses which corresponded to the starting location chosen.

Prior to loading, another step became convenient. This was the linking of user program to subroutines, or of separately written or translated user programs to each other, resulting in a single program for loading. Symbolic names defined in one of the modules to be linked could be referenced in another module which was prepared separately without access to the definition. The required resolution of intermodule symbolic references was provided by linkers.

The poor execution efficiency of interpreters led to a desire to perform generative translation, yet without losing the extended source-language capabilities of existing interpreters. This most difficult of the language translation requirements was met by the compiler. In fact, the earliest successful compiler particularly stressed target-language efficiency to enhance its chances of adoption. For quite a few years compilers were limited to problem-oriented languages designed for restricted fields of application, usually either business or numeric calculation. More widely applicable languages subsequently became available, and so have the corresponding compilers.

1.6 FUNCTION AND IMPLEMENTATION

In describing software, it is important to distinguish, as it is for hardware, among *architecture, implementation,* and *realization**. The architecture, or *function*, of a program is *what* the program does, as specified in its external description. The implementation is *how* the program performs that function, how it is organized internally. The realization is the *embodi-*

---

*Brooks [1975, p. 49] discusses the application to software engineering of this important insight due to Blaauw [1966, 1970].

ment of that organization in the particular language in which it is written and on the particular machine on which it runs.

The realization of translators is intimately bound with techniques of programming, and is dependent upon the details of specific languages and machines. To avoid excessive dependence on those matters, we shall concentrate on function and implementation. The choice of function does not dictate the choice of implementation. As for most programs, there is more than one way to implement the desired function. Indeed, different philosophies of translator design emphasize characteristics which result in widely varying implementations. Among the characteristics which influence implementation, or are consequences of the implementation, are the following.

> Translation speed
> Translator size
> Simplicity
> Generality
> Ease of debugging in source language
> Target-language code speed
> Target-language code size

The various characteristics cannot in general be established independently; for example, efficiency of compiled code is usually obtained at the expense of compiler time and space.

In the following chapters we shall examine both the functions of the principal types of translators, and the details of how generation and interpretation are performed. In discussing implementations, we shall not attempt to cover all possible approaches, but shall concentrate instead on typical forms of implementation. This will be particularly true for compilers. Because their function is the most complex of all the translators, compiler implementation shows the widest variety. Entire large books have been written on compiler design, and the material on compilers in this book must necessarily be illustrative rather than exhaustive.

FOR FURTHER STUDY

Two good overviews of system software, both considerably more detailed than this opening chapter, are Chapter 3 of Gear [1974] and Chapter 12 of Freeman [1975]. For the early history of translators, good sources are Knuth [1962] and Rosen [1964, 1967a, 1969].

Chapter 2

ASSEMBLY

2.1 ASSEMBLERS AND RELATED PROGRAMS

The simplest assembler program is the *load-and-go* assembler. It accepts as input a program whose instructions are essentially in one-to-one correspondence with those of machine language, but with symbolic names used for operations and operands. It produces as output a machine-language program in main storage, ready to be executed. The translation is usually performed in a single pass over the input program text. The resulting machine-language program occupies storage locations which are fixed at the time of translation and cannot be changed subsequently. The program can call library subroutines, provided that they occupy other locations than those required by the program. No provision is made for combining separate subprograms translated in this manner.

The load-and-go assembler forgoes the advantages of modular program development. Among the most important of these are (1) the ability to design, code, and test different program components in parallel; and (2) the restriction of changes to only applicable modules rather than throughout the program. Because some program development costs rise faster than proportionally to the length of a program component, another benefit of modularization is reduction of these costs. Most assemblers are therefore designed to satisfy the desire to create programs in modules. These *module* assemblers, also called "routine" or "subprogram" assemblers (cf. Barron [1972]), generally embody a two-pass translation. During the first pass the assembler examines the assembler-language program and collects the symbolic names into a table. During the second pass, the assembler generates code which is not quite in machine language. It is rather in a similar form, sometimes called "relocatable code" and here called *object code*. The program module in object-code form is typically called an *object module*.

The assembler-language program contains three kinds of entities. *Absolute* entities include operation codes, numeric and string-valued constants,

9

and fixed addresses. The values of absolute entities are independent of which storage locations the resulting machine code will eventually occupy. *Relative* entities include the addresses of instructions and of working storage. These are fixed only with respect to each other, and are normally stated relative to the address of the beginning of the module. An *externally defined* entity is used within a module but not defined within it. Whether it is in fact absolute or relative is not necessarily known at the time the module is translated.

The object module includes identification of which addresses are relative, which symbols are defined externally, and which internally defined symbols are expected to be referenced externally. In the modules in which the latter are used, they are considered to be externally defined. These external references are resolved for two or more object modules by a linker. The linker accepts the several object modules as input and produces a single module ready for loading, hence termed a *load module.*

The load module is free* of external references and consists essentially of machine-language code accompanied by a specification of which addresses are relative. When the actual main storage locations to be occupied by the program become known, a relocating loader reads the program into storage and adjusts the relative addresses to refer to those actual locations. The output from the loader is a machine-language program ready for execution. The over-all process is depicted in Fig. 2.1.

If only a single source-language module containing no external references is translated, it can be loaded directly without intervention by the linker. In some programming systems the format of linker output is sufficiently compatible with that of its input to permit the linking of a previously produced load module with some new object modules.

The functions of linking and loading are sometimes both effected by a single program, called a *linking loader.* Despite the convenience of combining the linking and loading functions, it is important to realize that they are distinct functions, each of which can be performed independently of the other.

In this chapter we examine in some detail the function and implementation of those assemblers which provide neither macro processing nor conditional assembly. Those functions are presented in Chapters 4 and 5, respectively. Because of its importance, the standard two-pass assembler is presented in detail, followed by a briefer description of two one-pass assemblers. Before describing a full-function two-pass assembler, however,

---

*This is an oversimplification. The module may still contain so-called *weak* external references which will actually not be made during the ensuing execution.

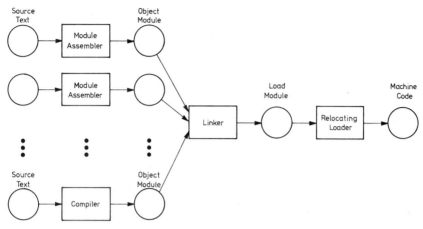

Figure 2.1   Program Translation Sequence

we concentrate on basic aspects of assembly by examining first a rudimentary assembler.

2.2   RUDIMENTARY TWO-PASS ASSEMBLER

2.2.1   *Function*

The program of Fig. 2.2, although written in a hypothetical assembler language for a mythical computer, contains the basic elements which need to be translated into machine language. For ease of reference, each instruction is identified by a line number, which is *not* part of the program. Each instruction in our language contains either an operation specification (lines 1–15) or a storage specification (lines 16–21). An operation specification is a symbolic operation code, which may be preceded by a label and must be followed by 0, 1, or 2 operand specifications, as appropriate to the operation. A storage specification is a symbolic instruction to the assembler. In our assembler language, it must be preceded by a label and must be followed, if appropriate, by a constant. Labels and operand specifications are symbolic addresses; every operand specification must appear somewhere in the program as a label.

Our machine has a single accumulator and a main storage of unspecified size. Its 14 instructions are listed in Fig. 2.3. The first column shows the assembler-language operation code and the second gives the machine-language equivalent (in decimal). The fourth column specifies the number

Line	Label	Operation	Operand 1	Operand 2
1		COPY	ZERO	OLDER
2		COPY	ONE	OLD
3		READ	LIMIT	
4		WRITE	OLD	
5	FRONT	LOAD	OLDER	
6		ADD	OLD	
7		STORE	NEW	
8		SUB	LIMIT	
9		BRPOS	FINAL	
10		WRITE	NEW	
11		COPY	OLD	OLDER
12		COPY	NEW	OLD
13		BR	FRONT	
14	FINAL	WRITE	LIMIT	
15		STOP		
16	ZERO	CONST	0	
17	ONE	CONST	1	
18	OLDER	SPACE		
19	OLD	SPACE		
20	NEW	SPACE		
21	LIMIT	SPACE		

Figure 2.2   Sample Assembler-Language Program

Operation code Symbolic	Machine	Length	No. of operands	Action
ADD	02	2	1	$ACC \leftarrow ACC + OPD1$
BR	00	2	1	branch to OPD1
BRNEG	05	2	1	branch to OPD1 if ACC $<$ 0
BRPOS	01	2	1	branch to OPD1 if ACC $>$ 0
BRZERO	04	2	1	branch to OPD1 if ACC $=$ 0
COPY	13	3	2	$OPD2 \leftarrow OPD1$
DIVIDE	10	2	1	$ACC \leftarrow ACC \div OPD1$
LOAD	03	2	1	$ACC \leftarrow OPD1$
MULT	14	2	1	$ACC \leftarrow ACC \times OPD1$
READ	12	2	1	$OPD1 \leftarrow$ input stream
STOP	11	1	0	stop execution
STORE	07	2	1	$OPD1 \leftarrow ACC$
SUB	06	2	1	$ACC \leftarrow ACC - OPD1$
WRITE	08	2	1	output stream $\leftarrow OPD1$

Figure 2.3   Instruction Set

of operands, and the last column describes the action which ensues when the instruction is executed. In that column "ACC", "OPD1", and "OPD2" refer to contents of the accumulator, of the first operand location, and of the second operand location, respectively. The length of each instruction in words is 1 greater than the number of its operands. Thus if the machine has 12-bit words, an ADD instruction is 2 words, or 24 bits, long. The table's third column, which is redundant, gives the instruction length. If our mythical computer had a fixed instruction length, the third and fourth columns could both be omitted.

The storage specification SPACE reserves one word of storage which presumably will eventually hold a number; there is no operand. The storage specification CONST also reserves a word of storage; it has an operand which is the value of a number to be placed in that word by the assembler.

The instructions of the program are presented in four fields, and might indeed be constrained to such a format on the input medium. The label, if present, occupies the first field. The second field contains the symbolic operation code or storage specification, which will henceforth be referred to simply as the *operation*. The third and fourth fields hold the operand specifications, or simply *operands*, if present.

Although it is not important to our discussion to understand what the example program does, the foregoing specifications of the machine and of its assembler language reveal the algorithm. The program uses the recursion relation $f_i = f_{i-1} + f_{i-2}$, implemented by the assignment NEW ← OLD + OLDER, to compute the so-called *Fibonacci numbers* (0, 1, 1, 2, 3, 5, 8, ..). The program prints all numbers beyond the zero, but not exceeding the positive integer limit read in on line 3 of the program, and then prints that limit. The astute reader will observe that the program could be improved. For example, the loop could be rewritten to require only one branch. Nevertheless, the forward branch (line 9) is an important component of many longer assembler-language programs and it has been left in this short example on purpose.

Now that we have seen the elements of an assembler-language program, we can ask what functions the assembler must perform in translating it. Here is the list.

Replace symbolic addresses by numeric addresses.
Replace symbolic operation codes by machine operation codes.
Reserve storage for instructions and data.
Translate constants into machine representation.

The assignment of numeric addresses can be performed, except by a load-and-go assembler (which we are not now considering), without foreknowledge of what actual locations will eventually be occupied by the assembled program. It is necessary only to generate addresses relative to the start of the program. We shall assume that our assembler normally assigns addresses starting at 0. In translating line 1 of our example program, the resulting machine instruction will therefore be assigned address 0 and occupy 3 words, because COPY instructions are 3 words long. Hence the instruction corresponding to line 2 will be assigned address 3, the READ instruction will be assigned address 6, and the WRITE instruction of line 4 will be assigned address 8, and so on to the end of the program. But what addresses will be assigned to the operands named ZERO and OLDER? These addresses must be inserted in the machine-language representation of the first instruction.

2.2.2 *Implementation*

The assembler uses a counter to keep track of machine-language addresses. Because these addresses will ultimately specify locations in main storage, the counter is called the *location counter*, although "address counter" would be more accurate terminology. Before assembly, the location counter is initialized to zero. After each source line has been examined on the first pass, the location counter is incremented by the length of the machine-language code which will ultimately be generated to correspond to that source line.

When the assembler first encounters line 1 of the example program, it cannot replace the symbols ZERO and OLDER by addresses because those symbols make *forward references* to source-language program lines not yet reached by the assembler. The most straightforward way to cope with the problem of forward references is to examine the entire program text once, before attempting to complete the translation. During that examination, the assembler determines the address which corresponds to each symbol, and places both the symbols and their addresses in a *symbol table*. This is possible because each symbol used in an operand field must also appear as a label. The address corresponding to a label is just the address of the first word of the machine-language code for the line which that label begins. Those addresses are supplied by the location counter. Creation of the symbol table requires one pass over the source text. During a second pass, the assembler uses the addresses collected in the symbol table to perform the translation. As each symbolic address is encountered in the second pass, the corresponding numeric address is substituted for it in the object code.

Two of the most common logical errors in assembler-language programming involve improper use of symbols. If a symbol appears in the operand field of some instruction, but nowhere in a label field, it is *undefined*. If a symbol appears in the label fields of more than one instruction, it is *multiply defined*. In building the symbol table on the first pass, the assembler must examine the label field of each instruction to permit it to associate the location counter value with each symbol. Multiply-defined symbols will be found on this pass. Undefined symbols, on the other hand, will not be found on the first pass unless the assembler also examines operand fields for symbols. Although this examination is not required for construction of the symbol table, normal practice is to perform it anyhow, because of its value in early detection of program errors.

There are many ways to organize a symbol table. Although the manner in which the symbol table is implemented is of considerable practical importance, it is not immediately relevant to the present discussion. We shall simply treat the symbol table as a set of (symbol,address) pairs, and assume the existence of procedures for insertion, search, and retrieval. In the illustrations which follow, the set of pairs is represented by a linear list in the order in which the symbols are first encountered. Symbol table organization is discussed in Section 6.4.

The state of processing after line 3 has been scanned is shown in Fig. 2.4. During processing of line 1, the symbols ZERO and OLDER were encountered and entered into the first two positions of the symbol table. The operation COPY was identified, and instruction length information from Fig. 2.3 used to advance the location counter from 0 to 3. During process-

Line	Address		Label	Operation	Operand 1	Operand 2
1	0			COPY	ZERO	OLDER
2	3			COPY	ONE	OLD
3	6			READ	LIMIT	

(a) Source text scanned

Symbol	Address	
ZERO	- - -	
OLDER	- - -	
ONE	- - -	Location counter: 8
OLD	- - -	
LIMIT	- - -	Line counter: 4

(b) Symbol table; Counters

Figure 2.4 First Pass After Scanning Line 3

ing of line 2 two more symbols were encountered and entered in the symbol table, and the location counter was advanced from 3 to 6. Line 3 yielded the fifth symbol, LIMIT, and caused incrementation of the location counter from 6 to 8. At this point the symbol table holds five symbols, none of which yet has an address. The location counter holds the address 8, and processing is ready to continue from line 4. Neither the line numbers nor the addresses shown in part (a) of the figure are actually part of the source-language program. The addresses record the history of incrementation of the location counter; the line numbers permit easy reference. Clearly, the assembler needs not only a location counter, but also a *line counter* to keep track of which source line is being processed.

During processing of line 4 the symbol OLD is encountered for the second time. Because it is already in the symbol table, it is not entered again. During processing of line 5, the symbol FRONT is encountered in the label field. It is entered into the symbol table, and the current location counter value, 10, is entered with it as its address. Figure 2.5 displays the state of the translation after line 9 has been processed.

Line	Address	Label	Operation	Operand 1	Operand 2
1	0		COPY	ZERO	OLDER
2	3		COPY	ONE	OLD
3	6		READ	LIMIT	
4	8		WRITE	OLD	
5	10	FRONT	LOAD	OLDER	
6	12		ADD	OLD	
7	14		STORE	NEW	
8	16		SUB	LIMIT	
9	18		BRPOS	FINAL	

(a) Source text scanned

Symbol	Address	
ZERO	---	
OLDER	---	
ONE	---	
OLD	---	
LIMIT	---	
FRONT	10	Location counter: 20
NEW	---	
FINAL	---	Line counter: 10

(b) Symbol table; Counters

Figure 2.5   First Pass after Scanning Line 9

The first pass continues in the same manner until line 14. There a label is encountered which is already in the symbol table, because it first appeared as an operand, on line 9. The symbol does not need to be entered again in the table, but its address, which has just become known, does. Each of lines 16–21 corresponds to one word of machine code, and the location counter is therefore incremented by 1 for each line. Each of these lines also includes a label, and the corresponding address for each is entered in the symbol table. At the end of the first pass, the state depicted in Fig. 2.6 has been reached.

The code generation is performed by our simple assembler during a second pass over the source text. Before starting the second pass, the line counter is reset to 1 and the location counter to 0. For each line of source code the assembler now produces a line of object code, which consists of the address, length, and text of the corresponding machine-language representation. The line and location counters are incremented as on the first pass. Line 1 is translated into 00 3   13 33 35 to indicate address 0, length 3 words, operation code 13, and operand addresses 33 and 35. The machine operation code is found in Fig. 2.3. This operation code table is fixed for all assemblies, being defined by the assembler and machine languages, and is part of the assembler program. The numeric addresses are found in the address fields of the symbol table entries for ZERO and OLDER. The symbol table is different, of course, for each assembly and is built during the first pass.

Successive lines are translated in the same manner. When line 5 is reached, a label is found. How is it treated on the second pass? It is ignored, because nothing in the machine code corresponds to the label field, and the address is given by the location counter. Thus the output corresponding to line 5 is 10 2   03 35. Lines 1–15, which contain operation specifications in the operation field, are all translated in this manner. Thus we see that whereas the first pass is concerned chiefly with advancing the location counter and building the symbol table, the second pass uses the symbol table to generate the object program.

But what about lines 16–21? For these the content of the operation field is a storage specification. The corresponding machine code is not an instruction. In fact, CONST specifies that its operand is to be placed in one word of machine code and SPACE specifies only that one word of machine code is to be reserved. Thus the object code produced from source line 16 is 33 1   00 and that corresponding to line 17 is 34 1   01. The content of the word corresponding to line 18 is not specified, and anything can be assembled. Using "XX" to represent an arbitrary value we can write the object code corresponding to line 18 as 35 1   XX. Figure 2.7 presents the object code which corresponds to the entire source-language program.

Line	Address	Label	Operation	Operand 1	Operand 2
1	0		COPY	ZERO	OLDER
2	3		COPY	ONE	OLD
3	6		READ	LIMIT	
4	8		WRITE	OLD	
5	10	FRONT	LOAD	OLDER	
6	12		ADD	OLD	
7	14		STORE	NEW	
8	16		SUB	LIMIT	
9	18		BRPOS	FINAL	
10	20		WRITE	NEW	
11	22		COPY	OLD	OLDER
12	25		COPY	NEW	OLD
13	28		BR	FRONT	
14	30	FINAL	WRITE	LIMIT	
15	32		STOP		
16	33	ZERO	CONST	0	
17	34	ONE	CONST	1	
18	35	OLDER	SPACE		
19	36	OLD	SPACE		
20	37	NEW	SPACE		
21	38	LIMIT	SPACE		

(a) Source text scanned

Symbol	Address	
ZERO	33	
OLDER	35	
ONE	34	
OLD	36	
LIMIT	38	
FRONT	10	Location counter: 39
NEW	37	
FINAL	30	Line counter: 22

(b) Symbol table; Counters

Figure 2.6   Result of First Pass

The XX can be thought of as a specification to the loader, which will eventually process the object code, that the content of the location corresponding to address 35 does not need to have any specific value loaded. The loader can then just skip over that location. Some assemblers specify anyway a particular value for reserved storage locations, often zeros. There

Address	Length	Machine code
00	3	13 33 35
03	3	13 34 36
06	2	12 38
08	2	08 36
10	2	03 35
12	2	02 36
14	2	07 37
16	2	06 38
18	2	01 30
20	2	08 37
22	3	13 36 35
25	3	13 37 36
28	2	00 10
30	2	08 38
32	1	11
33	1	00
34	1	01
35	1	XX
36	1	XX
37	1	XX
38	1	XX

Figure 2.7   Object Code Generated on Second Pass

is no logical requirement to do so, however, and the user unfamiliar with his assembler is ill-advised to count on a particular value.

The specifications CONST and SPACE do not correspond to machine instructions. They are really instructions to the assembler program. Because of this, we shall refer to them as *assembler instructions*. Another common designation for them is "pseudo-instructions". Neither term is really satisfactory. Of the two types of assembler instructions in our example program, one results in the generation of machine code and the other in the reservation of storage. Later we shall see assembler instructions which result in neither of these actions. The assembler instructions are given in a table available to the assembler. One organization is to use a separate table which is usually searched before the operation code table is searched. Another is to include both machine operations and assembler instructions in the same table. A field in the table entry then identifies the type to the assembler.

A few variations to the foregoing process can be considered. Some of the translation can actually be performed during the first pass. Operation fields must be examined during the first pass to determine their effect on the location counter. The second-pass table lookup to determine the machine operation code can be obviated at the cost of producing intermediate text which holds machine operation code and instruction length in addition to source text. Another translation which can be performed during the first pass is that of constants, e.g. from source-language decimal to machine-language binary. The translation of any symbolic addresses which refer backward in the text, rather than forward, could be performed on the first pass, but it is more convenient to wait for the second pass and treat all symbolic addresses uniformly.

A minor variation is to assemble addresses relative to a starting address other than 0. The location counter is merely initialized to the desired address. If, for example, the value 200 is chosen, the symbol table would appear as in Fig. 2.8. The object code corresponding to line 1 would be 200 3   13 233 235.

Symbol	Address
ZERO	233
OLDER	235
ONE	234
OLD	236
LIMIT	238
FRONT	210
NEW	237
FINAL	230

Figure 2.8   Symbol Table with Starting Location 200

If it were known at assembly time that the program is to reside at location 200 for execution, then full object code with address and length need not be generated. The machine code alone would suffice. In this event the result of translation would be the following 39-word sequence.

```
13    233   235    13    234   236    12    238    08    236    03    235    02
236    07   237    06    238    01   230    08    237    13    236   235    13
237   236    00   210    08    238    11    00    01    XX    XX    XX    XX
```

2.3   FULL TWO-PASS ASSEMBLER

2.3.1   *Functions*

Virtually all assembler languages incorporate more facilities for specifying machine function than does the rudimentary example presented in the previous section. We now examine the rich variety of functions which may be present. In Section 2.3.2 we discuss how each can be implemented in an assembler.

Symbolic Instructions. As we have seen, the operation code may be represented symbolically. The symbol used is often called a *mnemonic operation code*, or simply a *mnemonic*, because it is usually selected for its mnemonic significance. Thus ADD and LOAD, or even A and L, are more likely to be used for instructions which add and load than are, say XB5 and ZARF. Symbolic representation can be extended to other fields of the instruction, such as indexing and indirect addressing specifications. One useful extension is the so-called *extended mnemonic*. This has the form of a symbolic operation code, but designates more information than just the machine operation code. The IBM 360, for example, has a general-purpose operation code for branch on condition (mnemonic BC) which is specialized to a particular condition by a 4-bit mask field. The extended mnemonic BZ (branch on zero) specifies both the 8-bit operation code 01000111 and the 4-bit mask 1000.

Symbolic Addresses. A symbol selected by the programmer is used to refer to the location which an item will occupy when the program is executed. For an item which occupies more than one addressable location, the address of the first location is normally used. For example, if a 4-byte integer-valued field named PRESSURE occupies storage locations known to the assembler as 1836–1839 in a byte-addressed machine, then the address 1836 would be associated with the symbol PRESSURE. A standard, but unfortunate, terminology is to refer to the address as the "value" of the symbol. In discussing an assembly, one would then say "the value of PRESSURE is 1836" to refer to the address of the symbol. This must be distinguished from a reference to the numeric value of the operand (say, 1013) stored at the address (1836) designated by the symbol PRESSURE. To avoid this confusion, and to simplify reference to values of other attributes of a symbol than its address, "value" will not be used here in the specialized sense of "address".

Symbolic addresses are not limited to single symbols. Arithmetic expressions involving one or more symbols are often permitted, and are extremely useful. Examples of such *address expressions* are FRONT + 5, 4 * OFFSET + I, and PRESSURE − RESERVE. More complicated address expressions are permitted by some assemblers.

Storage Reservation. In most assembler languages it is not necessary to place a label on each storage reservation or constant definition. The use of address expressions in the source language or of indexing in the machine operations provides easy access to unlabeled locations.

An assembler instruction to reserve storage may specify directly the amount to be reserved. This is particularly common if the unit of allocation is fixed, as on most word-addressed machines. Thus one might have assembler codes RSF (reserve storage, first address) and RSL (reserve storage, last address) which require a label and one operand. The instruction ALPHA   RSF   23 would reserve a block of 23 words and associate the symbol ALPHA with the first word of the block. The instruction OMEGA   RSL   7 would reserve a block of 7 words, and associate the symbol OMEGA with the last word of the block.

If different units of allocation are used for different data types, it may be more convenient to specify quantities and units and rely on the assembler to compute the amount of storage required. The DS (define storage) operation of the IBM OS/360 assembler is of this type. The instruction WORK   DS   15D,6F causes 144 bytes to be reserved (fifteen 8-byte double words and six 4-byte full words). The address of the label WORK is the address of the first byte of the 144.

Data Generation. Data to be placed in the object code are usually encoded in the assembler-language program in a form in which they are easily written. Although a machine may encode numbers in binary, the programmer is likely to think of their values in decimal. It is necessary to specify, either explicitly or implicitly, both the source and the target encodings.

Near one extreme might be a machine with two data types and a restricted assembler language. The only data are one-word numbers in either fixed-point or floating-point binary encoding. The assembler language permits decimal encodings only; floating-point is to be used if and only if a decimal point is present. In this situation a single assembler instruction suffices. For example,

RATES   CONST   8000,0.22,12000,0.25,16000,0.28

would reserve storage for 6 words, the first of them labeled RATES, and generate fixed- and floating-point values in them alternately.

If several encodings are possible, it may be more convenient to provide a distinct assembler instruction for each type of conversion. Thus DECIMAL and OCTAL might require operands in decimal and octal, respectively, and implicitly specify their conversion to binary. If there are many different types of conversions, the language may be more tractable if a single assembler instruction is used in conjunction with type indicators. Thus the OS/360 assembler instruction DC (define constant) permits 15 types of conversions. For example, DC   F'5',H'−9',C'EXAMPLE' causes the generation of the integer 5 as a 4-byte full word, followed by the integer −9 as a 2-byte half word, followed by 7 bytes of characters. Repetition factors may be permitted, to assist in such specifications as that of a table all of whose values are initially zero.

Location Counters. The programmer is generally free to pick a nonzero origin for the location counter. An assembler instruction, perhaps called ORIGIN, has an operand to define the value of the location counter. In some assembler languages, this redefinition of the location counter can occur not only at the start of the source program, but at any point thereafter. That feature is useful chiefly with assemblers which provide two or more location counters.

Multiple location counters permit text to be permuted during translation. One example of a useful permutation is to write storage reservation and data generation specifications next to the associated source-language instructions, but to assemble data fields into a single area at the end of the program. Another is to interleave, in the source code, instructions to two or more processors (e.g. a machine and its I/O channels) but to segregate them in the object code.

Scope of Symbols. If two or more modules are to be combined after assembly, some symbolic addresses will be defined in one module and used in another. Most symbols, however, will be referenced only within the module in which they are defined. These symbols are said to be *local* to that module. A symbol defined within a module is called *global* if another module is to reference it. During the assembly of one module, the assembler can identify symbols used but not defined within the module. Each such use is either an error or a reference to a global variable whose definition must be supplied by another module during linking. The assembler cannot tell, however, whether a symbol which is defined in the module being translated will be referenced by another module. Yet this information must be transmitted by the assembler to the linker. Consequently, the assembler must itself be informed. One way is to mark the definition of each global symbol with a special tag. Thus

```
*RESULT   SPACE   1
```

might identify RESULT as external to the module, although internally defined. An alternative to the marker is an assembler instruction, say INTDEF. The sequence

```
RESULT   INTDEF
         SPACE   1
```

would have the same effect. The SPACE instruction can be given a label local to the module, as in

```
          RESULT    INTDEF
          ANSWER    SPACE  1
```

where the local symbol ANSWER can be used only within the module, whereas the global symbol RESULT can be used either within it or without. The advantage of providing a local label is that in some implementations the use of a global label may be more expensive. The alternative syntax

```
          INTDEF  RESULT
          ---
RESULT    SPACE  1
```

does not require adjacency of the definition of the label to its designation as global. It does not allow a local label, however, and it suffers from the irregular use of the operand field for symbol definition rather than for symbol reference.

To permit independent assembly of more than one module during a single invocation of the assembler, it is necessary to distinguish the beginning and end of each assembler-language program. Even if only one assembly is to be performed, assembler instructions, often START and END, are provided to delimit the source program. These can be thought of as constituting vertical parentheses which define the scope of local symbols.

Redefinable Symbols. A symbol whose address depends upon its context is said to be *redefinable*. It cannot be held in the symbol table in the usual manner, because different occurrences may be associated with different addresses. The most frequently used redefinable symbol has as its address the current value of the location counter; often an asterisk is used. A common use of such a symbol is in relative branching. Thus BR $*-6$, wherever it appears in the program, is a branch to an address which is 6 less than the current address.

Another extremely useful type of redefinable symbol is also called a *local label*, but with a more restrictive connotation than merely "non-global". Distinguished syntactically from other symbols, it is defined afresh each time it appears in the label field of an instruction. Any use of such a symbol in an operand field refers to the most recent definition. A particularly convenient variation is to permit the reference to be marked either as backward to the most recent definition or as forward to the next definition. If, for example, normal labels are restricted to begin with an alphabetic character, the decimal digits might be reserved as ten local labels. Thus 3B would be a reference to the closest previous occurrence of local label 3; and 1F, to the next forthcoming occurrence of local label 1.

A local label (under this stronger definition) can be thought of as having a scope restricted to only a portion of the module in which it is defined.

Base Registers. The specification of main storage locations by address fields of machine-language instructions is commonly performed in one of three ways. (1) The address field is a single number which refers directly to the storage location. This is *direct* addressing. (2) The address field is a single number which specifies the displacement of the storage location from the origin of the program segment. Before execution, the origin is placed in a base register by the operating system. During interpretation of the instruction at execution time, the displacement is automatically added to the base register content to yield the storage location. Because the instruction does not refer explicitly to a base register, this is *implicit-base* addressing. (3) The address field is a pair of numbers, of which one designates a base register and the other constitutes the displacement. This is *explicit-base* addressing.

If the target machine employs direct addressing, any storage location is addressable. If it employs implicit-base addressing, addressability is a consequence of limiting the length of program segments to the number of locations that can be distinguished by the displacement. If, however, the target machine employs explicit-base addressing, two constraints impose a burden on the assembler in ensuring that all program locations will be addressable. One is that the displacement field is usually shorter than for implicit-base addressing, because some bits must be used to designate the base register. This means that the portion of storage addressable from one explicitly-named base register is often smaller than that addressable under implicit-base addressing. The other constraint is the key requirement that any register used as a base contain a suitable value at execution time. Clearly, the assembler cannot control what instruction will be executed to provide this value. The programmer, however, can write an instruction to load a base register. He must inform the assembler of what value will be in the base register at execution time, to permit it to generate addresses relative to the base register content. If there are multi-purpose registers which can serve either as a base or in another capacity, the programmer must indicate which registers are to be used as base registers.

For the IBM 360-370, the assembler instruction USING specifies a register as being available for use as a base, and states its execution-time content. The assembler instruction DROP withdraws the register from the list of those available for use as bases. Thus USING *,12 states that register 12 can be used as a base register and promises that its content will be the address of the current line. (That assembler instruction would typically be preceded by the machine instruction BALR   12,0 to load the appropriate number at execution time into register 12, thus fulfilling the promise.)

If several registers have been made available for use as bases, the assembler, in addressing a given symbol, can use any base register for which the address displacement falls within the acceptable bounds. Consequently, the choice of base register is not fixed for the symbol, and is not among its attributes.

Symbol Attributes. One attribute we have seen is the address. This is the address of the start of the field to which the symbol refers. The address of each symbol is stored in the symbol table. Other attributes are normally stored there, too.

A particularly important attribute is whether a symbol is absolute or relative. This information is used by the loader in determining whether an adjustment is necessary when the load module is read into storage. It is used by the linker to determine the relocatability attribute of addresses which incorporate external references. Even within the assembler it is used to determine the relocatability attribute of address expressions.

If multiple location counters are permitted, the identity of the location counter to use for a symbol is another of its attributes. The location counter identity is used by the assembler to determine the origin with respect to which the symbol's relative address is to be generated.

The length attribute of a symbol is usually the length of the field named by the symbol. Different conventions for defining the length attribute are used in different assembler languages. Thus the storage reservation instruction ALPHA   RSF   23 for a word-addressed machine might imply for the symbol ALPHA a length of 1 or a length of 23. The length attribute is used primarily in variable-field-length instructions to specify the length of the operands in the absence of an explicit length specification.

Some assembler languages permit references to symbol attributes. References to the length of a symbol may be explicit, as in L(ALPHA), or implicit in using ALPHA as an operand in a variable-field-length instruction. An attribute to which reference can often be made explicitly is the address of a symbol. This permits the programmer to specify a constant whose value will be the execution-time location associated with an assembler-language symbol. Such a constant is known as an *address constant* and is typically written A(FRONT) if FRONT is the symbol to whose location reference is made. The indirect addressing which results can be used in passing parameters, in implementing list structures, and in providing for base addressing.

Alternate Names. The provision of symbolic names for other fields of the instruction than storage addresses is often convenient and valuable. Register designations, shift amounts, field lengths, and address displacements are usually encoded numerically in the assembler-language instruction. Program readability can often be enhanced by representing these numeric values symbolically. Thus a programmer might wish to use FR4 rather than 4 to name a floating-point register, and COMP, INCR, and LIMIT, rather than 8, 9, and 10, to name loop-control registers which hold comparand, increment, and limit. Assemblers which offer this *definitional* facility may use any of a variety of syntactic forms. Perhaps the most straightforward is the following use of the defined symbol as the label and the defining quantity as the operand.

```
FR4      SET    4
COMP     SET    8
INCR     SET    9
LIMIT    SET    10
```

Some assemblers offer a more general form of this facility, in which the operand may itself be a symbolic expression. Thus ZIP SET ZAP defines ZIP as a symbol whose attributes are set to equal the attributes which ZAP has at the point where the SET instruction is encountered. A subsequent change in the attributes of ZAP does not affect ZIP. This is analogous to call by value (see Section 3.5.2). Moreover, it is possible to redefine ZIP subsequently by use of another SET instruction. Except in the macro assemblers discussed in Section 5.4, the attributes of the defining expression will not change unless it incorporates a redefinable symbol. If the defining expression is just a numeric constant, the attribute is the value of the constant.

An apparently similar, but actually quite distinct, form of alternate naming caters to the dubious practice of two programmers independently preparing programs which are to be combined prior to assembly, yet using different names for the same entity. To avoid the tedious replacement of all occurrences of the name used in one of the programs, a *synonym* or name *equivalence* facility is provided in some assemblers. Thus ZIP EQU ZAP specifies that the symbols ZIP and ZAP are to be considered equivalent symbols throughout the program. Their attributes are the same. Thus whenever ZIP is used, the effect is the same as if ZAP had been named instead. This is analogous to call by name (see Section 3.5.3). It should be noted that in at least one system the mnemonic code EQU is used not for name equivalence, but for the definitional facility which we have called SET.

Alternate symbolic names for operation codes can be provided by EQU, although the use of a distinct instruction for this purpose offers some advantages in processing. Thus the programmer who prefers MULT to the standard MD for double-precision floating-point multiplication on the IBM 360-370 can code MULT   OPSYN MD to make MULT synonymous with MD whenever it is used as the operation code.

Each of the foregoing alternate naming facilities defines a symbol. It may or may not be required that the definition precede any use of a symbol so defined. Whether that requirement is imposed is dictated by whether lack of the definition will prevent the assembler from properly advancing the location counter during the first pass. The counter is not advanced, of course, when the SET, EQU, or OPSYN itself is encountered. Less restrictive alternate naming facilities can, of course, be provided at the cost of requiring more than two passes.

Literals. Often a programmer may wish to specify not the address of an operand but rather its value. In an instruction to increment a counter by 2, for example, the programmer may prefer just to write the constant "2" without concern for where that operand is located. An operand specified in this manner, with its value stated literally, is called a *literal*. Although several different instructions might include the same literal, usually only one copy of each literally specified value needs to be generated. The literals are placed together in a *pool* to avoid inserting each literal constant between instructions.

The literal pool is typically generated at the end of the object code. In some assembler languages, however, the programmer can control the placement of the pool. An instruction, perhaps LITORG, specifies that the pool of literals appearing up to that point in the text is to be placed at the address specified, usually the current value of the location counter. For machines with explicit-base addressing (e.g. IBM 360-370), this may be needed to ensure the addressability of literals. A literal pool generated subsequently includes only those literals which have been specified since the previous pool generation.

The assembler language must provide a distinction between numeric literals and numeric addresses, and between character literals and symbolic addresses. One way to distinguish is to use a different instruction format; another is to use a special symbol to mark a literal. Some literals, such as those with a decimal point or an exponent designator, are self-marking and would not need the special symbol. Even so, use of an explicit distinction permits a uniform implementation of all literals.

Error Checking. An assembler usually checks the source program for several different types of errors. One of the most important is the undefined symbol, which appears as an operand but nowhere as a label. Such an occurrence can be either rejected as an error or assumed to be an external symbol. If the assembler language requires external symbols to be identified, then undefined symbols can be caught at assembly time. Otherwise, they are not caught until linkage is attempted.

A symbol which occurs as a label more than once has a different location counter value associated with each occurrence. Even if its other attributes are the same for each occurrence, its address is not. The resulting error is a multiply-defined symbol.

The detection of undefined and of multiply-defined symbols makes use of inter-statement context, as recorded in the symbol table. Many other invalidities can be checked during examination of one instruction alone. Among these are nonexistent operation codes, wrong number of operands, inappropriate operands, and a variety of syntax errors. Some aspects of the checking process may be simpler if the source language is constrained to a fixed, rather than a free, format.

Listing. The object code output is written onto a machine-readable medium, such as punched cards, paper tape, or magnetic disk. The programmer may require a human-readable listing of both source and object code, preferably side by side. To assist in debugging, the symbol table and a *concordance* or *cross-reference* table are usually printed. The symbol table lists each symbol together with its address, and perhaps other attributes. The cross-reference table indicates for each symbol where in the source program it is defined (used as a label) and where it is accessed (used in an operand specification). The two tables are usually sorted in alphabetic order for ease of use. Often they are combined in a single table, as in Fig. 2.9, which shows a listing of the assembly performed in Section 2.2. Such a listing can be produced, of course, by a separate listing program which accepts the source code, object code, and symbol table as inputs. Alternatively, it can be produced by the assembler itself during its second pass.

Error messages are an important component of the listing. Some assemblers group the error messages at the foot of the source-language program. Many programmers prefer, however, to have any message which is associated with a single source instruction printed next to that instruction. Even if this is not done, the message must at least identify the erroneous instruction. Some error messages, however, do not apply to a specific instruction and should not be interleaved with the program text.

A facility for comments is often provided. One method is to use a word or character reserved for the purpose (e.g. an asterisk in card column 1 to make the entire card a comment). Another method of identifying comments is to use an assembler instruction (say, COMMENT or REMARK) which specifies that the ensuing text is to be skipped by the assembler. The

Line	Label	Operation	Operand	Operand	Address	Length	Machine code
1		COPY	ZERO	OLDER	00	3	13 33 35
2		COPY	ONE	OLD	03	3	13 34 36
3		READ	LIMIT		06	2	12 38
4		WRITE	OLD		08	2	08 36
5	FRONT	LOAD	OLDER		10	2	03 35
6		ADD	OLD		12	2	02 36
7		STORE	NEW		14	2	07 37
8		SUB	LIMIT		16	2	06 38
9		BRPOS	FINAL		18	2	01 30
10		WRITE	NEW		20	2	08 37
11		COPY	OLD	OLDER	22	3	13 36 35
12		COPY	NEW	OLD	25	3	13 37 36
13		BR	FRONT		28	2	00 10
14	FINAL	WRITE	LIMIT		30	2	08 38
15		STOP			32	1	11
16	ZERO	CONST	0		33	1	00
17	ONE	CONST	1		34	1	01
18	OLDER	SPACE			35	1	XX
19	OLD	SPACE			36	1	XX
20	NEW	SPACE			37	1	XX
21	LIMIT	SPACE			38	1	XX

Address	Symbol	Definition	References
30	FINAL	14	9
10	FRONT	5	13
38	LIMIT	21	3 8 14
37	NEW	20	7 10 12
36	OLD	19	2 4 6 11 12
35	OLDER	18	1 5 11
34	ONE	17	2
33	ZERO	16	1

Figure 2.9   Assembly Listing

amount to be skipped may be fixed (e.g. the rest of the line) or specified as an operand. It can even be determined by the presence of another assembler instruction which terminates skipping. Neither of these methods is convenient for placing comments adjacent to program text. Such a capability can be provided in a number of ways. One is to reserve a field on each line for comments. Another is to reserve a character to indicate that the remainder of the line is a comment. Yet another is to treat as commentary all characters beyond the rightmost required field.

Assembler instructions may also be provided for control of the listing format, especially if the format of the source-language program is fixed.

Other options may include the printing of optional items, or even the suppression of part or all of the listing itself.

Assembler Control. Because assembler instructions other than those which reserve storage or define constants do not cause the generation of object code, there is not a one-to-one correspondence between source and object text. Consequently even an assembler for a machine in which all data and instruction lengths are fixed and equal (e.g. one word) requires two position counters, one for lines of source text and the other for addresses in the object program.

Some assembler instructions, such as those for alternate names, must be obeyed during the first pass of the assembler. Others, such as those for listing control, must be obeyed during the second pass. Yet others, such as scope delimiters, affect both passes. Sometimes a function specified by an assembler instruction can be implemented on either pass. An example is the generation of constants.

Repetitive Assembly. Sometimes a sequence of source-language statements are nearly identical to each other. This occurs commonly in the construction of tables. Much of the tedium of writing the full source code can be relieved by the provision of an assembler instruction, say REPEAT or ECHO, which causes one or more subsequent source lines to be assembled repeatedly with minor variations. Thus

```
                    REPEAT  2,(1,10)
         ARG$       CONST   $
         FCT$       SPACE
```

might cause the group of two instructions to be repeated with the substitution, on each successive repetition, of the next digit in the range (1,10) for each occurrence of '$' in the group. This repetitive assembly would have the same effect as assembling the 20 following instructions.

```
         ARG1       CONST   1
         FCT1       SPACE
         ARG2       CONST   2
         FCT2       SPACE
                    ---
         ARG10      CONST   10
         FCT10      SPACE
```

This facility is but a special case of a much more powerful facility, to be discussed in Chapter 4 and in Section 5.4, for generating source code at assembly time.

2.3.2   *Implementations*

The many functions described in the foregoing sections can be implemented straightforwardly in a two-pass assembler. As in our rudimentary assembler, Pass 1 is still concerned chiefly with symbol table construction and location counter management. Pass 2 still produces the object code and, if one is to be provided, the listing. The complexity of each pass depends, of course, on just which functions are selected. The basic actions for symbol table construction are listed in Fig. 2.10.

A major exception to the rules of that figure occurs if a symbol encountered as a label has no attributes to be entered into the table. How can this occur? If the associated operation is SET (define) or EQU (synonym). For the SET operation, the defining expression is evaluated and its attributes (e.g. address and relocatability mode) are entered into the table. This evaluation is similar to the evaluation of an address expression, which is described in the discussion of Pass 2. It is customary in a two-pass assembler to restrict the defining expression to contain no symbols which have themselves not yet been defined. Because of this restriction, the SET operation is most often used only to give symbolic names to constants.

If the label with no attributes is encountered in a synonym instruction EQU, it is possible to determine its attributes if the defining symbol has itself been previously defined. Because there is no guarantee, however, that referents of synonyms are defined in advance, a different approach is used uniformly for all occurrences of EQU. The label is entered into the symbol table and marked as being of type "EQU". The defining symbol is also placed in the same symbol table entry, perhaps in the address field if there is room. At the conclusion of Pass 1, the symbol table is scanned, and the defining symbol in each EQU type entry is replaced by a pointer to the table entry for the defining symbol. Thus all symbols defined as each other's synonyms are linked into a chain.

Whether or not a synonym function is provided, the symbol table can be scanned after the conclusion of Pass 1 for symbols without attributes.

Where encountered	Already in table?	Attributes in table?	Action taken
label	no		enter symbol and attributes
label	yes	no	enter attributes
label	yes	yes	*ERROR*: duplicate definition
operand	no		enter symbol
operand	yes		none

Figure 2.10   Rules for Constructing Symbol Table

These are flagged either as undefined symbols or as external symbols, accordingly as the explicit identification of external symbols is required or not. An alternative to the table scan after Pass 1 is to wait until Pass 2, when the absence of definition is obvious.

Location counter management is much simpler than symbol table construction. For a START operation the location counter is set either to the default (usually zero) or to a specified address; for an ORIGIN operation, to the specified address. For SPACE and CONST operations, the appropriate length is computed (if indeed any computation is necessary) and added to the location counter value in preparation for the next line. For other assembler instructions the location counter value remains unchanged. For a machine instruction, the instruction length is added to the location counter value. If instructions are of variable length, the operation code table will need to be consulted. For machines with storage alignment restrictions (e.g. IBM 360-370), an amount may need to be added to the location counter *before* associating its value with the current source line. If multiple location counters are provided, the foregoing description should be interpreted as referring to the location counter in use. The assembler instruction to change location counters merely selects the counter to be incremented subsequently.

Although location counter management and symbol table construction are the chief responsibilities of Pass 1, certain other functions are mandatory during that pass, and still others may optionally be performed during Pass 1 rather than Pass 2. A mandatory function which was not explicitly described in Section 2.3.1 is nevertheless implicit in any translation. This is the scanning of the source-language text to determine what it says. Both lexical and syntactic analysis are involved; they are discussed, not only for assemblers but for other translators as well, in Chapter 6.

Another mandatory function of Pass 1 is to examine operation fields sufficiently to determine the instruction length, which must be added to the location counter. If an operation code synonym facility (OPSYN) is provided, each OPSYN must be processed during the first pass to make the length of the defining instruction available. The OPSYN processing requires that an operation table entry be made either with a pointer to the defining operation code or with a duplicate of the table entry for the defining operation code. The remainder of operation code processing is optional during Pass 1, but is often included either a) if operation table lookup is performed anyway, or b) to effect the space saving of replacing the mnemonic operation code by the machine operation code. During Pass 1, then, the operation code may or may not be translated; determination of its format (if multiple formats exist) may or may not be performed.

Errors detected during Pass 1 must be recorded for incorporation in the listing. The generation of constants does not require a completed symbol table, and can be performed during either pass. The space required by the constants, however, does need to be determined during Pass 1 because of its effect on the location counter. Constant fields in an instruction often require little or no data conversion and may well be generated during Pass 1 if the instruction format has been determined.

Although it is possible to defer all processing of literals until Pass 2, unless LITORG is provided, it is usually more convenient to build the literal pool during Pass 1. Each time a literal is encountered, it is entered in a literal table, unless it is a duplicate of a literal already entered. Suppose that the character "@" marks a literal and that the following literals occur in the program in the order shown: @−1000, @1, @'TABLE', @12.75, @1, @3. Then the literal table might be organized as in Fig. 2.11, where lengths are given in bytes. Of course, it is not mandatory to eliminate duplicate literals, and some assemblers do generate a value for each occurrence of a given literal. The first literal of the pool can be assigned the address given by the value of the location counter at the conclusion of the first pass. Subsequent literals are assigned addresses determined by the lengths of the preceding literals.

Pass 1 typically transforms the source program into an *intermediate text* for input to Pass 2. Labels can be omitted, because code generation makes no use of them. Other symbols can be replaced, if desired, by pointers to the symbol table. The replacement is performed as each symbol is encountered, and is possible only if the symbol table construction algorithm does not change the position of a symbol once it has been entered. Although the use of pointers may result in some space savings, its chief advantage is elimination of table searching during Pass 2. In a similar manner, literals can be replaced by pointers to the literal table. Of course, if a source listing is to be produced, these labels, symbols, and literals cannot be discarded.

Although the symbols are no longer needed during Pass 2 for generating

Length	Value
4	−1000
4	1
5	'TABLE'
8	12.75
4	3

Figure 2.11 Example of Literal Table

code, they do serve another purpose, production of the concordance. This lists each symbol, the number of the source line on which it is defined, and the number of each line on which it is referenced. The attributes of each symbol are usually included also. For maximum usefulness, the concordance should be in alphabetic order. The required sorting of the symbol table can be performed at any time after the conclusion of Pass 1. A convenient time for an assembler which uses magnetic or paper tape is during tape rewind. If multitasking facilities are provided, sorting a copy of the symbol table can be assigned to a separate task to be executed concurrently with Pass 2. If symbols have been replaced by pointers in the intermediate text, sorting the symbol table will invalidate the pointers unless special action is taken. One solution is to keep an unsorted copy of the table for use in Pass 2. Another solution is based on use of the permutation vector generated by the sort process. An extra symbol table field stores, at a symbol's original position in the table, a pointer to its new position.

During Pass 2 the actual object code is generated. As the source (or intermediate) text is passed for a second time, the location counter is advanced just as it was during Pass 1. This time the purpose is not to assign addresses to symbols, but rather to incorporate addresses in the generated code. Operation codes are translated and instruction formats determined, to the extent that these functions were not carried out during Pass 1. Symbolic addresses which consist of a single symbol are easily handled. For a machine with direct or implicit-base addressing, the symbol is merely replaced by its location counter value from the symbol table. For a machine with explicit-base addressing, a base register table is used. Whenever a USING instruction is encountered during Pass 2, the number of the specified register and the promised value of its content are entered in the table. They remain until the content is changed by another USING or the register is deleted in response to a DROP. The symbol's location counter value *locn* is compared with the register content values *regc* listed in the base register table. There should be a register such that the displacement $disp = locn - regc$ falls in the appropriate range (0 to 4095 for the IBM 360-370). The value of *disp* and the number of the register are assembled into the object code. If there is more than one such register, then any one of them can be selected.

Addresses which correspond to redefinable local labels are easily generated during Pass 2 (or even Pass 1), provided that they are limited to backward references. For processing efficiency it is customary to use a fixed set of reserved symbols for this purpose. A fixed-size local label table holds the location counter value most recently associated with each redefinable symbol. Table lookup, whether for symbol redefinition or for address generation, is performed directly. Because no hashing or scan is required, this gains speed over use of the regular symbol table. Moreover, the existence of the small table of redefinable symbols permits substantial reduction in the size of the regular symbol table. This size reduction increases speed of access to regular symbols also.

Forward references to redefinable symbols cannot be resolved by the normal Pass 2 mechanism, because entries in the local label table are not fixed. The methods of Section 2.4 can be applied, however, as can the technique used in the UNISAP assembler for the Univac I. That assembler, apparently the first to provide redefinable local labels, used magnetic tape for the input, intermediate, and output texts. After the first pass, the intermediate text had to be repositioned for what we have described as Pass 2 processing. Instead of rewinding, the assembler made an extra pass, reading the intermediate tape backward. During this backward pass, what were originally forward references could be processed in the same manner as were backward references on a forward pass.

Address expressions are evaluated after lookup has determined the location counter value associated with each symbol. Thus LIMIT+3− FRONT in the context of the sample program of Section 2.2 would be evaluated as 31, and that value would be used in the instruction address field. A check must also be made that the address expression is not malformed with respect to relocatability; Chapter 8 explores that matter further.

Each reference to a literal is replaced by the address assigned to the corresponding entry in the literal table. The address correspondences can be established either between passes, or as the literals are encountered during Pass 2.

Other instruction fields, such as shift amounts, index register designations, and lengths, are usually stated explicitly as constants or as symbolic names which have been defined to represent constants. These are easily encoded. Sometimes an implicit specification (e.g. length in IBM 360-370) requires an attribute to be obtained from the symbol table.

The generation of data is another important responsibility of Pass 2. There is almost always a conversion from source-language encoding to machine encoding. The input form is generally a character string, composed perhaps of decimal digits, the period, plus and minus signs, and perhaps the letter E. The output form may be the machine encoding of a long-precision floating-point number, a short-precision integer, or a string of bits or of characters. For a rich assembler language, the description of data may well be expressed in what really amounts to a sublanguage of considerable size. The volume of assembler program code which performs the conversions may be very substantial indeed.

Whenever a CONST (or DC) instruction is encountered, the specified constant is generated at the attained point in the object code. For a SPACE (or DS) instruction, the assembler need only emit a directive to the loader to advance the location. As an alternative, the assembler can generate the required amount of fill, usually binary zeros. After the END instruction has been reached, the entries in the literal table are converted to machine encoding and appended. The alternative is to convert each literal as it is encountered, place the machine-representation literals in the literal table, and append the completed literal table to the end of the object code.

In generating the listing, the assembler needs access to the original text. It is possible, of course, to list the source text during Pass 1 and the object code during Pass 2, but the correspondences between the two representations then become difficult to establish. The listing normally includes source text image with line or sequence numbers, object code with location counter values, error messages, and a concordance. Assembler instructions which control printing may or may not be omitted from the listing, depending on the assembler. Whether to print them may itself be an option controlled by an assembler instruction! Much simpler for the assembler, of course, is to pass the needed files to a separate lister.

The object code produced by the assembler is still often called an object "deck", and may be said to be "punched" even on a system which uses backing storage rather than cards to hold the assembler output. The object code contains basically three kinds of information: machine-language code for the computer, address and relocation information for the loader, and a global symbol table for the linker. This last item may be a single table which includes both the symbols used within the module but not defined therein, and the symbols defined within the module and marked as being global. Alternatively, a separate table may be produced for each.

The organization of the assembler program must provide for a number of data structures. Among them are the following.

Pass 1 program
Pass 2 program
Source text
Intermediate text
Object text
Listing (if produced)
Symbol table
Global symbol table
Redefinable symbol table (if the function is provided)
Literal table
Machine instruction table

Assembler instruction table
Base register table (if explicit base registers are used)

The major differences among translation program organizations are determined by the choice of data structures to keep in main storage. The names of these choices customarily use the word "core" to refer to main storage, because of the widespread use of coincident-current magnetic cores to implement main storage. For many modern machines the term is technically not correct, but its brevity is appealing.

The *text-in-core* organization keeps the texts and tables in main storage and the programs in backing storage. Segments of the programs are brought in as needed. This organization is not very suitable for a two-pass program structure, but is often used for compilation programs, which may be composed of dozens of *phases*.

The *translator-in-core* organization keeps the Pass 1 and Pass 2 programs in main storage, along with the tables. The texts reside in backing storage. This organization is more suitable for an assembler, because the texts need to be accessed only serially, whereas such is not true of the program.

The *all-in-core* organization is just what its name implies. It is applicable, however, only if there is room for everything. This organization is typical of load-and-go assemblers, which are discussed in Section 2.4.1. It can be used, given enough space, for a two-pass assembler.

A typical organization for a two-pass assembler combines the translator-in-core approach with the provision of space for only the currently active pass. The texts are maintained in backing storage. The program starts with the Pass 1 program and tables in main storage and, after the termination of Pass 1, overwrites the Pass 1 program with the Pass 2 program, which has been waiting meanwhile in backing storage. The total main storage requirement is minimized by making the programs for the two passes approximately equal in size. This is accomplished by suitable allocation of those functions which can be performed on either pass.

2.4 ONE-PASS ASSEMBLERS

The translation performed by an assembler is essentially a collection of substitutions: machine operation code for mnemonic, machine address for symbolic, machine encoding of a number for its character representation, etc. Except for one factor, these substitutions could all be performed in one sequential pass over the source text. That factor is the forward reference. The separate passes of the two-pass assembler are required to handle forward references without restriction. If certain limitations are imposed, however, it becomes possible to handle forward references without making two passes. Different sets of restrictions lead to the one-pass module assembler and to the load-and-go assembler. These one-pass assemblers are particularly attractive when secondary storage is either slow or missing entirely, as on many small machines. The manual handling of punched cards or paper tape between passes is eliminated by eliminating a pass.

2.4.1 *Load-and-Go Assembler*

The *load-and-go* assembler forgoes the production of object code to generate absolute machine code and load it into the physical main storage locations from which it will be executed immediately upon completion of the assembly. The following restrictions are imposed by this mode of translation. (1) The program must run in a set of locations fixed at translation time; there is no relocation. (2) The program cannot be combined with one which has been translated separately. (3) Sufficient space is required in main storage to hold both the assembler and the machine-language program. Load-and-go assemblers are rather attractive for most student jobs, which are typically small and subject to frequent change.

Because the assembled program is in main storage, the assembler can fill in each forward reference as its definition is encountered. To do this, it is necessary to record the references to each undefined symbol. Because the number of such references is unpredictable, it is most convenient to organize the information as a chain. Each element of the chain includes a sign (to indicate whether the undefined symbol appears positively or negatively), the main storage location of the corresponding address field in the assembled program, and a pointer to the succeeding element in the chain for the same symbol. The last element includes a null pointer; a pointer to the first element (the head of the chain) occupies the symbol table entry for the undefined symbol.

The first occurrence of an undefined symbol causes the symbol to be entered in the symbol table, marked as undefined, with a pointer to a one-element chain. Each successive occurrence causes a new element to be inserted between the symbol table entry and the head of the previously created chain. The operand field which contains an undefined symbol is replaced in the assembled program by the value of those parts of the address expression other than undefined symbols. That value is zero, of course, if the operand consists of the undefined symbol alone. Figure 2.12

shows a portion of an assembler language program which makes forward references. Location counter values have been supplied. They are labeled "location" rather than "address" because for a load-and-go assembler they really do refer to physical storage locations.

The generated code (based on Fig. 2.3), symbol table, and undefined symbol chains are shown in Fig. 2.13 as they stand after the STORE instruction has been translated. In the illustration, chain elements are assumed to require two words each, with space starting at location 120 available for the chain. Other implementations of the chain are also possible.

Location	Label	Operation	Operand 1
12		READ	PV
--		---	
47		LOAD	PV
49		ADD	THERM+1
51		STORE	PV
--		---	
92	PV	SPACE	
93	THERM	CONST	386.2
94		CONST	374.9

Figure 2.12   Input to Load-and-Go Assembler (location added)

Location	Machine code
12	12 00
--	---
47	03 00
49	02 01
51	07 00

(a) Assembled program

Symbol	Marker	Address
PV	undefined	126
THERM	undefined	124

(b) Symbol table

Location	Sign	Address	Pointer
120	+	13	null
122	+	48	120
124	+	50	null
126	+	52	122

(c) Undefined symbol chains

Figure 2.13   Data Structures after Translation of Location 51

When the definition of a previously referenced symbol is finally encountered, its storage location is added to or subtracted from the machine code which has already been generated at the location specified in each element of the associated chain, as directed by the element's sign field. When the end of the chain is reached, the mark in the symbol table entry is reset from "undefined" to "defined", and the pointer to the first chain element is replaced by the symbol's absolute location, which is the now-known location counter value. The space occupied by the undefined symbol chain is returned to the available space list for further use. The generated code and symbol table are shown in Fig. 2.14 as they stand after the symbol THERM has been processed. The entry "XX" for the machine code generated at location 92 indicates that the content of that location is unspecified.

A particularly economical implementation of the chain of undefined symbols stores the pointers within the partially translated program itself. The operand field which contains an undefined symbol is replaced in the assembled program by a pointer to the previous use of that symbol. Because this precludes making any provision for other parts of an address expression, a further restriction is necessary. Undefined symbols may then not appear in address expressions. Thus BR REPLACE+6 is permitted only if REPLACE occurs as a label earlier in the source program.

Although there is, to be sure, no full Pass 2, the load-and-go assembler is not really a pure one-pass assembler. The chain-following actions really do constitute partial second passes. Because the portions of the program which they examine are necessarily still in main storage, the cost often associated with a conventional second pass is nevertheless avoided.

Location	Machine code	Symbol	Marker	Address
12	12 92	PV	defined	92
--	---	THERM	defined	93
47	03 92			
49	02 94			
51	07 92			
--	---			
92	XX			
93	386.2			

(a) Assembled program   (b) Symbol table

Figure 2.14   Data Structures after Translation of Location 93

2.4.2 *One-Pass Module Assembler*

A *module* assembler, unlike a load-and-go assembler, produces not machine code, but rather object code which can later be linked and loaded. The one-pass module assembler purports to accomplish this in a single pass, despite forward references. The strategy is to rely on the pass which will eventually be made over the program by the loader, and to use that as the second assembler pass for those functions which just cannot be performed in one pass. Thus more work is imposed on the loader, but the assembler requires only one pass. The restriction typically imposed on source programs is the prohibition of forward references other than branches. Thus data areas precede the instructions which reference them, and literals cannot be used.

Each undefined symbol must occur in a branch address. It is entered in a *branch-ahead table* along with its sign and the address of the instruction address field in which it appears. If several branches are expected to refer to the same undefined symbol, the branch-ahead table could be implemented as a collection of chains similar to the undefined symbol chains described in Section 2.4.1. Because the number of branches to undefined symbols is usually not great, however, it is probably simpler to omit the pointers and just use a conventional table. Each time a label is encountered, the symbol and its attributes are entered into the symbol table. The branch-ahead table is then scanned for all occurrences of that symbol. For each occurrence, the assembler first generates a directive to the loader to adjust the corresponding address field when the program is loaded, and then deletes the entry from the branch-ahead table.

FOR FURTHER STUDY

Barron [1972] is an excellent short book on simple and macro assemblers, loaders, and linkers. Its Chapters 2, 4, and 6 are devoted particularly to assemblers. Two good brief treatments of assemblers are Chapter 4 of Ullman [1976] and Section 8.3 of Brooks and Iverson [1969], which is insightful but specialized to the IBM 360. More extensive presentations are in Chapter 9 of Gear [1974] and Chapter 4 of Graham [1975].

EXERCISES

2.1 What program development costs rise faster than proportionally to the length of a program component?

2.2 Rewrite the program of Fig. 2.2 in a form which makes no forward references to either instructions or data.

2.3 Assemble the following program manually, showing the resulting object code and the symbol table. Use starting location 100.

```
              READ    N
              COPY    ONE     FACT
              COPY    ONE     IDX
HEAD          LOAD    N
              SUB     IDX
              BRZERO  ALL
              BRNEG   ALL
              LOAD    IDX
              ADD     ONE
              STORE   IDX
              MULT    FACT
              STORE   FACT
              BR      HEAD
ALL           WRITE   FACT
              STOP
N             SPACE
IDX           SPACE
FACT          SPACE
ONE           CONST   1
```

2.4 Disassemble the following object code manually, showing a possible assembler-language representation and the symbol table. Be a careful detective in analyzing the last line.

```
        00      3       13 22 23
        03      2       12 24
        05      2       03 24
        07      2       05 21
        09      2       06 23
        11      2       01 15
        13      2       00 03
        15      2       03 24
        17      2       07 23
        19      2       00 03
        21      1       11
        22      1       00
        23      2       08 03
```

2.5 Let @ mark a literal and A(symbol) be an address constant. Using Fig. 2.3, show the generated code which corresponds to the following source text.

```
              LOAD    @A(FRONT)
              ADD     @3
              STORE   NEXT
FRONT         CONST   99
NEXT          SPACE
```

2.6   Explain why the four occurrences of "XX" cannot be omitted from the end of the machine code in the last paragraph of Section 2.2.2.

2.7   Write an address expression to designate the start of the Jth full word of the six full words in the area reserved by the IBM 360 Assembler instruction WORK   DS   15D,6F   (see "Storage Reservation" in Section 2.3.1).

2.8   Let @ mark a literal and A(symbol) be an address constant. Using Fig. 2.3, show the generated object code which corresponds to the following source text. (The program is not intended to be useful.)

```
                READ    OFFSET
                LOAD    OFFSET
                ADD     @A(FAR)
                STORE   NEAR
                BR      FAR+1
        NEAR    SPACE
        OFFSET  SPACE
        FAR     CONST   A(NEAR)
```

2.9   Let EQU be a synonym facility, SET a definition facility, and ∗ the current value of the location counter. Explain (a) the difference between the following instructions, and (b) how each can be implemented in a two-pass assembler.

```
        BACK6   EQU     *-6
        BACK6   SET     *-6
```

2.10   Consider the chain of symbols which are defined by a synonym facility to be equivalent. Why is the chain usually not constructed during Pass 1 as the symbols are read?

2.11   Let OPSYN be the operation code synonym facility mentioned in the third paragraph under "Alternate Names" in Section 2.3.1.
a) How is it distinct from EQU or SET?
b) How can it be implemented?
c) Why is it advantageous to require *all* occurrences of OPSYN to precede *any* instructions?

2.12   What are the advantages and disadvantages of holding symbolic operation codes in the main symbol table?

2.13   Let LITORG be an instruction to assign the current location counter value as the origin of a literal pool. Design an implementation of literals, including LITORG, and state precisely and fully what actions are performed during each pass. Make sure that your implementation is capable of handling the following situation (where @ marks a literal).

```
        ---      @A(PLACE)
        ---
        LITORG
        ---
PLACE   ---
```

2.14 Design an implementation of literals (without LITORG) which does all the processing on Pass 2.

2.15 [Donovan] Explain how to process LITORG on Pass 1 only, given that address constants are not permitted.

2.16 Suppose that a program contains both the literal @3 and an instruction C3 CONST 3. Is it permissible to assign the same location to the literal as to C3?

2.17 How can an assembler be designed to permit the use in a literal of a symbol defined by the SET instruction to represent a given value, as in the following?

```
LIMIT   SET     4
        ---
        ADD     @LIMIT
        ---
LIMIT   SET     6
        ---
        DIVIDE  @LIMIT
```

2.18 If the intermediate text contains pointers to the symbol table, can the symbols themselves be dropped from the table before Pass 2?

2.19 [Donovan] To permit a two-pass assembler to generate code for absolute loading (i.e. without relocation), the assembler instruction ABS has been defined. Its one operand specifies the execution-time physical location of the origin of the module being assembled. Where may the ABS instruction appear in the source program? On which pass(es) would the ABS be processed and how?

2.20 How can literals be processed by a load-and-go assembler?

2.21 Consider the translation of the program of Fig. 2.2 by a load-and-go assembler. Assume starting location 0. Show the data structures, as in Figs. 2.12-2.14,
a) after the translation of line 5;
b) after the translation of line 14;
c) after the translation of line 21.

2.22 Consider the translation of the program of Fig. 2.2 by a load-and-go assembler which uses the implementation described in the penultimate paragraph of Section 2.4.1. Assuming starting location 100, show the symbol table and the assembled machine-language program

a) after the translation of line 5;
b) after the translation of line 18.

2.23 Let the operand in location 50 of Fig. 2.12 be changed to THERM. Illustrate the implementation described in the penultimate paragraph of Section 2.4.1 by showing the assembled program and symbol table
a) after the translation of location 50;
b) after the translation of location 92.

2.24 Why must a one-pass module assembler forgo literals?

2.25 How can a one-pass module assembler handle branches to external symbols?

Chapter 3

PROGRAM MODULES

A computer program is often constructed of a number of subprograms or *modules*, which may be written more or less independently of each other and can often be translated separately and combined after translation. In discussions of software engineering, the term "module" often denotes an assignment in the division of programming responsibility or a unit in the subdivision of the functional specifications of a program. It will be used here in a more limited sense to denote a program unit which could be translated independently of other units. Examples include a procedure in Algol, Pascal, or PL/I, a user-defined function in APL, and a "control section" in IBM 360–370 assembler language. Several properties of such modules affect the translation process. Among them are the degree of reusability of a module, the structural relations among modules, the way a module is invoked, and the type of correspondence of formal to actual parameters.

3.1 DEGREES OF REUSABILITY

The extent to which a program module can be executed more than once with the same effect each time is known as its degree of *reusability.* Four degrees of reusability are distinguished. A module may be *nonreusable, serially reusable, reenterable,* or *recursive*. The classification of a module is determined both by its source-language formulation and its ultimate machine-language representation. A *nonreusable* module does not incorporate initialization of values changed by the module. Each execution of the module may therefore yield a different result. A *serially reusable* module does incorporate the required initialization. If one execution of it is terminated before another is begun, each execution will have the same result. A *reenterable* module is a serially reusable module which incorporates no modification of itself during execution. Consequently, multiple instances of execution will yield the same result even if one instance has not terminated before the next has begun. A *recursive* module is a module having the property that one cause of multiple instances of execution is the module itself.

Source-language differences corresponding to the four levels of reusability are shown in the procedures of Fig. 3.1. Each procedure is intended to return the value of n factorial $(1 \times 2 \times .. \times n)$ for a nonnegative integer argument n. Procedure F is nonreusable. It returns the correct value only if the global variables i and r both have value 1 when F is invoked. If they do have these values, then F (3) will indeed return the correct value 6. But a second call F (3) which is preceded by setting i and r to values other than 1 will return an incorrect value. The resulting lack of reproducibility is a disqualification for most programs, but there is at least one application for which it is not only welcome but mandatory. A pseudorandom number generator must indeed yield reproducible *sequences* of numbers to permit testing and debugging, but successive calls to the generator must certainly not always return the same value. A more homely example is an input routine, which delivers different data upon each invocation.

```
procedure F (n) integer
    integer n
    begin
        while i < n do
            i ← 1 + i
            r ← i × r
        return r
    end

                Nonreusable
```

```
procedure FA (n) integer
    integer n
    begin
        i ← 1
        r ← 1
        while i < n do
            i ← 1 + i
            r ← i × r
        return r
    end

                Serially Reusable
```

```
procedure FAC (n) integer
    integer n
    integer i, r
    begin
        i ← 1
        r ← 1
        while i < n do
            i ← 1 + i
            r ← i × r
        return r
    end
                Reenterable
```

```
procedure FACT (n) integer
    integer n
    integer r
    begin
        r ← if n < 2
            then 1
            else n × FACT (n−1)
        return r
    end

                Recursive
```

Figure 3.1   Programs for Computing n Factorial

Procedure *FA* incorporates the initialization of *i* and *r*. It is serially reusable; a second call *FA* (3) will return the same value 6 as does the first, regardless of any changes which may occur to the values of *i* and *r* between executions of *FA*. Suppose, however, that execution of *FA* (3) is suspended within the loop but just prior to entering the loop body with both *i* and *r* equal to 2, and that the call *FA* (4) is then executed in its entirety, while execution of the first call remains suspended. The effect of executing this second call will be to set *i* to 4 and *r* to 24, returning the correct value. Execution of the first call, *FA* (3), would then resume from the loop body, incrementing *i* to 5 and assigning 120 to *r*. The condition $i < n$ would not be satisfied, and execution of the first call, *FA* (3), would terminate with a return of the incorrect value 120. The reusability of the module is thus seen to be serial reusability only.

Procedure *FAC* is reenterable, because it can be reentered by a second instance of execution before termination of a prior instance, yet without producing incorrect results. This feat is accomplished by making values changed by the module *local* to the module. This is indicated in most programming languages by placing declarations of variables within the module, as is done for *i* and *r* in the example. A repetition of the previous scenario, in which the execution of *FAC* (3) is suspended to permit the evaluation of *FAC* (4), succeeds because *each* instance of execution of *FAC* has its own copies of the variables named *i* and *r*. A reenterable program can thus be shared by many users. Separate data areas are required for each user, but a single copy of the procedure code suffices. A reenterable module is therefore sometimes called a "pure" procedure; another common designation is "reentrant". Even if sharing is not contemplated, reenterable code is normally preferred over code which is only serially reusable, because it is usually easier to read and to verify.

Procedure *FACT* is recursive because it calls itself. Execution of *FACT* (3) invokes another instance of *FACT* with 2 as the argument, and this second execution results in the call *FACT* (1). The nesting of invocations stops at this point, because *FACT* (1) is evaluated as 1 without the issuance of a further call of *FACT*. Because each instance of *FACT* has its own value for the formal parameter *n*, the three instances of execution do not interfere with each other. Thus the second instance, with $n=2$, receives the value 1 from the call *FACT* (1), multiplies it by 2, and returns the product 2 as the value of *FACT* (2) requested by the original instance of *FACT* with argument 3. The parameters passed from one instance of execution to another, as well as the return address of each instance, must not be modified during execution. In practice, most recursive modules, like *FACT*, are fully reenterable. Anything which can be computed recursively – with the possible exception of some functions not classed as "primitive recursive" –

can also be computed iteratively. The programming may nevertheless be considerably easier if recursion is used. The Towers of Hanoi provide a good example, as do many algorithms for traversing binary trees.

Reentrant and recursive execution require that the changeable information associated with a partially executed module be stored separately for each instance of execution, or activation, of the module. The storage area used is called an *activation record*. All activations of a module share a common area of fixed information, but each has a distinct activation record. The reentrant execution of three activations of a module is depicted in Fig. 3.2.

The state of each activation can be determined by use of a conceptual *state word* which holds (1) the address, in the fixed area, of the next instruction to be executed by that activation, and (2) the location of the corresponding activation record. During execution of a module, the pointers which constitute the state word are stored in the processing unit. The instruction counter holds the instruction address; the activation record address is held in a base register or other easily accessible location. When processing

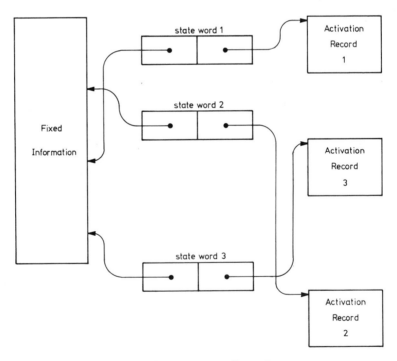

Figure 3.2   Reentrant Execution

is interrupted, the instruction address is stored in the activation record. The operating system maintains the list of activation record addresses to assist in making transitions between activations.

The use of a stack of activation records to implement recursion is diagrammed in Fig. 3.3. A procedure P has invoked the recursive program of Fig. 3.1 with the call $FACT$ (3). An activation record is shown for P; virtually all detail has been suppressed. The call $FACT$ (3) has created the adjacent activation record for $FACT$ with the value 3 assigned to the parameter n, but no values associated yet with either $FACT$ $(n-1)$ or r. The number 7 is the address* of the instruction (number of the statement in Fig. 3.1) from which execution is to resume in the same first activation of $FACT$ after execution of the recursive call $FACT$ (2) has terminated.

The activation record for $FACT$ is stacked above that for P with a back pointer to permit control to be returned to P after execution of $FACT$ has terminated. The second call, $FACT$ (2), has created the second activation

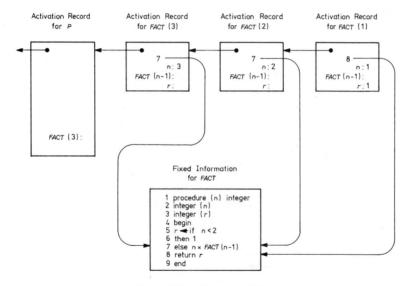

Figure 3.3 Recursion Stack

---

*This is a simplification, of course, because processing resumes from *within* statement 7. If we assume $FACT$ to have been translated before execution, then processing resumes not merely from within a statement, but from a particular machine-language instruction. The activation record would hold not the numeral 7, but rather the location of that instruction.

record for *FACT*, identical to the first except for the pointer used to direct return of control not to *P* but to the first activation of *FACT*. The third activation record for *FACT* was created when the second executed the call *FACT* (1). The status of that third *FACT* module is shown after the value 1 has been assigned to *r* but before the return of control at statement 8. When control is returned, that value 1 will be placed in the cell allocated for *FACT* $(n-1)$ in the previous activation record, and the second instance of execution will resume at the multiplication in statement 7. The record of the third activation of *FACT* can then be deleted, i.e. popped off the stack. Subsequent assignment of 2 to *r* in the second activation of *FACT* will permit that activation to terminate and the first to resume. Eventually the value 6 will have been computed for *FACT* (3) and delivered to procedure *P*. The stack of activation records for *FACT* will have shrunk back to empty, its state prior to the call *FACT* (3).

The management of activation records for recursive or reenterable modules must be performed directly by the assembler-language programmer, but the user of a higher-level language expects the translator to handle the details automatically. It is particularly important in allocating space for the different activation records of a recursive routine to ensure that they are indeed assigned different locations in storage, even though all invocations but the first may be performed by executing the same calling sequence. This is typically accomplished by issuing, when the recursive call is encountered at execution time, a request to the operating system to provide a distinct storage area. In an assembler-language program, the programmer may either include such requests to the operating system, or manage a stack for the parameters and return addresses.

Recursion is not limited to one procedure calling itself directly. If *A* calls *B* and *B* calls *A*, then one call of *A* can ultimately engender another call of *A*, and the property of recursion holds for *A* (as it does also for *B*). A formal definition of recursion among a set of modules is possible, but it will be adequate for us to consider the call structure to be recursive if there exists a module whose execution can result in a call of itself.

A call statement existing in a program text may or may not actually be executed when the program is run. It is thus possible to distinguish between a *potential* call (existing in the text at translation time) and an *actual* call (performed at execution time), hence between potentially and actually recursive modules. The detection of potential recursion is possible at translation time, and is performed most readily if all of the modules are compiled at one time. This detection by the compiler is obviated, however, if each recursive module is declared by the programmer to be recursive.

3.2 BLOCK STRUCTURE

Many programming languages are endowed with a feature known as *block structure*, which controls the scope of names and also subdivides programs into modules. The provision of block structure restricts the program extent within which an identifier is known, the so-called *scope* of the identifier. Because different locations in the program lie within the scopes of different sets of identifiers, they are said to have different *environments*. The program text is explicitly divided by the programmer into units generically called *blocks*, although various names are used for the blocks in different languages. Examples are BEGIN blocks in PL/I, procedures in Algol, and user-defined functions in APL. Some languages (e.g. PL/I) have more than one type of block.

Two blocks in the static text of the program are either disjoint, having no portion in common, or nested, one block completely enclosing the other. This *static nesting* of blocks in the text is distinct from the *dynamic nesting* of block activations during execution. The program of Fig. 3.4(a) illustrates both kinds of nesting. There are 3 blocks, procedures *A*, *B*, and *C*. In the static text, blocks *B* and *C* are disjoint, and each is enclosed in block *A*. If block *A* is activated first and all the calls shown are executed, then *A* will activate *C*, which will in turn activate *B*. When *B* has finished executing, it will return control to *C*, and *C* will eventually return control to *A*. Thus the dynamic nesting changes dynamically with time, reaching a maximum depth of 3 while *B* is active.

The static nesting structure of text embedding can be represented by a fixed tree of blocks in which the ancestor of each block other than a root is the immediately enclosing block. The tree need not actually be drawn as a directed graph, and the notation of Fig. 3.4(b) is often convenient. The dynamic nesting structure of activations can be represented by a stack of activation records which grows upon entry to an inner level of dynamic nesting and shrinks on exit therefrom. A single diagram can capture the dynamic stack at only one moment; the one chosen in Fig. 3.4(c) is that during execution of block *B*.

If an identifier is known anywhere within a block, it is known throughout the block. Thus the block is the unit for determining scope of identifiers and for describing the environment. An identifier which is either declared within a block or named as a formal parameter of the block is obviously known, and is said to be *local* to that block because knowledge of it derives from within the block. A local identifier is not known outside the block to which it is local. Alternatively, knowledge of an identifer may be imposed

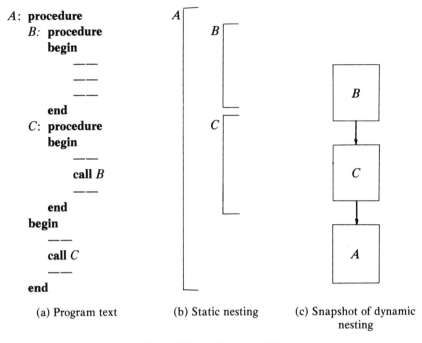

(a) Program text   (b) Static nesting   (c) Snapshot of dynamic
                                                           nesting

Figure 3.4   A Block-Structured Program

on a block from outside the block. Such an identifier is said to be *global* with respect to that block, although it may be local to some enclosing block. An identifier of which a block has no knowledge may be termed *unknown* to the block.

The rules for determining scope of identifiers vary somewhat among block-structured languages, but it is possible to describe a typical set of rules, based on static nesting. Subject to an exception about to be described, an identifier is local to the block in which it is declared (or named as a formal parameter), global to all blocks directly or indirectly nested within that block, i.e. *contained* inside it and unknown elsewhere. Thus in Fig. 3.5(a) the variable x is local to block A and global to the other four blocks. Variable y, on the other hand, is local to block B, hence unknown to A and C, and global to D and E. The scope of either variable is the set of blocks to which it is not unknown.

The exception to the foregoing rule occurs when an identifier local to a given block has the same name as an identifier local to a contained block. The identifier which is local to the inner block can be thought of as *masking*

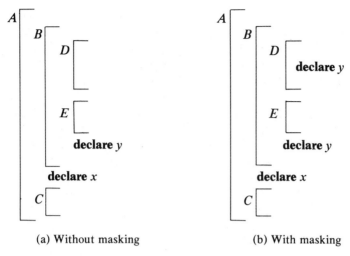

(a) Without masking   (b) With masking

Figure 3.5   Scope of Identifiers

knowledge of the other identifier, which would otherwise be global to the inner block. Thus in Fig. 3.5(b) the variable y declared in block B is no longer global to D, as it is in (a), because it is masked by the variable y declared in D. There are two distinct identifiers y in the program. The scope of one is blocks B and E; the scope of the other is block D. Both identifiers y are unknown in blocks A and C.

In determining the environment of a block it is necessary to proceed from that block outward through successive levels of static nesting. Consider references within block D of Fig. 3.5(b) to identifiers x and y. Because y is local to D, the description of y is immediately available. Identifier x, on the other hand, is not local to D, and it is necessary to look outside D to find its description. The immediately containing block B is examined, but no description of x is found. The description of y which does occur in B is not relevant to the search, because of masking; it describes a variable other than the y which is referenced within D. The search for x continues with examination of the next outer block A, where the description is indeed found.

Just as representation of the dynamic nesting of activations is required at execution time to permit control to be returned from a dying block to its activator, so is representation of the static nesting of blocks necessary at execution time for accessing nonlocal identifiers. One possible solution is to consider the activation records as the nodes of the active portion of the static tree structure and to supply for each a *static link* to point to its enclosing ancestor. To show the dynamic stack structure a *dynamic link* can be used. These two sets of links are illustrated in Fig. 3.6. The static program structure is shown in (a). It is assumed that blocks *A, B, C, D,* and *E* are activated in that sequence and that *E* is a procedure which calls itself recursively. The execution-time representation is depicted in (b) at a time during execution of the third instance of *E*. The dynamic links are shown on the left, the static links on the right. The set of static links which can be followed from the currently active record constitutes the *static chain*.

An alternative to the static chain is the *current-environment vector,* or *display*. This is a variable-length vector of pointers to the currently accessible activation records, ordered by level in the static tree structure. The

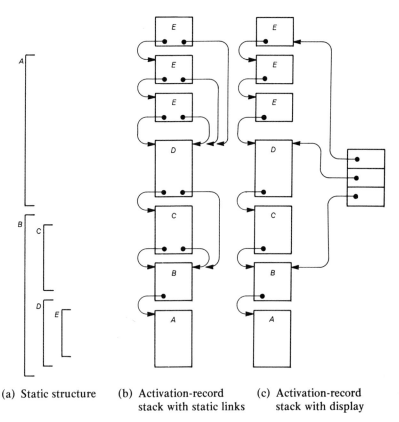

(a) Static structure   (b) Activation-record   (c) Activation-record
                              stack with static links   stack with display

Figure 3.6   Run-Time Representation of Nesting

activation-record stack of Fig. 3.6(b) is redrawn in Fig. 3.6(c) with a display instead of a static chain.

The program translator must generate code to use the dynamic link in returning control and to use the environment representation (display or static chain) in accessing nonlocal identifiers. It must also generate code to set the appropriate pointer values on entry to each newly activated block, and to reset them on exit. This matter is examined further in Chapter 7.

3.3   MODES OF ACTIVATION

A program module can be activated in at least six ways, almost each of which is associated with a different type of module. The simplest module is the *BEGIN block* of PL/I. Execution begins when the instructions in the block are encountered by normal progression from earlier instructions. Execution terminates when normal progression leads to an instruction outside the block. A major purpose of the BEGIN block is to provide nesting in the static text of the program, thus delimiting the scope of source language names. Even more important is the deferral of storage allocation for AUTOMATIC variables. For these purposes, a separate activation record is required. It is created upon entry to the BEGIN block, stacked above the activation record of the enclosing block, and deleted upon exit from the BEGIN block.

A widely used type of module is the *subroutine*, with which all but the greenest of computer programmers are familiar. Associated with the subroutine, or *called procedure*, is a *calling block* to which it is subordinated in an asymmetric relation of dependence. Execution begins upon specific naming of the called procedure by the calling block and, upon termination, control is returned to the caller. An activation record for the called procedure is created upon invocation, stacked above that for the calling block, and destroyed upon termination. For intermodule communication, parameters can be passed from the calling to the called module. The mechanisms for invoking a subroutine, passing parameters, and returning control are referred to collectively as *subroutine linkage*. Issues in subroutine linkage are treated in Section 3.4.

The *interrupt function module* is also invoked asymmetrically, either explicitly or, more commonly, in response to the occurrence of some stated condition during execution of the calling block. The archetypal example is the ON unit of PL/I, activated by the SIGNAL statement or by detection of the status associated with an ON condition. There are no parameters. The principal problem in programming with interrupt function modules is the opacity of programs which incorporate them. The principal problem in translating programs which incorporate interrupt function modules is the need to make references which transgress the usual limits of scope. Consider, for example, the following fragment of program text.

```
A: BEGIN;
   ---
   ON condition-name ...
   ---
   CALL B;
   ---
END A;
B: PROCEDURE;
   ---
   condition-name occurs
   ---
```

The activation record for block B must incorporate a reference to the interrupt function module in block A, even though the text within block A is not in B's environment. This permits an activation record for the ON unit to be constructed if the ON condition is raised. Moreover, if block A contains two calls of B, each preceded by a different ON unit, then the reference must be different for each call.

Unlike the subroutine, which is subordinate to its caller, the *coroutine* is a module coordinate with other modules. Whereas a subroutine *call* creates an activation record for the subroutine, and return of control from the subroutine to its caller destroys the activation record, a coroutine *resume* neither creates nor destroys an activation record. Execution of the coroutine is merely resumed from wherever it last left off, rather than from a fixed entry or reentry point. Its activation record must therefore store the current restart point. Coroutine invocation is thus seen to be symmetric.

Because coroutines are symmetric, and the management of a stack is asymmetric, coroutine activation records cannot share a stack. Instead, each coroutine activation record occupies the bottom of its own stack, which grows and shrinks as the coroutine invokes its own subroutines or enters BEGIN blocks, and as those modules activate yet others or terminate. Thus the execution-time representation of coroutines requires multiple stacks.

Creation of a coroutine activation record is caused by an initial invocation distinct from the resume. This initial call may be termed an *allocate* because it allocates an activation record. Deletion of the coroutine activation record may occur either automatically upon the coroutine executing its last instruction or explicitly as the result of a *free* command in another module, typically the one which caused the activation record to be created.

Parameters can be passed to a coroutine, just as they can to a subroutine, but at a choice of times. The values of actual parameters can be passed in the allocate call, or else in the first resume which follows allocation. It may even be possible to pass parameters with each resume.

The original illustration of coroutines [Conway, 1963] is a program for printing characters read from cards, with the substitution of the single character "↑" for each occurrence of the character pair "**", which represents exponentiation. An "asterisk squasher" coroutine interacts with a coroutine which provides the next input character.

Coroutines can sometimes be substituted for a multipass algorithm. Figure 3.7 depicts in (a) an algorithm which makes three successive passes over a sequential file. In the coroutine implementation (b), coroutine *A* resumes coroutine *B* when Pass 1 would have written a record to the first intermediate file; coroutine *B* resumes *A* when Pass 2 would have read a record and resumes *C* when Pass 2 would have written a record to the second intermediate file; coroutine *C* resumes *B* when Pass 3 would have read a record. The one-pass coroutine algorithm saves the time needed to pack, write, read, and unpack the intermediate data records. It requires enough space, however, to hold all the programs at once. Some algorithms, of course, are essentially multipass and cannot conveniently be replaced by coroutines.

Coroutines provide synchronization among interleaved cooperating processes. The processes may appear to be concurrent, but are not, because

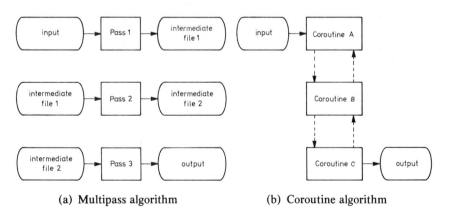

(a) Multipass algorithm   (b) Coroutine algorithm

Figure 3.7   Alternative Algorithms

only one is in execution at a time. Coroutines do provide, however, for the efficient simulation of concurrent processes and are so used in the language SIMULA, where the coroutines are known as *classes* or *activities*. Simple examples in which coroutines are clearly more efficient than subroutines are difficult to produce; meaningful examples tend to be rather complex. This is perhaps one reason why other languages do not provide coroutines, and why the use of coroutines appears to be a neglected art.

A fifth mode of activation can be superimposed on subroutines or coroutines. Each module, instead of issuing a call, return, or resume command, issues instead a *scheduling* command. This is a request to the operating system's process scheduler for a call, return, or resume to be issued. Use of this control program component to determine execution sequence can result in greater efficiency of resource utilization. In this mode, program modules are often called *events*, and scheduling information for each event whose execution has been requested is an *event notice*. Whenever execution of one event ceases, control is passed to the scheduler, which examines the event notices and selects one event for execution. The search over all event notices can be traded for extra processing time earlier to insert each event notice into an *event queue*, ordered on some criterion, such as simulated time, or a dispatching priority. Event queues provide for global supervision of the scheduling of module activation.

Events are executed consecutively as the result of scheduled invocations. Unscheduled sequencing, a sixth mode, may be used instead when multiple processing units are available to provide true concurrency rather than only interleaving. A module can invoke another module to be executed in parallel with the instruction sequence which follows the invocation, often termed an *attach* invocation. In this situation, the sequence of execution of the different modules is unspecified, whereas for coroutines it is specified by the resumes and for events by the scheduler. This absence of sequence specification raises important problems of synchronization, solutions to which are discussed in books on operating systems.

The attachment of a module in parallel is represented by the bifurcation of the activation-record stack. Both the original parent module and the newly attached child module can continue to invoke subroutines, each on its own partial stack. If a child attaches children of its own, further bifurcation results. The partial stacks may or may not have independent lives, depending upon whether a child module is required to expire before its parent. When either a parent or its child terminates, the previously forked stack loses a tine.

Another form of concurrent execution is specified by such constructions as the **cobegin-coend** pair of some languages. Because the enclosed parallel instruction streams share the same environment, it might appear that distinct activation records are not needed. But synchronization statements within those streams may require one stream to become temporarily inactive. It is thus appropriate to have for each stream a different activation record, even though all incorporate the same values of the static link and dynamic link.

3.4 SUBROUTINE LINKAGE

When one module calls or resumes another, it communicates information by means of parameters and preserves enough status information to permit its own resumption. This activity is termed *linkage*, and must not be confused with the "linkage" performed by the linker in binding intermodule symbolic references. The linkage with which we are concerned here is performed at execution time, by executing instructions which have been prepared by the translator. Although linkage applies to coroutines as well as to subroutines, the ensuing description is couched in terms of subroutines. The changes required for coroutines are for the most part straightforward.

The four most common ways to transmit and receive parameters are the following. A *common data* area for parameters can be shared by both calling and called routines. The use of storage which is global to the two routines requires that both use the same names or addresses, which are external references, to access the parameters. The advantage of using such global variables for communication is simplicity. Disadvantages are the need to know external names, the time to translate external references, and, in some systems, particularly those with explicit-base addressing, restrictions on addressability.

Processing unit *registers,* if available in the machine, provide another locus for parameters. This, too, permits simple communication as long as the registers are not needed for other purposes. Disadvantages are that several registers are likely to be needed for frequently used values such as increments and limits, for the return address, and perhaps for base-register addressing. The consequence may be fewer available registers than parameters to be passed.

All parameters for one call can be grouped into a *parameter area* in storage, and its starting address passed to the called routine. This has the advantages of keeping the registers free and of being easy to implement. The need to pass an address is at worst a minor disadvantage, and the use of a parameter area is often attractive.

A *shared stack* of parameters works as follows. The calling routine transmits the parameters by pushing them onto the stack. The called routine receives the parameters by popping them from the stack. Prior to returning control, it can push them back on if necessary. Subroutines nested dynamically at multiple levels can share a single stack. Advantages of the shared stack are that it can consume less storage space than separate parameter areas and that it is convenient for recursive calls. One disadvantage is the execution time required. A more serious disadvantage is the need to provide either an implicitly addressed stack mechanism in the hardware or else software stack manipulation with a fixed address.

Whatever method is used to communicate parameters, it is usually also necessary, for all but the simplest routines, to save the calling routine's program status when a subroutine is called and to restore it upon return from the subroutine. A program's status information includes: (1) its register contents; (2) its instruction counter setting, condition bits, timer request, and interrupt status; (3) its regions of main storage and, if paging or segmentation is used, the associated tables and backing storage; (4) logically associated operating system storage, such as job queue entries; and (5) outstanding I/O requests and the positions of noncyclic I/O devices and volumes.

Fortunately, when subroutine calls are issued, the vast majority of this information is not in danger of loss. Usually, only the register contents need be saved and a return address passed. To save the necessary information, two things are required: an owner of space to hold the information and an agent to perform the storing and restoring. The two possibilities for each are the calling and called routines. If the agent is the caller, the save-restore code for *each call* must be written in the caller. Alternatively, a single copy of that code, which is invoked as needed, can be used. Of course, that one copy then becomes another subroutine, although a very limited one. If the agent is the called routine, the save-restore code must be incorporated there, but often one copy will suffice. The most that will be required is one copy of the save code per entry point and one of the restore code per return point.

If the storage area is owned by the routine which is not the agent for storing and restoring, the agent needs to learn the storage area's location. Suppose first that the called routine owns the space and the caller is the agent. The storage space could be provided by convention at a fixed distance from the beginning of the called routine. More flexible would be to put there a pointer to the storage area. Then if multiple entry points are used, multiple storage areas would be obviated by provision of a pointer at the same fixed offset relative to each entry point. Suppose, on the other hand, that the caller owns the space and the called routine is the agent. The caller can pass the storage area location to the called routine in the same manner as it passes the parameters. Because only one call by a given routine can be outstanding at a time, a separate storage area is not needed for each call in the calling routine. If the routine is recursive, one storage area is needed per activation.

Each programming system has a subroutine linkage convention which is not only adopted for use among components of the operating system, but also imposed on the users, because of the interactions between their programs and the operating system. An attractive solution for multiple-register processing units is for the calling routine to own the space, the called routine to do the work, and one of the registers to point to a parameter area. Whatever solution is chosen, however, the translation programs are involved in two ways. As elements of the programming system they must use its linkage convention in their own functioning. As translators they must produce user programs which employ that convention.

3.5 PARAMETER CORRESPONDENCE

A *formal parameter* of a subroutine or coroutine procedure is an identifier, within that procedure, which is replaced, during execution of the procedure, by another identifier or by an expression. The replacing identifier or expression is the corresponding *actual parameter*. The formal parameters are named in the definition of the procedure. Thus A and B are formal parameters of P in the following.

SUBROUTINE P (A,B)	[Fortran]
procedure P(A,B)	[Algol]
P: PROCEDURE (A,B);	[PL/I]
∇ A P B	[APL]

The actual parameters are named in the invocation of the procedure. Thus the statements

CALL P (X,Y∗Z)	[Fortran]
P (X,Y∗Z)	[Algol]
CALL P (X,Y∗Z);	[PL/I]
X P Y×Z	[APL]

all specify the variable X as the actual parameter corresponding to the formal parameter A of procedure P, and the expression Y times Z as the actual parameter corresponding to the formal parameter B. An actual parameter expression may be a constant, as in CALL P (X,5). Whether a constant is handled as a variety of expression or is treated specially depends on the language. The most important distinction in actual parameters, however, is whether or not they are variables.

When a procedure is invoked, the calling module passes to it an explicit or implicit list of addresses of the actual parameters. The called procedure copies these addresses, if necessary, into its own activation record and uses them to establish the correspondences between actual and formal parameters. The nature of the correspondences depends upon the programming language and, for some languages, upon the programmer's choice. Three principal types of correspondence are described in the following sections.

3.5.1   Call by Reference

Under the *call by reference* correspondence, the calling module first determines whether the actual parameter is an expression. If so, it evaluates the expression and places the value in a temporary location. The calling module calculates, if necessary, the address of the actual parameter variable, constant, or temporary location. It then passes that address to the called procedure, which uses it to make *reference* to the actual parameter. Call by reference is therefore also termed "call by address". An example is given by the following procedure.

procedure P (a,b) {call by reference}
begin $a \leftarrow b*4$ **end**

If P is invoked by execution of the call statement

$P(x[i], y)$

the calling module will calculate the addresses of $x[i]$ and y and pass them to P, perhaps in storage locations with symbolic addresses ADDR1 and ADDR2. The code for $a \leftarrow b*4$ might then be

```
LDIND    ADDR2
MULT     @4
STIND    ADDR1
```

where LDIND and STIND are load and store instructions which access storage with the use of one level of indirect addressing. For the IBM 360-370, which uses explicit-base addressing, the instruction LDIND ADDR2 could be written as the pair

```
        L       R1,ADDR2
        L       R6,0(R1)
```

which follows the convention of using the predefined synonym Ri for i in referring to a general register. The first instruction of the pair can be omitted if the actual parameter address is passed in register 1 rather than in a storage location. Call by reference is thus seen to be easy to implement. It is the normal type of correspondence in PL/I.

Suppose that our example procedure were invoked by the call $P(x+2, y)$, where the formal parameter a to which an assignment is to be made corresponds not to a variable but to an expression. What happens? The calling module evaluates the expression $x+2$, stores its value in a temporary location, and passes the address of that location in ADDR1. The called procedure correctly multiplies the value of y by 4 and stores the result in the temporary location allocated to $x+2$. But that temporary location is not accessed again, and the value computed by P is lost.

Suppose next that the actual parameter corresponding to a is a constant. The assignment of value will overwrite the constant, yielding incorrect results if the constant is used later in the program. This insidious error, actually possible in Fortran, is easily prevented by using a temporary location to hold a constant actual parameter, as should be done for any expression other than a variable.

3.5.2 Call by Value; Call by Result

Under the *call by value* correspondence, the called procedure keeps its own location to correspond to the formal parameter. As for call by reference, the calling module passes the address of a variable or of a temporary location which holds the value of a constant or other expression. The called procedure takes the *value* stored at that address and copies it into its own location, which is then used like any other local variable. The called procedure cannot change an actual parameter, not even a variable, because it does not write into the caller's storage. In an alternative implementation, the calling module, rather than the called procedure, makes the copy. In determining where to place the copy, it might use a location at a fixed offset from the entry point, or follow a pointer from such a location. The key distinction, however, is not which module makes the copy, but rather the fact that a copy is made.

The code to implement call by value includes not only instructions to execute the body of the procedure, but also a prolog to initialize the local copies of actual parameters. For the example procedure

procedure P (a,b) {call by value}
begin $a \leftarrow b*4$ **end**

The following code might be used

```
LDIND   ADDR1 ⎫
STORE   A     ⎬  prolog
LDIND   ADDR2 ⎪
STORE   B     ⎭
---
---
---
LOAD    B     ⎫
MULT    @4    ⎬  body
STORE   A     ⎭
```

Call by value avoids the indirection in each parameter access at the price of extra storage (particularly expensive for arrays) for copies of the actual parameters. It is the normal type of correspondence for "arguments" in APL. Because call by value provides only one-way communication from the calling module to the called procedure, it is not practiced in isolation. To transmit information back to the caller, the procedure may be a function procedure which returns a value, or it may use a type of correspondence other than call by value for one or more of the other parameters.

Under the *call by result* correspondence, as for call by value, the called procedure has a location which corresponds to the formal parameter. This location is used like any other local variable, except on termination of the procedure. The actual parameter address, passed at invocation time, is used by the called procedure at termination to deliver the *result* from the local location to the actual parameter location in the calling module's storage. Call by result is the normal type of correspondence for return of "results" in APL, and it is a natural type to use in conjunction with call by value.

The implementation of call by result is straightforward. The code for the procedure body includes the initialization of the location which corresponds to a parameter called by result. It is followed by an epilog to store the terminal value in the location of the actual parameter. For the example procedure

$$\textbf{procedure } P \ (a,b) \quad \{\text{call } a \text{ by result, } b \text{ by value}\}$$
$$\textbf{begin } a \ \leftarrow \ b * 4 \ \textbf{end}$$

the code might be

```
LDIND   ADDR2 ⎫
STORE   B     ⎬  prolog (for b)
              ⎭
---
---
---
LOAD    B     ⎫
MULT    @4    ⎬  body
STORE   A     ⎭
---
---
---
LOAD    A     ⎫
STIND   ADDR1 ⎬  epilog (for a)
              ⎭
```

If the value of the local variable corresponding to the formal parameter is *both* initialized upon entry to the procedure *and* delivered upon exit therefrom, the parameter correspondence is termed *call by value result*. This type of correspondence was introduced as an option in Algol W and is also available in Algol 68. Call by result is sometimes designated "call by reference result" to distinguish it from call by value result. Implementation of call by value result requires both a prolog and an epilog for the same variable. It therefore uses more space than does call by reference, and more time on both procedure entry and exit, in return for using less time in making each access to the parameter. It might seem that the difference is one of implementation alone and does not extend to the effects of the two types of correspondence. That such is not the case is illustrated by the program of Fig. 3.8. Invocation of *PRINT* will write the value 3 if the parameter x is passed by reference, but the value 2 if x is passed by value result. The difference arises from the nonlocal reference by *INCR* to the variable which is also the actual parameter of the call.

3.5.3 Call by Name

Under the *call by name* correspondence, each occurrence of the *name* of the formal parameter is considered to be replaced textually by the actual

```
procedure PRINT
    integer y
    procedure INCR (x)
        integer x
        begin
            y ← 1
            x ← x+2
        end
    begin
        y ← 0
        INCR (y)
        write y
    end
```

Figure 3.8   Program to Illustrate Parameter Correspondence

parameter. This type of correspondence is therefore sometimes called the "replacement rule". Such a rule, which is the standard type of correspondence in Algol 60, appears very elegant – pure textual substitution is to be performed – but it holds traps for the unwary.

One trap is illustrated by

$$\textbf{procedure } P \ (a,b) \quad \{\text{call by name}\}$$
$$\textbf{begin } a \gets 1; \quad b \gets b+1; \quad a \gets 2; \quad b \gets b+2 \textbf{ end}$$

when invoked by the call

$$P \ (i,x[i])$$

because the result is *not* to increment $x[i]$ by 3 while setting i equal to 2. The replacement rule specifies that for this invocation of P the statements to be executed are

$$i \gets 1$$
$$x[i] \gets x[i] + 1$$
$$i \gets 2$$
$$x[i] \gets x[i] + 2$$

and it is seen that both $x[1]$ and $x[2]$ will be incremented, whereas $x[i]$ will not (unless i had value 1 or 2 at the moment of invocation).

A second trap is that the actual parameter substituted into the text of the *called* procedure has a meaning specified in the *calling* module. The identifier *i* which appeared in the foregoing call is not to be confused with an identifier *i* which is known to the called procedure but unknown to the caller.

Call by name cannot be implemented efficiently by actually performing the text substitution which defines its effect. It would be necessary to execute the procedure body interpretively at execution time because there is no practical way to generate at compilation time the code which would result from an arbitrary call. Instead, object code compiled for the procedure includes for each formal parameter a separate routine to evaluate the corresponding actual parameter. This routine, called a *thunk* for historical reasons, belongs to the body of the called procedure, not to a prolog. It is invoked for *each* reference made in the body to the corresponding formal parameter, and returns the address of the value of the actual parameter. The thunk must first save the environment of the called procedure and reestablish the environment of the calling module, then evaluate the actual parameter in the caller's environment, and finally reinstate the called procedure's environment. The evaluation of the actual parameter may entail a further call (by name) which results in further stacking of environments before a return is possible. For the call in the foregoing example, the translator must generate thunks to evaluate the addresses of *i* and of *x*[*i*] and it must ensure that the addresses of the thunks are available to the code for the procedure body.

Call by name is obviously no favorite of compiler writers. The simplicity of its operational definition – textual substitution – has sometimes been mistaken for conceptual elegance. Not only is call by name awkward and costly to implement, but its use greatly increases the difficulty of proving program correctness. Call by name has not survived into any important modern language.

FOR FURTHER STUDY

Section 10.3 of Stone [1972] includes an example of a recursive routine written in assembler language. Rice [1965] is a thoughtful note on recursion and iteration. Many of the issues covered in this chapter are treated at length in Chapter 4 of Wegner [1968], particularly the activation-record stack, block structure (4.5, 4.9), and modes of module activation (4.9, 4.10). Modes of module activation are also discussed in Sections 5-4 and 6-8 of Pratt [1975]. Some attention to block structure is paid in Section 3.5 of McKeeman, Horning, and Wortman [1970], Chapter 11 of Elson [1973], and the article by Berthaud and Griffiths [1973]. Griffiths [1974a] offers a clear explanation of displays and of static and dynamic links.

The original description of coroutines is in Conway [1963]. Brief explanations are to be found in Wegner [1968, sect. 4.10.3], Stone [1972, sect. 7.2], Knuth [1973, sect. 1.4.2], and Pratt [1975, pp. 159–163]. A more extensive treatment is offered by Sevcik [1975]. Subroutines and linkage conventions are mentioned in Sections 7.1 and 7.3 of Stone [1972] and Section 1.4.1 of Knuth [1973].

Modes of parameter correspondence are discussed briefly by Elson [1973, sect. 5.5], more fully by Gries [1971, sect. 8.7], Stone [1972, sect. 7.3.2], Ullman [1976, sect. 6.10], and Aho and Ullman [1977, sect. 2.11], and at greater length yet by Pratt [1975, sect. 6-9, 6-10] and Rohl [1975, sect. 12.6–12.12]. The implementation of thunks is described in Ingerman [1961].

EXERCISES

3.1   Consider the program *FAC* of Fig. 3.1. Let an execution of *FAC*(3) be suspended, as discussed for *FA* in the third paragraph of Section 3.1, to permit the evaluation of *FAC*(4). Show the activation records of both instances of *FAC* at the moment at which the execution of *FAC*(4) is about to enter the loop body for the third time.

3.2   Write in a suitable high-level notation (which may be, but doesn't have to be, a real programming language) a two-parameter recursive routine which computes the product of one parameter, the multiplicand (MC), by the other parameter, a (positive integer) multiplier (MP), using only repeated addition of the MC and decrementation of the MP by unity. Number the statements. Let the routine be called with MC=10 and MP=4. Draw the stack of activation records at its maximum size, showing the content of each. State all calls which are generated and all results which are returned.

3.3   Diagram the execution-time static chain when procedure Q, nested within procedure P and called by P, calls itself.

3.4   Show the activation-record stack, using both a display and a full set of static links, during the execution of procedure C of this PL/I program. Do not show any detail within an activation record.

```
A:  PROCEDURE;
    CALL E;
    D:  PROCEDURE;
        CALL C;
        C:  PROCEDURE;
            PUT SKIP LIST ('IN C');
            END C;
        END D;
    E:  PROCEDURE;
        CALL B;
        B:  PROCEDURE;
            CALL D;
            END B;
        END E;
    END A;
```

3.5 Consider the following program in some procedure-oriented language.

```
Procedure M
    Procedure P1
        Begin Block B
            Call P2
        End B
        Call P2
    End P1
    Call P2
    Call P1
    Procedure P2
        Call P3
        Procedure P3
        End P3
    End P2
End M
```

a) Describe each stage in the life of the activation-record stack as procedure M is executed, once using a static chain and once using a display. Do not show any detail within an activation record.

b) Is every static link needed at each stage? Why or why not?

c) Explain how to construct the static chain corresponding to a given execution-time display and *vice versa*.

3.6 Exhibit and explain the subroutine linkage convention for your operating system.

3.7 Design a coroutine linkage convention for the operating system you use. Exhibit the actual program code.

3.8 Code subroutines for printing x^2, where x is a parameter called
a) by reference;
b) by value.
Assume (1) that your machine has a "multiply indirect" instruction, and (2) that you may not pass x in a register.

3.9 Write for your computer the subroutine code required to execute: $I := I + 1$, where I is a formal parameter called by value result. Incorporate a full prolog and epilog.

3.10 Write an OS 360 Assembler language subroutine to increment I by 1, J by 2, and K by 3, where I, J, and K are full-word formal parameters called by value result. Use the standard linkage convention, accounting for the fact that your subroutine does not itself call another. Save and restore the contents of all registers; set the return code to zero. Assume that the calling routine has placed the three actual parameters (not just their addresses) in the parameter list.

3.11 Suppose that you are programming in a language which offers for *each* parameter, independently of the other parameters, the choice between the *two* following modes of correspondence: (a) call by value, value result, or result, as appropriate to the direction in which the information is to be transmitted; and (b) call by reference. Describe the costs of each and the circumstances under which you would prefer each choice to the other, and justify your claim. Note that the question does not ask for an analysis of subchoices under (a).

3.12 Why is the PL/I statement CALL P((A)), where A is an actual parameter identifier, sometimes said to be a "call by value"?

3.13 [Gries] Manually execute the following program five times, once under each of the following assumptions, indicating the final values (which may or may not be defined) in $v(3)$ and $v(4)$. Consider the formal parameter a to be called
a) by reference;
b) by value;
c) by value result;
d) by result;
e) by name.

```
begin
    integer k
    integer array v

    procedure P (a)
        integer a
        begin
            a ← a+1
            v[k] ← 5
            k ← 3
            a ← a+1
        end

    v[3] ← 6
    v[4] ← 8
    k ← 4
    call P (v[k])
end
```

Chapter 4

MACRO PROCESSING

4.1 FUNCTION

A subroutine of the standard type discussed in Section 3.3 has been known historically as a *closed subroutine*. It is characterized by the incorporation of only a single copy of its text in the complete program. Its execution is triggered by execution of the program statement which calls the subroutine. Parameters passed to the subroutine tailor its function within limits established when the subroutine was constructed. Closed subroutines thus reduce the over-all size of a program, as well as the effort of writing it, by permitting a call statement to serve as an abbreviation for an entire subroutine.

The savings in space and effort cost time, however, for calling the closed subroutine, for passing and accessing parameters, and for returning from the subroutine. The *open subroutine*, also known as "in-line code", offers a faster alternative at the cost of space and effort. A copy of the open subroutine is written in the program in place of a call of a closed subroutine. Modifications of the text of the open subroutine, performed not at execution time but rather at programming time, tailor its function as desired by the programmer. Multiple copies of specialized program text are thus incorporated in the program, rather than a single copy of generalized text.

The tedium of writing many identical or nearly identical copies of the same text is readily transferred from the programmer to the computer. Translation programs have been developed to assist in the repetitive and/or parameterized generation of program text. If the desired text is to be in a programming language, the assisting translator is usually called a *preprocessor*. If the text is to be in an assembler language, the assisting translator is called a *macro processor*. If the translator is not specialized to generating text in a particular language, it may be called a *string processor* (referring to arbitrary text strings) or a *macro generator*.

Whether the application is to programming languages, assembler languages, or arbitrary strings, the required processing is much the same. We shall adopt uniform terminology regardless of the application, using *macro* for a specification of how program text is to be generated and *macro processor* for a translator which accomplishes the task. Macro processing is described, both in this chapter and in the next, primarily in terms of the application to assembler-language programming. This permits us to use the hypothetical assembler language of Chapter 2 in illustrating macro processing. The techniques described are not limited to assembler-language text, however, but are applicable in general.

The assembler-language programmer often finds himself repeating groups of instructions. One group might increment a counter in storage, a second might extract characters from variously specified positions of a card image, and a third might perform fixed-point arithmetic with specified scaling and rounding. By using a single instruction, called a *macro instruction*, to represent each such group of assembler-language instructions, the programmer is spared the tedium of repetitive coding. Moreover, the macro instructions can be thought of as statements in a higher-level language which is particularly useful to the programmer, because he himself has defined them. Sometimes the designers of the programming system can anticipate that many programmers might wish to have certain instruction sequences available. Examples include calling sequences for the routines which provide system services such as input and output, process synchronization, and storage allocation. Macros provided in the programming system for all users are called *system macros*.

The output of a macro processor is usually a program in the source language of another translator. Its input will then contain both program text which is ready for the subsequent translation and *macro definitions* which are to be *expanded* into such text. The definition of a macro consists of a *prototype* statement, which names the macro and its formal parameters, and a *skeleton* (also called "template" or "body"), which serves as a model of the output to be generated.

Because the same source language is used both for statements within macro definitions and for those without, macro definitions must be explicitly distinguished from the surrounding text. This is most readily done by the use of delimiters. Two syntactic forms of delimiter use are common. The opening delimiter may be combined with the prototype statement, as in Fig. 4.1(a). There the pseudo-instruction MCDEFN serves as the opening delimiter; the name of the macro instruction (INCR) occupies the label field, and its parameters (L and A) appear in the operand field. The closing delimiter is MCEND. Figure 4.1(b) illustrates a prototype which is not commingled with a delimiter; there MCDEFN is separate from the prototype. The skeleton is identical to that of the previous example. The pseudo-instruction END could be used as the closing delimiter for macros as well as for assembler-language text. Its use would be unambiguous, because of nesting, but then END could not appear in the skeleton, and the macro processor would be unable to generate an END instruction.

The skeleton can be thought of as an open subroutine which is inserted into the program text at the point of call. Indeed, the use of a macro is termed a *call*. It is signaled by the appearance of a macro instruction, such as those which are shown following each of the two definitions of Fig. 4.1. Observe how each call corresponds to the prototype of the definition to which it refers. Replacement of a macro instruction by the skeleton, with actual values substituted for the parameters, is known as *macro expansion*. Figure 4.1(c) shows the result of expanding either call.

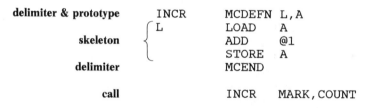

(a) Macro definition and macro call

(b) Alternative definition and call

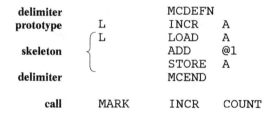

(c) Macro expansion

Figure 4.1 Macro Processing

4.2   PARAMETER SYNTAX

During expansion, the actual parameters named in the call are substituted for the formal parameters which appear in the skeleton and are named in the prototype. Both actual and formal parameters are, of course, character strings. The correspondence of formal parameter occurrences in the skeleton to their occurrences in the prototype is fixed by the macro definition and can be established at the time the definition is processed. The substitution of actual values depends on the call, and must be accomplished separately for each call. If the prototype and the call each include several parameters, it is necessary to identify which actual parameter corresponds to which formal parameter.

Two syntactic approaches to parameter identification are in widespread use: positional and keyword. *Positional* parameters are distinguished by the position which they occupy in the list of parameters. Positional parameters are used in Fig. 4.1(a). The two formal parameters, L and A, are stated in a list in the operand field. The actual parameters of the call, MARK and COUNT, are also given as a list in which adjacent entries are separated by a syntactic marker (here, the comma). The first actual parameter, MARK, is substituted for the first formal parameter, L; the second actual parameter, COUNT, is substituted for the second formal parameter, A. In general, the ith actual parameter is substituted for the ith formal parameter.

Use of the empty character string (or of blanks) as an actual parameter is often termed *omission* of the parameter. Suppose we wish to call the macro defined in Fig. 4.1(a) without specifying a label. If the syntactic markers are left in the parameter list, the omission becomes evident. Thus the call

```
          INCR     , COUNT
```

would cause

```
          LOAD     COUNT
          ADD      @1
          STORE    COUNT
```

to be generated. The omission of two successive parameters from the middle of a longer list would leave three consecutive commas. The omission of a parameter can sometimes be positionally evident if there is no list. In Fig. 4.1(b) the formal parameter L occupies the label field. If a prototype is restricted to having at most one parameter in its label field, then omission of that actual parameter from the call is evident. The call

```
INCR    COUNT
```

would specify, under those conditions, the expansion just given.

It is possible to establish positional correspondence without use of the prototype. Formal parameters in the skeleton can be given a syntactic form which refers to a position in the actual parameter list. Thus &SYSLIST(i) in an IBM 360-370 macro skeleton is replaced by the ith operand of the call.

If the number of parameters is large, it can be difficult to remember the correct sequence, or to provide the right number of commas for omitted parameters. This can be remedied by the use of *keyword* parameters. The macro call specifies for each actual parameter not just the value, as under positional syntax, but also the name of the corresponding formal parameter. The customary keyword syntax is *formal=actual*. The formal parameters are identified by their appearance in the prototype, with or without the syntactic mark =. The actual parameters can appear in the call in any order, because each is accompanied by the name of the corresponding formal parameter. A macro definition with four keyword parameters (L, A, B, and C) is presented in Fig. 4.2. Note, incidentally, the use of a syntactic marker (here, the period) to separate the literal indicator @ from B, thus permitting the latter to be recognized as a parameter. The call

```
INCR    L=MARK,A=COUNT,B=1,C=COUNT
```

would result in the expansion already shown in Fig. 4.1(c).

Parameter correspondence independent of the prototype can be established for keyword parameters as well as for positional parameters. The mere use of the formal parameter name in the skeleton is enough to establish the correspondence; identification of a character string as a parameter is accomplished by the syntactic mark (the = in our examples). Thus the skeleton

```
L=          LOAD     A=
            ADD      @.B=
            STORE    C=
```

could replace that of Fig. 4.2.

The processing previously shown for an omitted actual parameter resulted in replacement of the formal parameter by a fixed default value, blanks.

Figure 4.2   Macro Definition with Keyword Parameters

Arbitrary default values can be specified instead, whether positional or keyword syntax is used for calls. Thus the definition of Fig. 4.3 specifies blanks as the default for L, 1 as the default for B, and ACCUM as the default for both A and C. The definition satisfies the requirements of either parameter syntax. For this definition, a macro processor using positional parameter syntax in calls would expand INCR   MARK,COUNT,,COUNT into the assembler-language text shown in Fig. 4.1(c). A macro processor using keyword parameter syntax in calls would expand

INCR   C=COUNT,L=MARK,A=COUNT

into the same text. Unlabeled text to increment the content of ACCUM by 2 would be generated from the positional syntax call INCR   ,,2, or from the keyword syntax call INCR   B=2.

The simplicity of positional correspondence and the flexibility of keyword correspondence can be enjoyed together. It is perfectly feasible to use one syntax for some of the parameters and the other for the remainder. This requires a convention, in the prototype, to enable the macro processor to determine which syntax applies to which parameter.

If a macro skeleton includes a label which is not supplied as a parameter, each call of the macro will generate a distinct occurrence of that label. If the macro is called more than once, the generated assembler-language program will then contain a multiply-defined symbol. To avoid this error, many macro processors maintain a count of the number of times a macro call is expanded, which can be appended (in character string form) to generated labels. The attachment can be performed automatically. Alterna-

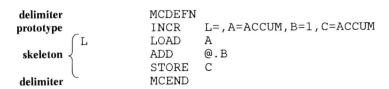

Figure 4.3   Macro Definition with Default Values

tively, the count can be provided as the actual value corresponding to a system-defined formal parameter, say SER. Thus the string MASS.SER in the skeleton for the macro instruction REVISE might be replaced by MASS0023 in the first expansion of REVISE and by MASS0036 in the second expansion of REVISE. This would occur if the two calls of REVISE were the 23rd and 36th to be expanded by the macro processor.

A somewhat different problem of generation is represented by comments. Readability of macro processor input is often enhanced by comments which explain the skeleton, but whose presence is not desired in the generated text. Such comments must be differentiated syntactically from those which are indeed to be generated.

We have mentioned syntactic devices to distinguish generation-time from execution-time comments, to identify parameters, and to separate a string, such as @.B or MASS.SER, into its component parts. Some assemblers, those for IBM 360-370 in particular, use a syntactic marker (& as the first character) to distinguish parameters of macros from execution-time symbols. This helps to accentuate for the reader the different binding times* of the two classes of symbols. The distinction is not logically required by the macro processor, however, as long as the parameters are required to be present in the prototype.

4.3   TWO-PASS IMPLEMENTATION

A straightforward implementation of the macro processor is possible if each macro is defined only once. We assume that a macro is restricted to contain neither another macro definition nor a macro call. Two passes over the program text suffice, the first to collect the definitions and the second to expand the calls.

During Pass 1 the macro processor simply copies instructions from input text to intermediate text until it encounters the opening delimiter of a macro definition. At this point it enters *definition mode*. All succeeding instructions of the definition are entered in a *macro-definition table*. The macro definition is copied only into this table, and not to the intermediate text. Although it is possible to copy these instructions into the table unchanged, the subsequent expansion of each call of the macro is simplified if some editing is performed. Each formal parameter in the skeleton can be replaced by the number which gives the position of the formal parameter in the prototype's parameter list. Thus the macro definition of Fig. 4.4(a)

*The concept of binding time is discussed in Section 5.1.

```
           MCDEFN
SPOT       ABSDIF A,B,C                SPOT        ABSDIF A,B,C
SPOT       LOAD   A                    #0          LOAD   #1
           SUB    B                                SUB    #2
           BRPOS  ST.SER                           BRPOS  ST.SER
           LOAD   B                                LOAD   #2
           SUB    A                                SUB    #1
ST.SER     STORE  C                    ST.SER      STORE  #3
           MCEND                                   MCEND
```

      (a) In input text   (b) In macro-definition table

Figure 4.4   Macro Definition Editing

could be stored in the macro-definition table as shown in Fig. 4.4(b). There
the symbol # serves as a syntactic marker to distinguish a parameter reference from an ordinary symbol. The label parameter was assigned the
number 0. The opening delimiter is not needed in the table, because the
table is known to contain macro definitions. The closing delimiter is included to mark the end, however, because the length of the definition is
not fixed.

When the prototype is encountered, its operation field (the macro name)
can optionally be stored in a *macro-name table*, to be used during Pass 2
to distinguish macro calls from other text. If this is done, the prototype
may be omitted from the edited definition. After the closing delimiter is
entered in the macro-definition table, the macro processor leaves definition
mode to resume copying. If system macros are provided, their definitions
are incorporated in the macro-definition table and their names in the
macro-name table prior to use of the macro processor.

During Pass 2 the macro processor reads as input the intermediate text
prepared by Pass 1. Macro definitions are no longer present, but macro
calls are. The operation field of each instruction is compared with entries
in the operation table or in the optional macro-name table. If it is not a
macro name, the instruction is copied unchanged to the output text. If the
operation field is a macro name, then a macro call has been encountered
and the macro processor enters *expansion mode*. The corresponding prototype is found, either by searching the macro-definition table, or by following
a pointer which was placed in the macro-name table when the definition
was collected during Pass 1. By comparing the call with the prototype, the
macro processor prepares a list of the actual parameters to be substituted.
For the definition in Fig. 4.4(b), the call

        ABSDIF   INPRES,OUTPRES,PRESSURE

would establish the following list (assuming 8-character label and operand fields).

```
#0      '        '
#1      'INPRES  '
#2      'OUTPRES '
#3      'PRESSURE'
```

Positional parameters are identified by counting; keyword parameters are identified by comparing the parameter names in the call with those in the prototype. For omitted parameters, default values are placed in the list.

The macro processor now copies the instructions of the skeleton into the output text, replacing each occurrence of #i by the ith value in the list of actual parameters, and each occurrence of .SER by the serial number of the expansion. When the closing delimiter is encountered, the macro processor leaves it uncopied, discards the actual-parameter list, and returns from expansion mode to copy mode.

The advantages of this two-pass division of labor are that space requirements are modest, only the tables and the program for one pass being needed in storage, and that forward references are permitted—a macro call can precede the associated definition in the text. Forward references to macro definitions in the input text are not as important, however, as forward references to symbols in assembler-language text, because requiring macros to be defined before use imposes no hardship. Passing the text twice then incurs unnecessary cost. A more fundamental disadvantage of this implementation is that it does not permit macros to be redefined.

4.4   ONE-PASS IMPLEMENTATION

It is not unusual to expect multiple calls of one macro during a single invocation of the macro processor. What is less obvious is the desirability of multiple definitions of a macro. Each macro definition with the same name as an existing definition is considered to be a redefinition of the correspondence between a call and its expansion. One of the many uses of redefinition is to override system macros. If redefinition is allowed, it is necessary to expand each macro call according to the most recent definition of its macro. It is therefore no longer appropriate to defer macro expansion until all macro definitions have been collected.

The required processing can be effected in a single pass over the input text. Forward references can no longer be permitted; *every* call must be of a previously defined macro. As stated earlier, this is not a serious restriction.

Because macro definitions are assumed to contain neither macro calls nor other macro definitions, the macro processor can never be in both definition mode and expansion mode at the same time. It is either in one of those two modes or in copy mode. The actions during these three modes are precisely those described in Section 4.3. The algorithm is presented in Fig. 4.5. In this and succeeding algorithms, an instance of *opcode* will be recognized as a "prototype" if it is read from the first line of a macro definition or from a line which follows the delimiter MCDEFN. It will be recognized as a "macro name" only if it names a macro but is not recognized as a prototype.

The major effect of permitting macros to be redefined is upon the organization of the macro-definition table. There is no guarantee that any definition of a macro will not require more space than its previous definition. This precludes rewriting a new definition in the place of its predecessor. The space occupied by a superseded definition can be liberated, unless a facility is desired for reverting to a previous definition, as in overriding a system macro only temporarily. One way to organize the macro-definition

$d \leftarrow$ **false** {definition-mode switch}
$e \leftarrow$ **false** {expansion-mode switch}
read *line* from *input*
while *line* $\neq$ **empty do**
    if d **then** {in definition mode}
        case *opcode* **of**
            prototype:
            'MCEND': $d \leftarrow$ **false** {leave definition mode}
            other: replace ith formal parameter by '#i'
        write *line* to *macro definition*
    else {in copy mode or expansion mode}
        case *opcode* **of**
            prototype:
            macro name: $e \leftarrow$ **true** {enter expansion mode}
                      PREPARE actual-parameter list
            'MCDEFN': $d \leftarrow$ **true** {enter definition mode}
                      ALLOCATE macro definition in table
            'MCEND': $e \leftarrow$ **false** {leave expansion mode}
                      DISCARD actual-parameter list
            other: **if** e **then** replace '#i' by *actual-parameter list* [i]
                      write *line* to *output*
    if e **then** {in expansion mode}
        read *line* from *macro definition*
    else read *line* from *input*

Figure 4.5 Macro Processing without Nesting

table is to chain definitions, as shown in Fig. 4.6. In definition mode, the macro processor places each new definition at the head of the chain. In expansion mode, it scans the chain for a definition of the called macro; the first definition it encounters is the most recent. The definitions in the chain may, but need not, be contiguous. An alternative to linking all the definitions in a single chain is to use a separate chain for each macro name, with a macro-name table pointing to the current definition. Reversion to the previous definition is accomplished easily with either chaining discipline.

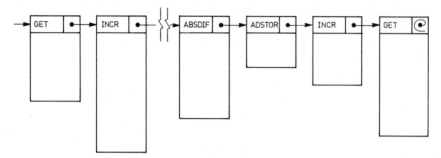

Figure 4.6   Chained Macro-Definition Table

Two approaches to macro identification are possible. One is to search the operation table for the current instruction's operation field. If it is not found, it is assumed to be a macro call, and the macro-definition table chain is searched for the most recent definition. The other approach is to search the macro-definition table first. Only if the operation field is not found is the operation table searched. The advantage of this second approach is that it permits existing operation codes to be redefined by the programmer. It incurs the cost of searching the entire macro-definition table even for a regular operation code for which no macro has been defined.

The searching time under either approach can be greatly reduced by the provision of a macro-name table with separate chains for each macro name. The distinction between the two search strategies dictates whether the macro-name table is searched before or after the operation code table.

4.5   NESTED DEFINITIONS

If the restrictions imposed in Section 4.3 are removed, then the skeleton of one macro (A) may contain a definition of another macro (B), as in

Fig. 4.7. The definition of B is said to be *nested* within that of A. It is important to realize that the act of defining macro A does *not* define macro B. The definition of A merely specifies that the text into which a call of A is to be expanded includes a definition of macro B. Thus it is a *call* of macro A which causes macro B to be defined. Each subsequent call of A also defines B. Because the text of B may include formal parameters of A, each call of A with different actual parameters can result in B being redefined. The level of nesting of macro definitions is not limited to one. Macro B, for example, might incorporate the definition of a third macro C, which could not be called until after a call of B had effected the definition of C.

The inner macros MULTSC and DIVSC of Fig. 4.8 are intended to provide fixed-point multiplication and division, scaled to the arbitrary radix point position RP. The instructions SHIFTL and SHIFTR are assumed to shift the accumulator content left and right, respectively, by the number of positions given in the operand field. If operation at radix point 3 is desired for a while, the call SCALE 3 is written and its expansion augments the macro-definition table by the versions of MULTSC and DIVSC shown in Fig. 4.9. If radix point 5 is desired later, the call SCALE 5 redefines the two inner macros.

Nested macro definitions can be implemented by the one-pass macro processor of Section 4.4, extended by two modifications. One modification ensures that an exit from definition mode is not caused by the closing delimiter of an *inner* macro. In definition mode, a *definition-level counter* is incremented by 1 for each opening delimiter encountered and decremented by 1 for each closing delimiter. If the counter is set to 0 before entry to definition mode, then the later reduction of its value to 0 is the signal that definition mode has ended. For example, in defining the macro

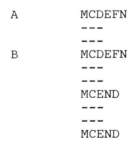

Figure 4.7 Nested Macro Definitions

```
MCDEFN
SCALE   RP
MCDEFN
MULTSC  A,B,C
LOAD    A
MULT    B
SHIFTR  RP
STORE   C
MCEND
MCDEFN
DIVSC   A,B,C
LOAD    A
DIVIDE  B
SHIFTL  RP
STORE   C
MCEND
MCEND
```

Figure 4.8   Macro to Generate Scaled Arithmetic Macros

SCALE (Fig. 4.8), the sequence of values of the counter will be 0, 1, 2, 1, 2, 1, 0.

The other modification precludes confusing the formal parameters of one macro with those of another macro nested within it. Inner macro B may have a formal parameter U, which is identical in name to a formal parameter U of outer macro A. When A is called with corresponding actual parameter R, occurrences of U within A are to be replaced by R, *except* for those which are also within B. This is because the property that U is a formal parameter of B is not to be upset by the coincidental choice of the same name for a formal parameter of an enclosing macro. Just as in block-structured programming languages, the declaration within macro B of U as a formal parameter masks the parameter U of macro A. Thus an occurrence of U within the skeleton of B is not bound by assignment of a value to A's formal parameter U during a call of A. On the other hand, if macro A has also a formal parameter V, but B does not, then an occurrence of V

```
MULTSC  A,B,C          DIVSC   A,B,C
LOAD    A              LOAD    A
MULT    B              DIVIDE  B
SHIFTR  3              SHIFTL  3
STORE   C              STORE   C
MCEND                  MCEND
```

Figure 4.9   Macro Definitions Generated by SCALE   3

within the skeleton of B is indeed bound to the value assigned to V during a call of A. Consequently, when the definition of A is processed, the editing of formal parameter occurrences must distinguish among those bound at the different levels of macro nesting.

A convenient solution is provided by the use of a *formal-parameter stack* (often called "macro-definition stack", a term which can lead to confusion with a stack-organized macro-definition table) to assign *pairs* of numbers to parameters entered in the macro-definition table. As definition level d is entered, the name of its ith formal parameter is placed on the stack, together with the number pair (d,i). Every symbol in the entire macro definition is compared with the stack entries, starting with the most recent, until a match is found. If the symbol occurrence in the text is associated with the pair (d,i), then as it is copied to the macro-definition table it is replaced by $\#(d,i)$. If the symbol is not found in the formal-parameter stack, it is copied unchanged. When the closing delimiter is encountered, the stack entries for the current level are discarded. The stack is thus empty when definition mode is entered, and is again empty when definition mode is left. The formal-parameter stack is created and used only during definition mode processing of the *outermost* macro of a set of nested definitions. Figure 4.10 shows three nested definitions, the maximum extent of the formal-parameter stack, and the result of editing the nested definitions. The arrow shows where the stack top was during editing of the enclosed line of input text.

Formal-parameter stack		Input text		Macro-definition table entry	
top		MCDEFN			
		X	A,B,C,D	X	A,B,C,D
G	3,4		A,B,C,D		#(1,1),#(1,2),#(1,3),#(1,4)
E	3,3	MCDEFN		MCDEFN	
C	3,2	Y	A,B,E,F	Y	A,B,E,F
A	3,1		A,B,C,D		#(2,1),#(2,2),#(1,3),#(1,4)
F	2,4 ←	MCDEFN		MCDEFN	
E	2,3	Z	A,C,E,G	Z	A,C,E,G
B	2,2		A,B,C,D		#(3,1),#(2,2),#(3,2),#(1,4)
A	2,1		E,F,G,H		#(3,3),#(2,4),#(3,4),H
D	1,4	MCEND		MCEND	
C	1,3		E,F,G,H		#(2,3),#(2,4),G,H
B	1,2	MCEND		MCEND	
A	1,1		E,F,G,H		E,F,G,H
bottom		MCEND		MCEND	

Figure 4.10   Formal Parameters in Nested Definitions

During expansion mode, the actual parameters of the call replace the called macro's formal parameters, which are identified by having level 1 in the number pairs #(1,i). Each embedded macro definition is appended to the macro-definition table, with the level number of all remaining formal parameter references decremented by 1. Consequently, the newly defined macros have the levels of their formal parameters now set to 1 and are ready to be called in their turn. Text not within an embedded macro is generated in the normal manner. The algorithm is given in Fig. 4.11.

Figure 4.12 illustrates the operation of the algorithm by showing a 10-line input text and the steps in macro processing. The parameter names indicate which are formal and which are actual. Line numbers have been

```
d ← 0      {definition-level counter}
e ← false  {expansion-mode switch}
read line from input
while line ≠ empty do
    case opcode of
        'MCDEFN': d ← d+1
                  if d=1 then ALLOCATE new macro definition
                         else write line to new macro definition
        prototype:  if not e then PUSH ith formal parameter and
                                       (d,i) on formal-parameter stack
                    if d>0 then write line to new macro definition
        macro name: e ← true
                    PREPARE actual-parameter list
        'MCEND':  if d=0 then DISCARD actual-parameter list
                         e ← false
                    else if not e then POP formal-parameter
                                          stack {level d}
                         d ← d−1
                         write line to new macro definition
        other:    if e then replace '#(k,i)' by
                            if k=1 then actual-parameter list [i]
                                   else '#(k−1,i)'
                  if (not e) and d>0 then replace each formal parameter
                                          by topmost corresponding '#(k,i)'
                                          from formal-parameter stack
                  if d=0 then write line to output
                         else write line to new macro definition
    if e then {in expansion mode}
            read line from old macro definition
                    named in current macro call
        else read line from input
```

Figure 4.11 Macro Processing with Nested Definitions

Line	Input
1	MCDEFN
2	A FORMAL1
3	LOAD FORMAL1
4	MCDEFN
5	B FORMAL2
6	STORE FORMAL2
7	MCEND
8	MCEND
9	A ACTUAL1
10	B ACTUAL2

(a) Source text

Line read	d	e	Line written	Macro definitions		Output	
1	0	false					
2	1	false	11	A	FORMAL1		
3	1	false	12	LOAD	#(1,1)		
4	1	false	13	MCDEFN			
5	2	false	14	B	FORMAL2		
6	2	false	15	STORE	#(2,1)		
7	2	false	16	MCEND			
8	1	false	17	MCEND			
9	0	false					
11	0	true					
12	0	true	18			LOAD	ACTUAL1
13	0	true					
14	1	true	19	B	FORMAL2		
15	1	true	20	STORE	#(1,1)		
16	1	true	21	MCEND			
17	0	true					
10	0	false					
19	0	true					
20	0	true	22			STORE	ACTUAL2
21	0	true					

(b) Successive actions

Figure 4.12 Macro Processing Trace

supplied for ease of reading. The values shown for d and e are those which hold prior to execution of the **case** statement.

Figure 4.13 shows the output text and new macro-definition table entry which result from the call X   P,Q,R,S to the macro defined in Fig. 4.10.

Output text	**New macro-definition table entry**		
P,Q,R,S	Y	A,B,E,F	
E,F,G,H		#(1,1),#(1,2),R,S	
	MCDEFN		
	Z	A,C,E,G	
		#(2,1),#(1,2),#(2,2),S	
		#(2,3),#(1,4),#(2,4),H	
	MCEND		
		#(1,3),#(1,4),G,H	
	MCEND		

Figure 4.13   Result of Call X   P,Q,R,S

In one interesting application of nested definitions the name of the inner macro is a formal parameter of the outer macro, as in Fig. 4.14. The purpose of CREATE is to define a set of macros, each bearing the name of a subroutine, and each to be expanded into a standard sequence for calling that subroutine. Thus the calls CREATE INSERT, CREATE DELETE, and CREATE REVISE would define three macros, INSERT, DELETE, and REVISE. A subsequent call DELETE LOCN would result in execution of the standard subroutine calling sequence with LOCN used as the location of the parameter list and DELETE as the location of the called subroutine. The algorithm of Fig. 4.11 does not, however, examine the operation code field of a prototype to determine whether it contains a formal parameter.

```
MCDEFN
CREATE  SUBR
MCDEFN
SUBR    PARMLIST
---
---     PARMLIST
---
BR      SUBR
MCEND
MCEND
```

Figure 4.14   Macro to Generate Subroutine Call Macros

4.6   NESTED CALLS

Just as the text of one macro definition can contain another definition, so can the text of a macro definition contain a macro call, as in

```
A           MCDEFN
            - - -
B
            - - -
            MCEND
```

where B is a macro instruction. When macro A is called, the call of macro B will be encountered, requiring the macro processor to suspend expansion of A and begin expansion of B. Thus the static nesting of a call within a definition engenders the dynamic nesting of a call within a call.

Nested calls are particularly convenient for defining macros in terms of other macros. The macro DISCR of Fig. 4.15(a) computes the discriminant $d = b^2 - 4ac$ of the quadratic polynomial $ax^2 + bx + c$, using arithmetic scaled to radix point 3. It includes three calls of the macro MULTSC defined in Fig. 4.9. If each call of MULTSC were expanded prior to its inclusion in DISCR, the definition of DISCR would appear as in Fig. 4.15 (b). The skeleton of this second definition includes 14 instructions as compared with 5 for the definition with embedded calls. The first definition is easier to write and easier to understand. An occasional drawback is the hiding of inefficiencies which are evident only in the longer form of the definition. Here, the adjacent instructions STORE TEMP1 and LOAD TEMP1 are clearly superfluous, and the instruction STORE TEMP2 can

```
                                        MCDEFN
                                        DISCR   A,B,C,D
                                        LOAD    A
                                        MULT    C
                                        SHIFTR  3
                                        STORE   TEMP1
                                        LOAD    TEMP1
                                        MULT    FOUR
                                        SHIFTR  3
          MCDEFN                        STORE   TEMP1
          DISCR   A,B,C,D               LOAD    B
          MULTSC  A,C,TEMP1             MULT    B
          MULTSC  TEMP1,FOUR,TEMP1      SHIFTR  3
          MULTSC  B,B,TEMP2             STORE   TEMP2
          SUB     TEMP1                 SUB     TEMP1
          STORE   D                     STORE   D
          MCEND                         MCEND
```

        (a) With nesting   (b) Without nesting

Figure 4.15   Use of Nested Calls

also be seen to be redundant. Nevertheless, the nesting of calls is a valuable facility.

Expansion of the call DISCR P,Q,R,S is most readily understood as the two-level process symbolized in Fig. 4.16. The first-level expansion replaces DISCR P,Q,R,S by the skeleton of Fig. 4.15(a), with the formal parameters A,B,C,D replaced by the actual parameters P,Q,R,S of the call. The second-level expansion replaces each call of MULTSC by the skeleton of Fig. 4.9, with formal parameters A,B,C replaced each time by the appropriate actual parameters. If the expansion were actually performed in two stages, it would be necessary to back up after the first-stage generation of STORE S and re-scan from MULTSC P,R,TEMP1. Even if only one level of static nesting of calls within definitions is permitted, there is no limit to the number of levels of the resulting dynamic nesting of calls within calls. Expansion of nested calls by multiple passes would therefore be extremely inefficient.

A single-pass implementation is used instead to keep track of dynamic nesting. An expansion which occurs conceptually in n stages is generated practically by stacking to depth n. Suppose that the call DISCR P,Q,R,S is encountered on line 38 of the input text. Comparison of the call with the prototype identifies P,Q,R,S as the actual parameters. These are placed on an *actual-parameter stack* (also called "macro-expansion stack") together with the number, 39, of the input text line from which code generation is to resume. The first line of the skeleton is then generated as MULTSC P,R,TEMP1. Table lookup determines this to be a macro call

Outer call	First-level expansion	Second-level expansion	
DISCR P,Q,R,S	MULTSC P,R,TEMP1	LOAD	P
		MULT	R
		SHIFTR	3
		STORE	TEMP1
	MULTSC TEMP1,FOUR,TEMP1	LOAD	TEMP1
		MULT	FOUR
		SHIFTR	3
		STORE	TEMP1
	MULTSC Q,Q,TEMP2	LOAD	Q
		MULT	Q
		SHIFTR	3
		STORE	TEMP2
	SUB TEMP1	SUB	TEMP1
	STORE S	STORE	S

Figure 4.16 Expansion of Nested Macro Calls

and the second level of expansion is entered. The actual parameters P,R, TEMP1 are stacked together with the number, 2, of the next line of the outer-level macro definition skeleton from which expansion is to resume. The inner macro definition is then expanded, using the actual parameter values from the top of the actual-parameter stack, until the closing delimiter is encountered. At this point the stack is popped. The actual parameters are discarded, and the line number is used to direct the continuation of expansion from line 2 of the skeleton of DISCR. After the last line, 5, of the skeleton of DISCR has been expanded, the closing delimiter causes the first stack entry to be popped, leaving an empty stack which signals departure from expansion mode, and normal processing resumes from input text line 39. Figure 4.17 shows the actual-parameter stack during expansion of the third MULTSC instruction.

In general, the depth of the actual-parameter stack serves as a *macro-expansion level* counter. As each level is entered, its actual parameters are stacked together with the location from which expansion is to resume in the macro definition at the next outer level. Each element of the actual-parameter stack thus contains the complete actual-parameter list for the call at the corresponding level. The actual parameters are used during expansion at the current level, then are discarded upon final exit from that level. Implementation of the stack entries requires considerable care, because the number of actual parameters can vary from one macro to another, and the length of each actual parameter can vary from one call to another.

If nested macro definitions are not allowed, the actual-parameter stack mechanism can be added directly to the simple one-pass macro processor of Section 4.4. If nested calls and nested definitions are both permitted, the mechanism can be added to the macro processor of Section 4.5. The two resulting programs are given in Figs. 4.18 and 4.19.

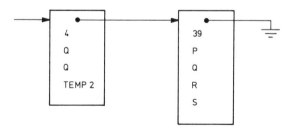

Figure 4.17   Actual-Parameter Stack During Processing of MULTSC Q,Q,TEMP2

```
d ← false   {definition-mode switch}
e ← 0       {expansion-level counter}
read line from input
while line ≠ empty do
    if d {in definition mode}
        then case opcode of
                prototype:
                'MCEND':   d ← false
                other:     replace ith formal parameter by '#i'
             write line to new macro definition
        else {in copy mode or expansion mode}
             case opcode of
                prototype:
                macro name: e ← e+1
                            PREPARE actual-parameter list
                            PUSH actual-parameter list
                                on actual-parameter stack
                'MCDEFN':   d ← true
                            ALLOCATE new macro definition
                'MCEND':    POP actual-parameter list {level e}
                                from actual-parameter stack
                            e ← e−1
                other:      write line to output
    if e > 0 then {in expansion mode}
             read line from old macro definition
                        named in current macro call
             replace '#i' by actual-parameter list [i]
                        from actual-parameter stack
        else read line from input
```

Figure 4.18   Macro Processing with Nested Calls

FOR FURTHER STUDY

Part 1 of Brown [1974] contains a good general treatment of macro processors, as do the books by Campbell-Kelly [1973], which devotes substantial space to a variety of applications, and by Cole [1976]. All three consider the macro processing of arbitrary text as well as of assembler-language programs, and they all describe several specific macro processors. Chapter 3 of Wegner [1968] is devoted to general-purpose macro generators, whereas Section 2.6 considers the application to assemblers. That section presents concisely the implementation of a macro assembler with nested calls and definitions. Section 8.5 of Brooks and Iverson [1969] embodies a treatment of parameter syntax which is careful, but restricted to

$d \leftarrow 0$ {definition-level counter}
$e \leftarrow 0$ {expansion-level counter}
read *line* from *input*
while *line* $\neq$ **empty do**
    case *opcode* **of**
        'MCDEFN': $d \leftarrow d+1$
                if $d=1$ **then** *ALLOCATE* new macro definition
                         else write *line* to *new macro definition*
        prototype: **if** $e=0$ **then** *PUSH i*th formal parameter
                           and (d,i) on *formal-parameter stack*
                if $d>0$ **then write** *line* to *new macro definition*
        macro name: **if** $d=0$ **then** {expand call}
                        $e \leftarrow e+1$
                        PREPARE actual-parameter list
                        PUSH actual-parameter list
                            on *actual-parameter stack*
                if $d>0$ **and** $e=0$ **then** replace each formal parameter
                                by topmost corresponding '#(k,i)'
                                from *formal-parameter stack*
                if $d>0$ **then write** *line* to *new macro definition*
        'MCEND':   **if** $d=0$ **then** *POP actual-parameter list* {level e}
                          from *actual-parameter stack*
                        $e \leftarrow e-1$
                  else {in definition mode}
                      if $e=0$ {but not expanding} **then**
                      POP formal-parameter stack {level d}
                    $d \leftarrow d-1$
                  write *line* to *new macro definition*
        other: **if** $e=0$ **and** $d>0$ **then** replace each formal parameter
                                by topmost corresponding '#(k,i)'
                                from *formal-parameter stack*
                  if $d=0$ **then write** *line* to *output*
                      else write *line* to *new macro definition*
    if $e>0$ **then** {in expansion mode}
            read *line* from *old macro definition*
                      named in current *macro call*
              replace '#(k,i)' by
                    if $k=1$ **then** *actual-parameter list* $[i]$
                            from *actual-parameter stack*
                      else '#$(k-1,i)$'
    else read *line* from *input*

Figure 4.19   Macro Processing with Nested Definitions and Calls

the IBM OS Assembler language. The original implementation of a macro assembler for that language is described in Freeman [1966]. Both McIlroy [1960] and Brown [1974, ch. 1.4] discuss macro processing for programming languages.

EXERCISES

4.1 Explain the similarities and differences between the use of macros at translation time and the use of subroutines at execution time.

4.2 Rewrite the complete macro definition of Fig. 4.2, using formal parameters in the skeleton only. Repeat for both positional and keyword syntax.

4.3 Let some of the parameters of a macro obey positional syntax, whereas others obey keyword syntax.
a) What are the constraints on the order in which parameters appear in the prototype?
b) What are the constraints on the order in which parameters appear in the call?
c) Is it possible to specify default values for parameters of both types? Describe a mechanism or explain why none is possible.

4.4 Given the macro definition

```
              MCDEFN
LABEL         MOD     DIVIDEND,DIVISOR,REMAINDR
LABEL         LOAD    DIVIDEND
HEAD.SER      SUB     DIVISOR
              BRPOS   HEAD.SER
              BRZERO  HEAD.SER
              ADD     DIVISOR
              STORE   REMAINDR
              MCEND
```

show (a) the edited macro definition as it might stand in the macro-definition table, and (b) the result of expanding the call

```
PUZZLE     MOD      COCONUTS,MONKEYS,LEFTOVER
```

during the seventeenth expansion performed by the macro processor.

4.5 Given the macro definition

```
              MCDEFN
              APPLY   OP,A,B,C
              LOAD    A
              OP      B
              STORE   C
              MCEND
```

show (a) the preprocessed macro definition as it might stand in the macro-definition table, and (b) the result of expanding the call

APPLY   DIVIDE,SUM,COUNT,MEAN.

4.6 Would coroutines provide a suitable implementation of the three modes (definition, expansion, and copy) of the one-pass macro processor of Section 4.4?

4.7 Rewrite the program of Fig. 4.5 to incorporate a single **case** statement.

4.8 Show the output text generated by a macro processor from the following input.

```
MCDEFN
OUTER   A=,B=
MCDEFN
INNER   A=,C=
LOAD    A
MULT    C
MULT    @4
STORE   *+4
BR      *+3
SPACE
LOAD    B
MULT    B
SUB     *-5
MCEND
STORE   A
MCEND
OUTER   B=BRAVO,A=DELTA
INNER   A=ALFA,C=CHARLIE
```

4.9 Continue the processing illustrated in Figs. 4.10 and 4.13.
a) Show the output text and new macro definition which result from the call
   Y   K,L,M,N.
b) Show the output text which results from the subsequent call
   Z   T,U,V,W.

4.10 Consider the definition of a macro B nested within the definition of macro A.
a) Can a call to macro B also appear within macro A? If not, why not? If so, explain any restrictions.
b) Can a call to macro B appear outside macro A? If not, why not? If so, explain any restrictions.

4.11 Will the use of entries of the form "$\#(d,i)$" in the macro-definition table work correctly if the definitions of macros B and C are both nested within that of A, but disjoint from each other?

4.12 It is desired to distinguish among identically named formal parameters of nested macro definitions which use keyword syntax. A friend proposes that each macro be edited when it is defined, by replacing each occurrence of each formal parameter P in the skeleton by P=, except within portions of the skeleton which are delimited by MCDEFN and MCEND. Is the friend's proposal satisfactory? If so, what makes it work? If not, what is needed instead?

4.13 Execute the program of Fig. 4.11 manually, using as input the following text, to which line numbers have been affixed. Show the macro-definition table entries and the output text generated, numbering their lines serially from 11 in the order of their creation. Show the sequence in which source-text and macro-definition lines are read, together with the values of d and e during reading.

```
 1.    MCDEFN
 2.    OUTER    PARM1
 3.    MCDEFN
 4.    INNER    PARM2
 5.    MULT     PARM2
 6.    MCEND
 7.    LOAD     PARM1
 8.    MCEND
 9.    OUTER    ARG1
10.    INNER    ARG2
```

4.14 Rewrite the program of Fig. 4.11 to permit the name of an inner macro definition to be a formal parameter of an outer definition.

4.15 Execute the program of Fig. 4.19 manually, using as input the following text, to which line numbers have been affixed. Show the macro-definition table entries and the output text generated, numbering their lines serially from 16 in the order of their creation. Show the sequence in which source-text and macro-definition lines are read, together with the values of d and e during reading.

```
 1.    MCDEFN
 2.    FIRST    A
 3.    LOAD     A
 4.    MCEND
 5.    MCDEFN
 6.    SECOND A
 7.    FIRST    X
 8.    MCDEFN
 9.    THIRD    A
10.    FIRST    A
11.    MCEND
12.    STORE    A
13.    MCEND
14.    SECOND Y
15.    THIRD    Z
```

4.16 Execute the program of Fig. 4.19 manually, using as input the following text, to which line numbers have been affixed. Show the macro definitions and the output text generated, numbering their lines serially from 21 in the order of their creation. Show the sequence in which source-text and macro-definition lines are read, together with the values of d and e during reading.

```
 1.    MCDEFN
 2.    ALPHA   W
 3.    MCDEFN
 4.    BETA    X
 5.    ADD     X
 6.    MCDEFN
 7.    GAMMA   Y
 8.    WRITE   Y
 9.    MCEND
10.    MCEND
11.    LOAD    W
12.    MCEND
13.    MCDEFN
14.    GAMMA   Z
15.    ALPHA   A
16.    BETA    B
17.    STORE   Z
18.    MCEND
19.    GAMMA   C
20.    GAMMA   C
```

Chapter 5

PROGRAM TRANSLATION

5.1 ATTRIBUTE BINDING

A key concept central to translation is that of *binding*. An attribute is said to be *bound* when its value is specified. The time at which the specification occurs is known as *binding time*. A source-language symbol for a variable, for example, has attributes subject to binding. Its type is usually bound at compilation time by the compiler's action controlled by a declaration statement. The variable's location in main storage is bound at load time by the loader's action controlled by a start address which may be supplied by the operating system. For a load-and-go assembler, however, the location is bound at assembly time. The variable's value is bound at execution time by the machine's action controlled by instructions which correspond perhaps to an assignment statement.

Observe that binding time is not necessarily the time at which the directive to bind is issued. Thus declaration statements and assignment statements are both present at compilation time, but only the former result in compilation-time binding. Observe also that a given attribute is not necessarily bound at a fixed time. The value of an assembler-language variable may be (1) bound at macro processing time; (2) fully bound at assembly time, by a CONST specification; (3) partially bound at assembly time, by synonymy with a second variable, whose value is specified later; (4) partially or fully bound at linking time, if the variable is externally defined; or (5) bound at execution time.

Although the attributes of symbols are those whose binding is of the greatest importance to translators, many entities other than symbols have attributes subject to binding at different times. The number of concurrently executing processes under an operating system may be fixed when the operating system is generated, or subject to change by the machine operator, or may vary dynamically during execution. The binding of the I/O medium for a data set may occur at compilation time or be deferred until devices need to be allocated prior to execution. The priority of different classes of interrupts may be built into the hardware, hence bound when the system is manufactured. Alternatively, it may be bindable by the operating system during execution.

In both operating systems and translators, late binding of an attribute provides flexibility. Thus scheduling-time specification of an I/O medium permits the programmer to test his program with a small card deck and then switch to a disk data file without recompiling. Execution-time binding of array sizes enhances the programmer's ability to process variable amounts of data. The price of late binding is complexity, because provision must be made earlier for the eventual appearance of any of several different specifications.

Early binding, on the other hand, offers simplicity at the price of rigidity. Compilation-time binding of array sizes simplifies both the function of the compiler and the management of storage at execution time. But the programmer must abide by his choice of array size or else recompile the program. Compilation-time specification of I/O devices precludes deciding for each run what medium to use for a data file. There is no need, however, to defer part of the translation until execution time, when it will be performed for each execution rather than only once per compilation.

Attribute binding and binding time should be borne in mind whenever systems of programs are built. Their role in translators influences not only the organization of different types of translators but also the implementation of translation mechanisms.

5.2 TRANSLATION MECHANISMS

The usual task in using a computer is to produce output results, given input data and a computer program. If the program is written in machine language, all that is needed is to let the program control the computer. If a different source language is used instead, translation becomes necessary. Two basic approaches to translation are available, *generation* and *interpretation.*

The generative approach to translation is depicted in Fig. 5.1. The source-language program is translated into a program in target language, usually machine language, and that resulting program is subsequently executed with input data to obtain the desired results. The two stages, translation and execution, are not only distinct conceptually but also separated in practice. Translation can precede execution by an arbitrary length of time.

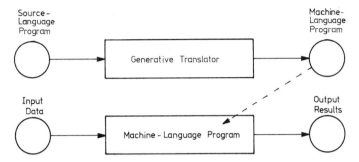

Figure 5.1   Generative Translation

Moreover, execution can be repeated for different input data without repeating the translation.

The machine on which the translation is performed, the *host* machine, is often the same as that which is to run the translated code. Thus a Fortran compiler for the Univac 1110 would normally be written to run on the Univac 1110. There is no requirement, however, that translators other than load-and-go translators and the loader be written to run on the machine for which they produce code. The prefix *cross-* designates a translator whose host and target machines are different. Thus an assembler for the Motorola 6800 which runs on the CDC 6600 is a *cross-assembler* and a PL/I compiler for the DEC PDP-11 which runs on an IBM 370 is a *cross-compiler*. Cross-translators are particularly convenient if the target machine is small relative to the space required by the translator, or if its operating system provides a poor programming environment to the user.

The interpretive approach to translation is symbolized in Fig. 5.2. The source-language program is translated into actions which use the input data to yield the output results; no machine-language form of the program is produced. Translation and execution are intimately linked. Translation time is deferred until execution time and the source-language program is translated each time it is executed.

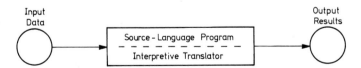

Figure 5.2   Interpretive Translation

A major advantage of generation over interpretation is the greater execution-time efficiency which results from not repeating the translation. Assemblers, linkers, loaders, and most compilers are among the translators which employ generation exclusively or primarily. Macro processors translate chiefly by generation. Some programs called "generators" are also among the translators based on generation.

A translator based on interpretation is an *interpreter*. Some writers use "interpreter" for a translator which performs some generation to obtain a text which is then executed by interpretation. We use the term here in the narrower sense associated with pure interpretation.

Translation by interpretation is deferred until data attributes have been bound. This makes interpreters particularly easy to construct, and they are therefore widely used despite execution-time inefficiencies. Virtually all translators for LISP and for unrestricted APL, and most of those for SNOBOL, are interpreters. At least one Fortran IV compiler for the DEC PDP-11 and the PL/I Checkout compiler for the IBM 360–370 generate first an intermediate-language program which is then executed interpretively. The GET and PUT routines of some operating systems are interpreters, although in others they are generated from information bound when an OPEN of the associated file is executed. Nearly all operating systems obey user commands by means of a program, the command language interpreter, which bears the name of the translation technique. Most conditional generators (see Section 5.3) incorporate a measure of interpretive execution. The processing unit of a computer is itself an interpreter for the machine language of the computer. This is particularly evident in those computers which implement the interpretation by microprogram.

5.2.1   *Interpretation*

The basic function of interpretation is to execute successive source-language statements by translating them into actions. The implementation of this function in an interpreter, whether built of hardware or software, is particularly straightforward. For each statement the same sequence of steps is performed.

1. Obtain statement.
2. Determine action.
3. Perform action.

Before examining interpretation by software, consider a familiar hardware interpreter, the computer executing a machine-language program. The execution (interpretation) sequence is the following.

1. Fetch an instruction (statement) from the location specified by the instruction counter (IC).
2. Advance the IC in preparation for the next fetch.
3. Decode the instruction.
4. Execute the instruction.

After step 4, the computer loops back to step 1 to continue executing the program. The normal sequential execution of instructions is modified by (successful) branch instructions, whose execution (on step 4) replaces the value which was set into the IC on step 2, and by halt instructions, which terminate the looping.

In a software interpreter, the cyclic operation is much the same. The looping action gives its name to the control mechanism of an interpreter, the *interpretive loop* (also "control loop"). Its four steps are similar to those of the computer interpreting machine language.

1. Fetch a source-language statement from the position specified by the statement counter (pseudo-IC).
2. Advance the statement counter.
3. Analyze the statement to determine what operation is to be performed, and upon what operands.
4. Execute the statement by calling a subroutine appropriate to the specified operation.

The structure of an interpreter is quite simple. There is a set of operation subroutines for performing the operations in the source language and an interpretive loop for sequencing the subroutines.

There is usually one subroutine for each instruction defined in the source language. Thus an interpreter for a three-address machine-type language (e.g. add A to B and store the result in C) would incorporate a subroutine for "add", one for "subtract", one for "branch", etc. On the other hand, a more complex language may have several instructions which call for related actions. Here, more subroutines than just one per statement type would help. Thus a PL/I interpreter might have an exponentiation subroutine which is called by an expression evaluation subroutine, which is itself called by an assignment subroutine when the statement $D = B**2 - 4*A*C$; is executed.

The interpretive loop selects the principal subroutine to be executed for each source-language statement. It also selects the operands. If these are specified symbolically, the interpretive loop needs to maintain a symbol table and assign actual storage locations to correspond to the symbols. To assist in determining the operands and the operations to be performed, the interpretive loop may call on other subroutines for lexical and syntactic analysis. Some of this analysis may be performed as a prelude to interpretation. Execution of the interpretive loop, once begun, continues until a source statement causes it to halt, either intentionally or as the result of an error. Otherwise, the interpretive loop accomplishes sequencing of source-language statements by updating the statement counter.

As an illustration, consider an interpreter for a three-address source language. Each statement includes an operation code, two operand addresses, and one result address. The program and data areas occupy the first 1000 storage locations in a decimal machine with words of 12 digits, which we number from 0 to 11. Digits 0-1 are the operation code, digit 2 is required to be zero, digits 3-5 and 6-8 are the first and second operand addresses, and digits 9-11 are the result address. Storage locations 1000-1999 are reserved for the interpretive subroutines, each of which is allocated 10 words beginning at the location obtained from the operation code (e.g. 63) by appending a one at the left and a zero at the right (e.g. 1630). The interpretive loop, which can be placed anywhere from location 2000 on, is shown in Fig. 5.3. The instruction set of Fig. 2.3 is used once again, augmented by the load and store indirect instructions introduced in Chapter 3, and also by a branch indirect instruction. The source-language program is assumed to begin at location 0.

```
                 LOAD     @0
                 STORE    STMTCNTR
    CONTROL      LDIND    STMTCNTR
                 STORE    INSTR
                 LOAD     STMTCNTR
                 ADD      @1
                 STORE    STMTCNTR
                 LDIND    INSTR[3..5]
                 STORE    OPD1
                 LDIND    INSTR[6..8]
                 STORE    OPD2
                 LOAD     INSTR[0..2]
                 ADD      @1000
                 STORE    SUBRADDR
                 BRIND    SUBRADDR
    STMTCNTR     SPACE    1 {statement counter}
    INSTR        SPACE    1 {source-language statement}
    OPD1         SPACE    1 {first operand}
    OPD2         SPACE    1 {second operand}
    SUBRADDR     SPACE    1 {address of subroutine}
```

Figure 5.3   Interpretive Loop

The address of the appropriate subroutine is found by using instruction digit 2 to provide the zero, and addition of 1000 to provide the one. Upon entry to the subroutine, the values of the two operands have been placed in locations OPD1 and OPD2. The subroutine places the result by use of the STIND instruction, and closes the loop by branching back to CONTROL. Figure 5.4 shows subroutines for multiplication and for branching on greater or equal.

In implementing this simple structure, storage must be provided for the interpreter program and its data. The former consists of the control loop and the operation subroutines; the latter consist of the source-language program and that program's data. Some tables may be required, too. The use of a symbol table for referencing symbolic operands has already been mentioned. Another table is convenient for source languages in which each statement specifies a single operation. This table lists the correspondences of subroutine names or addresses to operation codes.

Because translation is not performed until execution time, such operand attributes as location, type, and value are known. This information can be used directly by the translator, for example in accessing an element of an array of dynamically specified size. Another example, in APL, is a variable's type, which can change during execution. Generative translation of unrestricted APL is therefore virtually impossible, but interpretation is straight-forward. Better error diagnostic messages are another result of postponing translation time until operand attributes are bound.

The immediate availability of results at translation time aids in debugging the source-language program. So does having source-language names available at execution time. Another benefit, particularly if I/O facilities are limited, is the avoidance of the extra I/O which may be required by the two-stage operation of Fig. 5.1.

The basic interpreter can be augmented to record facts and statistics of execution. After all, the interpretive loop effects a trace of the source program. Study of the trace information can lead to improvements in the

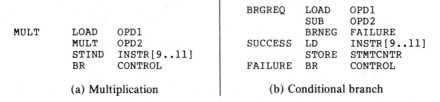

Figure 5.4   Operation Subroutines

program being interpreted. A special case is the machine *simulator*, an interpreter for the machine language of another computer, which may even be still unbuilt. Execution of the simulator usually includes study of the timing of the simulated machine. If that machine is currently under development, this study can assist in detailing its design.

Because no machine-language version of the program is produced, substantial space savings are possible. In fact, the source program and interpreter program together may well require less space than does the result of first translating the source program into machine language.

A major difference between interpretive and generative translation is that under the former a source-language statement is translated *each time* it is executed. This yields a small saving, to be sure, because the interpreter doesn't even examine source code which is not reached in a particular run. The principal effect, however, is the loss of time in repeatedly translating the statements of a source-language loop. This effect is further compounded by the overhead of performing sequencing operations in source language rather than in machine code. The net result is that interpretation is slow. Interpretive execution of a program typically takes between 20 and 100 times as long as execution of a machine-language version of the program. To be altogether fair, one must count the effort of producing that machine-language program, either by hand or as the result of compilation. Nevertheless, interpreters are not chosen for their execution efficiency. They are chosen instead for the space saving, for the ease with which they are constructed, and for the flexibility obtainable by deferring translation until execution time.

The inefficiency of interpretive programming can sometimes be mitigated by coding important sections of the program directly in the host computer's machine language, the *host language*. Correct execution of a host-language section is provided by *mode switching*. The last source-language statement which precedes the inserted host-language program is a mode-switching statement. Upon recognizing that statement, the interpreter stores enough of its own status to permit it to be resumed later, then branches to the inserted code. This work, diagrammed in Fig. 5.5(a), is easily performed by one of the interpreter's subroutines, to which the control loop passes as a parameter the address of the start of the host-language insert. The inserted code must terminate with restoration of the interpreter's status and a branch back to the interpretive loop, as shown in Fig. 5.5(b). The numbers on the arrows in the two figures indicate the temporal sequence of the corresponding transfers of control. An alternative to having a special mode switch subroutine in the interpreter is simply to treat the host-language insert as a user-written subroutine without parameters.

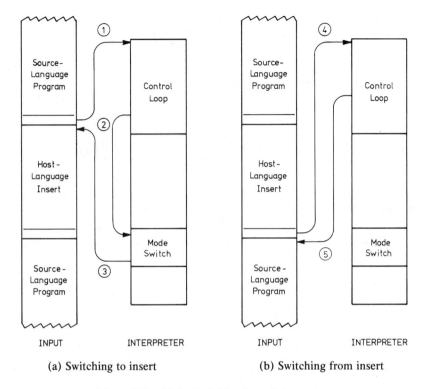

(a) Switching to insert	(b) Switching from insert

Figure 5.5   Mode Switching in an Interpreter

5.2.2   *Generation*

Just as execution of a process specified by the user is the objective of interpretation, so is it also the objective of generation. But whereas interpretation synthesizes actions to be performed immediately, generation synthesizes code to be executed later. The generation process itself is really just a matter of substitution; target-language code is substituted for source-language code. The complexity of the required substitution depends on the nature of the translation. The generation of a machine-language instruction from an assembler-language instruction is usually rather simple. The generation of machine-language text from a statement in a rich programming language is a much more complex process. Between these two extremes lie such generations as that of expanding a macro call into assembler-language statements.

As the first example of generation consider the translation of line 11 of the program of Fig. 2.6(a), using the symbol table of Fig. 2.6(b). Scanning the source text has identified the operation as COPY, operand 1 as OLD, and operand 2 as OLDER. The operation is looked up in the operation table (Fig. 2.3), which gives 13 as the value to be substituted for it. The two operands are looked up in the symbol table, which yields 36 and 35 as the corresponding values. The three numbers are combined into 133635, which is the instruction generated by the assembler.

The organization of the generator can be extremely simple. Assume that the lexical scanner assigns to variables *operand1* and *operand2* the symbols, if any, in the respective fields, and that a function procedure *LOCATION* returns the location of its one parameter, as determined from the symbol table. Then a search of the operation table is used to select a subroutine which corresponds to the assembler-language operation code. For COPY, that subroutine would be the following, where the comma is used to represent catenation.

$$word1 \leftarrow 13$$
$$word2 \leftarrow LOCATION \text{ (operand1)}$$
$$word3 \leftarrow LOCATION \text{ (operand2)}$$
$$code \leftarrow word1, word2, word3$$

If address expressions are permitted, the call to *LOCATION* would be replaced by one to an address evaluation routine which itself calls *LOCATION* as needed. If the assembler language includes extended mnemonics (see Section 2.3.1), the operation table entry specifies not only the text to be placed in the machine-language operation code field, but other portions of the instruction as well. If the fields of the machine-language instruction do not coincide with addressable words, as they do for the mythical computer of Chapter 2, it is necessary for the generator to piece together partial words, using whatever bit-manipulation facilities are available to it. If the generation of a constant is required, complicated conversions may be necessary, but the translation is conceptually still simple.

As a second example of generation, consider the enrichment of the assembler language by an add-to-storage instruction ADST. This instruction causes the content of the accumulator to be added to that of the storage location whose symbolic name is ACCUM. Although a new instruction has been added to the assembler language, the machine remains unchanged. The addition must still be performed by executing an ADD instruction, which will destroy the previous content of the accumulator. A specific storage location, named BACKUP, is therefore assumed available to hold a copy of that value. Each time ADST is encountered in the source program it is to be translated as if it had been replaced, before assembly, by the following four statements.

```
STORE    BACKUP
ADD      ACCUM
STORE    ACCUM
LOAD     BACKUP
```

The replacement could be performed either during a pre-pass of the entire text or upon recognition of ADST during Pass 1 of the assembler. Although the latter choice would often be adopted to avoid an extra pass of the text, the former will be assumed here for ease of description. The generation program, shown in Fig. 5.6, involves only substitution.

The new instruction ADST can be viewed, of course, as a parameterless macro. The macro processing technique of Chapter 4 serves to translate it whether it is user-defined or system-defined. In the implementation in that chapter, the text to be substituted is first stored in and subsequently read from a data structure, the macro-definition table, which is accessed by the translation program. In the implementation of Fig. 5.6, the text to be substituted is not merely accessed by, but actually embodied in, the translation program. This second technique is therefore restricted to system-defined macros, unless the translator is itself to be generated after the macro is defined.

If the macros have parameters, values of the actual parameters must be inserted in the appropriate positions of the text to be generated. The macro ABSDIF, defined in Fig. 4.4(a), serves as an example. Assume that the format

```
columns    1- 8     label
          10-15     operation
          17-33     operand(s)
```

is used for both input and output lines. The heart of the generation program might then be written as in Fig. 5.7. The comma is again used for catenation, and the details of character extraction have been suppressed in favor of an indexing-type notation. The global numeric variable *serial* holds the serial number of the current macro expansion. The procedure *CHAR* converts a numeric variable into a 4-character string. The procedure *LEXANAL* performs a lexical analysis of the character string named as its first parameter. It delivers to the variables *parm0*, *parm1*, etc., the eight-character string values of the label and of the other macro parameters, the total number of which is specified as the second parameter of *LEXANAL*.

```
read line
while line ≠ empty do
    if opcode = 'ADST'
        then write '            STORE   BACKUP'
             write '            ADD     ACCUM'
             write '            STORE   ACCUM'
             write '            LOAD    BACKUP'
        else write line
    read line
```

Figure 5.6 Parameter-Free Generation

A somewhat different organization would be for the generator to have the six output lines, with parameters not filled in, available as global data. The following would be used for ABSDIF.

```
'            LOAD                     '
'            SUB                      '
'            BRPOS    ST              '
'            LOAD                     '
'            SUB                      '
'ST          STORE                    '
```

In translating the ABSDIF instruction, the generator would make a copy of the foregoing lines and insert into the appropriate positions the symbols which appear as the parameters in the instruction.

Although this book is devoted to program translation, another kind of generation deserves brief mention. Sometimes the input to a generative translator is in the form not of an algorithm, but rather of a description of the desired result. The distinction is that an algorithm is composed of im-

```
if line [10.. 15] = 'ABSDIF'
    then serial ← serial + 1
         ser ← CHAR (serial)
         LEXANAL (line, 3)
         write         parm0,  '    LOAD     ' , parm1
                       '        SUB      ' , parm2
                       '        BRPOS    ' ,'ST', ser
                       '        LOAD     ' , parm2
                       '        SUB      ' , parm1
              'ST' ,ser, '     STORE    ' , parm3
```

Figure 5.7 System-Defined Parameterized Generation

perative statements which specify how a problem is to be solved. A result description, on the other hand, is composed of declarative statements which specify the problem, but not the method of solution. The requirements of generation are clearly different for the two types of source language.

Specifications for sorting data and for printing reports are often stated in nonalgorithmic form. A *sort generator* accepts descriptions of a file of data items and of the desired sequence, and generates a program to effect the sort. Figure 5.8 shows, for one particular sort generator, the required system commands (prefaced by //) and two statements which describe the record fields and sorting sequence. A *report program generator* (RPG), as one of its activities, accepts descriptions of a file of data items and of the desired printing format (see Fig. 5.9), and generates a program to effect the printing. These generators from nonalgorithmic source texts also perform system-defined substitutions, but their requirements are rather different from those of program translation, and will not be discussed further. We might observe in passing that queries to data base management systems and commands to operating systems, which are often handled by interpreters, are also often expressed in nonalgorithmic languages.

We have considered a system-defined parameterized macro for an assembler language, and seen how code could be generated to correspond to the choice of parameters. Because the correspondence was predefined, the generator code could be prepared ahead of time. Such advance preparation is not possible, however, if the user is permitted to define his own macros. Instead, construction of the generator code must be deferred until after the user-supplied definition has been encountered.

Suppose that the ABSDIF instruction, as previously described, is defined not by the system, but rather by the user. The generation program of Fig. 5.7

```
//SORT      EXEC  PGM=SORT
//SORTLIB   DD    DISP=SHR,DSN=SYS1.SORTLIB
//SYSOUT    DD    SYSOUT=A
//SORTWK01  DD    SPACE=(2298,50,,CONTIG),UNIT=SYSDA
//SORTWK02  DD    SPACE=(2298,50,,CONTIG),UNIT=SYSDA
//SORTWK03  DD    SPACE=(2298,50,,CONTIG),UNIT=SYSDA
//SORTOUT   DD    SYSOUT=A,DCB=(RECFM=F,BLKSIZE=80)
//SORTIN    DD    DSN=UNC.CS.E578C.BELLOVIN.TRANSACT,DISP=SHR
//SYSIN     DD    *
 SORT   FIELDS=(5,1,CH,A,1,3,ZD,D,7,6,ZD,A)
 RECORD  LENGTH=(80),TYPE=F
```

Figure 5.8   Example of Input to Sort Generator

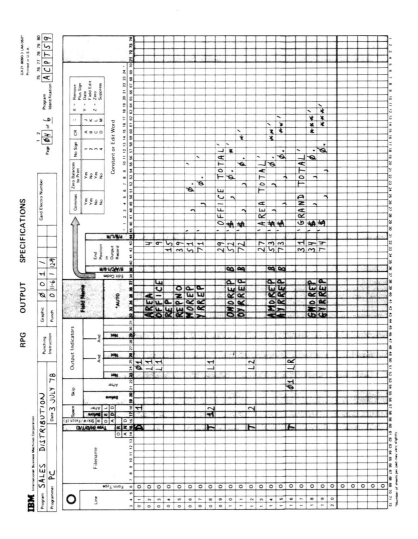

Figure 5.9   Example of Input to RPG

cannot be prepared in advance of encountering the user's definition; it must be constructed from the definition. Such construction can be performed by a system-defined program which accepts an arbitrary prototype, like

        SPOT   ABSDIF A,B,C

and a model of the corresponding text, such as the edited definition of Fig. 4.4(b), and generates a generator program which will replace the former by the latter. The generation mechanisms we have already seen are wholly adequate to this task. For example, the fragment

   if *line* [10..15] = 'ABSDIF'

would be generated from

   if *line* [10..15] = '

by insertion of the operation field of the prototype. Hence the code to perform the user-defined generation can itself be generated by a system-defined generation which occurs when the user's definition is processed. The task of user-defined generation has thus been reduced to the simpler task of system-defined generation.

Although this process involving two stages of generation is perfectly feasible, in practice it is rarely used in preference to the line-by-line technique of Chapter 4. Although a program to generate an entire user-defined macro expansion cannot be prepared in advance of the definition, a program to generate one line of an arbitrary macro expansion can be prepared and incorporated in the macro processor. The first stage of generation is in effect accomplished once when the macro processor is built and need not be repeated for every macro definition.

Another example of program translation is that of the PL/I preprocessor input

```
%DECLARE X CHARACTER, Y FIXED;
%X = 'Y+Z';
%Y = 5;
A = X;
```

to the following single statement.

```
A = 5+Z;
```

The three preprocessor statements (those marked by a % sign) can be used in the generation of a generator which substitutes $5+Z$ for X in the fourth statement. Although the process is similar in concept to the two-stage generation process for user-defined macros, the greater richness of PL/I and its preprocessor language render that type of implementation even more unwieldy. More satisfactory is a partially interpretive approach in which each preprocessor statement inserts, changes, or deletes entries in a preprocessor symbol table, and the regular statements are translated by an interpretation which uses the current symbol table entries. The foregoing example was chosen for its simplicity rather than its utility; most use of the PL/I preprocessor involves conditional generation, as illustrated in Section 5.3.1.

The generation of intermediate code such as the "quadruples"

```
SUB     A     B     T1
BRNEG   T1    -     +4
MULT    B     D     T2
ADD     T2    A     C
BR      -     -     +3
MULT    A     D     T3
ADD     T3    B     C
```

from the PL/I statement pair

```
IF A<B THEN C = B+A*D;
       ELSE C = A+B*D;
```

is typical of compilation. The syntactic and semantic complexity of most programming languages, as opposed to assembler languages and most macro processing, make it appropriate to treat compilation as a separate subject. Much of Chapter 6 and all of Chapter 7 are devoted to compilation.

5.3 CONDITIONAL GENERATION

5.3.1 *The Generation-Time Machine*

The preprocessor translation of

```
%DECLARE I FIXED;
%DO I=1 TO 10;
A(I) = B(I) + C(I);
%END;
```

into the ten PL/I statements

```
A(1)  = B(1)  + C(1);
A(2)  = B(2)  + C(2);
---
A(10) = B(10) + C(10);
```

treats the one regular source-text statement (the one with no % sign) in a manner which depends on specific values (here, 1 and 10) presented at generation time. This adaptation of the output text to generation-time conditions is known as *conditional* generation and often considerably augments the usefulness of a translator. Some assemblers, too, perform conditional assembly. The DAS assembler for the Varian 620/i offers conditional assembly as a means of specializing the generated code to either the 16-bit or the 18-bit version of the machine, as selected at assembly time. Another example is the REPEAT instruction presented in Section 2.3.1.

The most widespread application of conditional generation, however, is to macro processing. In particular, two functions which are dependent upon conditional generation markedly enhance the utility of macros. One is the validation of operands of macro instructions. The other is the generalization of a single macro-definition skeleton, especially over a variety of data types. These functions require that symbol attributes and means of testing them be available at generation time. Conditional macro processing, because of its importance, will serve as our illustration of conditional generation. The techniques presented are applicable, with little modification, to conditional assembly and conditional preprocessing.

What generation-time capabilities are required for conditional generation? The macro processor must be able to evaluate conditions and alter the flow of processing accordingly. Although mechanisms for iteration and selection could be provided in the language, typical facilities usually include only an unconditional branch, a conditional skip or branch, and labels to mark branch destinations. Normal sequential flow is maintained by the input-text line counter. Generation-time variables are also needed, both for temporary storage during expansion and for communication between macros. With facilities for manipulating these variables we complete the requirements for a computer system which operates at generation time, executing programs written in a language of macros with conditional generation. The "processing unit" of this system is implemented in software rather than hardware, but the *generation-time machine* is none the less real. Its existence serves as a reminder that we are able to perform any operation at any stage of translation, although not necessarily with equal ease at each stage.

5.3.2   *Conditional Macro Processor*

The implementation of a macro processor for a macro language with conditional facilities embodies an implementation of the generation-time machine. A closer look at the language of this machine will illustrate what further translation is required.

The generation-time variables are usually distinguished from other symbols by being declared explicitly. The declaration specifies both type and scope. The most common scopes are (1) global to all macro definitions and (2) local to the definition in which the declaration is encountered, and perhaps to definitions nested within that one. Because a macro processor is a text manipulator, character variables are a principal type. Numeric variables, especially integers for counting, and boolean variables, for recording conditions, are usually also provided. A simple declaration format might include the variable symbol in the label field, scope declaration (GLOBAL or LOCAL) in the operation field, and type specification (BOOL, CHAR, or INT) in the operand field. An example would be CNTR   LOCAL INT.

Expressions involving these variables can be formed using appropriate operations, typically arithmetic operations on integers, logical operations on booleans, substring and catenation on characters, and comparison on all three types. Assignment of the value of such an expression to a variable is accomplished by an assignment instruction, perhaps like CNTR   ASSIGN CNTR+1. The value of a relational expression which includes a comparison operation may be assigned to a boolean variable or used directly as a condition in a sequence control operation.

The sequencing operations usually available correspond to the **goto**, **if** *condition* **then goto**, and **return** statements of higher-level languages. The second one is alone sufficient, and might be written in a form such as

```
MCGOIF  (INDEX<N)%BEGIN
```

where %BEGIN appears as the label on the line of input text from which processing is to continue if the condition INDEX < N holds. An alternative to the conditional branch is the conditional skip, say SKIPIF or simply SKIP, which skips one line if the condition is satisfied, and therefore need not specify a label. An unconditional branch must be provided for use in conjunction with the conditional skip.

Generation-time labels must be distinguished from the execution-time labels previously encountered, because they are neither to be entered in the symbol table nor generated in the output text; they just mark positions in the input text. In our hypothetical language, both types of labels are defined by being used in the label field. Since neither type is declared and their positional use is the same, the distinction must be lexical. Here the character % is used as a lexical marker on generation-time labels. Sometimes both a generation-time label and an execution-time label are needed on a statement, but in most assembler languages only a single label field is provided. This impasse is solved by a dummy operation code which does nothing other than provide an extra input-text line on which a generation-time label can be hung. If that operation is NULL, the lines

```
%FRONT    NULL
ARG.CNTR CONST   CNTR
```

allow both labels to mark the same effective location.

Although the unconditional branch is a special case of the conditional branch, it is convenient to provide it explicitly. An example would be MCGO %FRONT. Macro expansion may terminate conditionally somewhere within the body of the macro definition. A branch to the closing delimiter would, of course, have the desired effect, but the provision of an expansion *terminator* distinct from the definition delimiter can be used instead to make the definition easier to read and write. An operation code such as MCEXIT can serve in this capacity.

Three examples of conditional macros are presented to illustrate the foregoing features. The first is a generalization of the repetitive assembly

```
        REPEAT 2,(1,10)
ARG$    CONST  $
FCT$    SPACE
```

discussed in Section 2.3.1. The call TABLE 1,10 of the macro defined in Fig. 5.10 would result in the expansion shown in Chapter 2.

The second example is a macro whose expansion delivers to the second argument a copy of the content of the first argument. Because the accumulator is used to effect the operation, its content is first saved in a temporary location and afterwards restored. Thus the expansion of MOVE X,Y is

```
STORE   TEMP
LOAD    X
STORE   Y
LOAD    TEMP
```

```
              MCDEFN
              TABLE    LOWER,UPPER
CNTR          LOCAL    INT
CNTR          ASSIGN   LOWER
%FRONT        NULL
ARG.CNTR      CONST    CNTR
FCT.CNTR      SPACE
CNTR          ASSIGN   CNTR+1
              MCGOIF   (CNTR≤UPPER)%FRONT
              MCEND
```

Figure 5.10   Table Generation Macro

If, however, either argument is named ACC, then the accumulator content is meant instead of a storage location. As a result, the call MOVE   ACC,Y yields the one-line expansion STORE   Y and the call MOVE   X,ACC produces LOAD   X. The macro is defined in Fig. 5.11, which uses a conditional skip but no branching to arbitrary lines of text. If conditional branches were used instead, two would suffice instead of four skips.

The third example generates code to add two *n*-element vectors which may be either fixed-point or floating-point. It is assumed that T(*symbol*) returns the data type of *symbol* as a character string, and that ADDFIX and ADDFLT are machine instructions for adding numbers of the two types. The starting addresses of the operand vectors are A and B; that of the result vector is C; zero-origin indexing is used. The mechanism for generating error messages is not specified. Figure 5.12 shows the vector addition macro. Note that if a call of VECADD precedes the definition of the symbol passed to it as an actual parameter corresponding to the formal parameter A, then T(A) is a forward reference to a symbol attribute. Note

```
MCDEFN
MOVE     A,B
SKIPIF   (A='ACC')  or  (B='ACC')
STORE    TEMP
SKIPIF   A='ACC'
LOAD     A
SKIPIF   B='ACC'
STORE    B
SKIPIF   (A='ACC')  or  (B='ACC')
LOAD     TEMP
MCEND
```

Figure 5.11   Value Copying Macro

```
                 MCDEFN
                 VECADD  A,B,C,N
INDEX            LOCAL   INT
TYPEA            LOCAL   CHAR
TYPEB            LOCAL   CHAR
TYPEA            ASSIGN  T(A)
TYPEB            ASSIGN  T(B)
                 MCGOIF  (TYPEA=TYPEB)%OK
                 {generate error message}
                 MCEXIT
%OK              NULL
INDEX            ASSIGN  0
%BEGIN           LOAD    A+.INDEX
                 MCGOIF  (TYPEA='FLOAT')%FLOAT
                 ADDFIX  B+.INDEX
                 MCGO    %BOTH
%FLOAT           ADDFLT  B+.INDEX
%BOTH            STORE   C+.INDEX
INDEX            ASSIGN  INDEX+1
                 MCGOIF  (INDEX<N)%BEGIN
                 MCEND
```

Figure 5.12   Vector Addition Macro

also the syntactic distinction between $A+$.INDEX in an operand field to be generated and INDEX$+1$ in a generation-time assignment. The period segregates INDEX as a generation-time symbol whose value, rather than the symbol itself, is to be generated. All macro processors must provide for this distinction, but they are not restricted to the particular convention illustrated here.

For another example of a forward reference to an attribute of an assembler-language symbol consider a set of programs to hash alphanumeric part numbers of various lengths. Each program hashes part numbers of one specific length and requires a mask twice as long as the part number and consisting of binary ones for the middle half of its length and zeros at the ends. A single macro is provided to generate that mask, whatever the required length. It is called by each of the hashing programs, which passes as an actual parameter the symbol which represents the part number. The macro definition must refer to the field length associated with that symbol, which will be defined only later in the text when the program which contains the macro call is reached.

Conditional assembler language is seen to resemble other higher-level languages. Variables are declared and their values assigned; subroutines (macros) are defined and invoked; expressions are evaluated and compared; sequence control is exercised. How should this language be translated? Generation of machine-language code to be incorporated in the conditional generator is attractive because of potential space savings. The input text line INDEX   ASSIGN INDEX + 1 could easily occupy 80 characters in a fixed-format conditional assembler program. It could be compiled to a load, add, store sequence which might be no more than 15% as long. Nevertheless, a separate generator (or compiler) is not generally used on macro definitions. Although historical reasons may be a primary cause, there is a good technical reason. An interpreter is easier to write, and it is probably not worth while to compile a macro definition which may be called only once, as many are.

Thus the instructions about how to generate are usually executed interpretively, the conditional macro processor racing around to generation-time labels as it executes the conditional and unconditional branches. To avoid the danger of endless looping during macro expansions, a limit can be imposed on the number of successful generation-time branches performed.

5.3.3 *Recursive Macros*

In Chapter 4, it was tacitly assumed that a nested macro definition or call would refer to a macro whose name was not that of the enclosing definition. Let us explicitly relax this restriction and examine the consequences. If the definition of macro A encloses a second definition of A, then the first call of A will result in A being redefined. The original definition will no longer be accessible; it contains the seed of its own destruction. In the example of Fig. 5.13(a) all of the text outside the inner pair of delimiters will be callable only once. Consequently, it is more satisfactory to define that text as a macro separate from the inner definition, and to assign different names to the two macros.

A different situation is shown in Fig. 5.13(b), where the definition of macro A includes a call of macro A. When A is first called, the expansion of A will generate a second call of A, whose expansion will in turn generate a third call, and so on. The self-perpetuating call of this recursive macro would appear to be even less useful than the self-destructive definition of Fig. 5.13(a). The recursion need not be infinite, however, if conditional generation is provided. An appropriate test within the macro can terminate the repetition after a finite number of calls. Such a test can be made, however, only if the expansion of one instance of the call can use information developed in the expansion of a previous instance. An example of such in-

```
A        MCDEFN                    A        MCDEFN
         - - -                              - - -
A        MCDEFN                             - - -
         - - -                     A
         MCEND                              - - -
         - - -                              - - -
         MCEND                              MCEND
```

   (a) Self-destruction   (b) Recursive call

Figure 5.13   Identical Names in Nested Macros

formation might be the number of instances expanded thus far. To communicate this information from one instance of a call to another, generation-time variables are needed. Thus the generation-time machine provides a mechanism for implementing the recursion.

Why would anyone want to write a macro which calls itself? Conditional macro language is the "machine language" of the generation-time machine. For that machine, as for others, recursion is a powerful programming tool. Moreover, macro processing in its most general form is arbitrary string manipulation. Programs for that application, as for any other, are sometimes more understandable in a recursive form than in an iterative form. The resulting processing tends to be more costly, but the benefits may be well worth the cost.

A recursive macro to reverse the characters of a string is presented in Fig. 5.14. If the string is longer than one character, the leftmost character is removed and the remaining characters are reversed by a recursive call of

```
         MCDEFN
         REVERS STRING
FIRST    LOCAL  CHAR
REST     LOCAL  CHAR
L        LOCAL  INT
L        ASSIGN LENGTH(STRING)
         MCGOIF (L=1)%DONE
FIRST    ASSIGN STRING[1]
REST     ASSIGN STRING[2..L]
         REVERS REST
STRING   ASSIGN REST,FIRST
%DONE    MCEND
```

Figure 5.14   Recursive Macro for String Reversal

the macro. The original leftmost character is then appended to the right. If the string is only one character long, no action is taken.

The sequence

```
        TOKEN      GLOBAL CHAR
        TOKEN      ASSIGN 'ABCD'
                   REVERS TOKEN
```

would result in the character string 'DCBA' being placed in the generation-time variable TOKEN. The original call of REVERS has the actual parameter TOKEN, whose value is the character string 'ABCD'. Expansion of REVERS issues a second call, with actual parameter REST, having value 'BCD'. The second call results in a third, with actual parameter also named REST, but with value 'CD', and the final call will have actual parameter REST with value 'D'. The occurrences of the generation-time variable REST at different levels of recursion are distinct, because each is local to a single instance of the macro, and they can hold different values. To pass the parameters correctly, the actual-parameter stack described in Section 4.6 is entirely adequate. No extra provision needs to be made for the recursive nature of the calls. It should be observed, however, that the actual parameter REST placed on the actual-parameter stack when the ith instance of REVERS calls the $i+1$st refers to the symbol REST at the ith level. Thus when '#1' is encountered in the macro definition being scanned at expansion level $i+1$, it is replaced by a reference to REST at level i.

5.4 MACRO ASSEMBLER

The combination of a macro processor with an assembler is the widely used translator known as a *macro assembler*. A straightforward implementation couples an assembler, which may or may not be conditional, with a distinct macro processor whose output serves as the assembler's input. An alternative approach is to embed macro processing within an assembler. This makes it possible to avoid duplicating actions and data structures common to both, and to tailor the macro processing more directly to the assembler-language application. Because of the restriction to a particular application, the resulting translator is sometimes called an *applied* macro assembler. The phrase "macro assembler" by itself does not make explicit whether the macro processing is performed independently of the assembly.

Implementation of an applied macro assembler may take either of two forms, macro processing during assembler Pass 1 or after Pass 1. To effect macro processing during Pass 1 of the assembler it is necessary only to incorporate the regular Pass 1 actions into the one-pass algorithm for the desired complexity of macro processing. Each of the four macro processing algorithms of Chapter 4 includes the statement "**write** *line* to *output*", which is executed whenever a line other than a macro call or a delimiter is encountered outside definition mode. That statement is simply replaced by normal Pass 1 processing. If *line* is a machine instruction, the location counter is advanced and symbol table management is performed. If *line* is an assembler instruction, the appropriate Pass 1 action is performed.

The chief advantage of embedding macro processing in the first pass of the assembler is to keep the total number of passes down to two. A corresponding disadvantage is that quite a lot must be packed into the first pass program, which may become unpleasantly large. Another drawback is that forward references to attributes of symbols not yet defined cannot be made during macro processing.

Some of these drawbacks disappear if the macro processing is deferred until after the completion of assembler Pass 1. Because macro definition is not begun until Pass 1 has built the symbol table, both macro definitions and macro calls can make forward references to attributes of symbols. Macro expansion does, however, cause insertions in the assembler-language program text, thus invalidating the location values in the symbol table. Other attributes, however, such as field length, name length, and relocatability mode, remain unchanged by the expansion process.

The IBM 360 Operating System Assembler (F-level) is an applied macro assembler of this type, and makes four passes. Pass 1 is essentially the first pass of the assembler, although some editing of macro definitions is performed. Pass 2 performs the macro processing, with reference to the symbol table. Pass 3 reconstructs the symbol table, incorporating symbols generated during Pass 2 and providing correct location values which reflect the expansion performed during Pass 2. The second pass of the assembler is Pass 4. The disadvantages of having to make several passes are counterbalanced by two major advantages. One is the language feature of permitting macros to refer forward to symbol attributes. The other is the reduction in program size for any given pass. In fact, meeting tight space constraints was a major design criterion of that macro assembler.

Extra passes are useful not only for processing macros within an assembler. A third assembler pass would permit forward references by the SET-type definitional facility. Other potential uses of a third pass are the optimization of index register assignments and such simple code optimization as removing the redundant STORE-LOAD pair from the second-level expansion in Fig. 4.16.

FOR FURTHER STUDY

The concept of binding is addressed briefly by Wegner [1968, sect. 1.1.7], Brooks and Iverson [1969, pp. 386–388], Freeman [1975, sect. 11.7.1], and Pratt [1975, sect. 2-7]. One of the best treatments is that of Elson [1973], who devotes Chapter 5 to the subject.

The process of generation is treated at least implicitly in all of the references on assemblers, macro processors, and compilers. A brief, but sound, explicit presentation is that in Section 8.5 of Brooks and Iverson [1969]. The contrast between generation and interpretation is presented carefully in Lee [1974, pp. 27–38]. Berthaud and Griffiths [1973] distinguish clearly between generative and interpretive translation in the implementation of a compiler. Interpreters appear to be described rarely. Two good expositions, however, are those of Brooks and Iverson [1969, sect. 8.2] and of Glass [1969].

EXERCISES

5.1   How does an interpreter handle forward references?

5.2   Identify one parameter which *must* be passed to the mode-switch subroutine.

5.3   Describe in detail a scheme for passing an arbitrary number of parameters between a source-language program being interpreted and a host-language insert.

5.4   Write a mode-switch subroutine to accompany the interpretive loop of Fig. 5.3.

5.5   Define, as is done in Section 5.2.2 for ADST, a new instruction called INCR, which increments the content of a storage location. Assume the operations of Fig. 2.3, but do not make use of BACKUP. There are two parameters. One parameter is the symbolic name of the storage location; a second parameter is written as the integer to be added. Write a generation program which will replace each occurrence of the INCR instruction by the appropriate lines of assembler-language code. Use whatever assembler features are appropriate.

5.6   Rewrite the definition in Fig. 5.11, using conditional branching rather than SKIPIF. Follow the syntax conventions of Chapter 5.

5.7   The macro defined in Fig. 5.12 is called by the statement
            VECADD   ADDEND,AUGEND,SUM,4
for which each of the first three actual parameters is known to be of type 'FLOAT'. Consider the printed lines to be numbered from 1 through 21.

State the sequence in which lines are read from the macro definition during expansion of the call, and show the output text generated.

5.8 Using the language defined implicitly in Section 5.3.2 with the substring notation of Fig. 5.14, write a definition for the following macro. The prototype is ROOM   NAME,LENGTH where NAME is a symbolic parameter and LENGTH a positive integer parameter. If the initial letter of the symbol is in the range I..N, the macro generates the stated integer number of occurrences of SPACE   1 and labels the first of them with the symbol. If the initial letter is different and the integer is even, the macro generates one-half the stated number of occurrences of SPACE   2 and labels the first of them with the symbol. If the initial letter is different and the integer is odd, the macro calls a parameter-free macro ERROR.

Repeat the exercise using a real macro assembler, if one is available to you.

5.9 Let the definition of macro A contain a call of macro B, and the definition of B contain a call of A. Are the macros recursive?

5.10 Write a recursive macro, in the source language of Chapter 5, to solve the problem of the Towers of Hanoi.

5.11 In an applied macro assembler, will macro processing after assembler Pass 1 work if a macro expansion redefines symbols defined by EQU or SET?

Chapter 6

INITIAL SOURCE-LANGUAGE PROCESSING

6.1 OVERVIEW

Before generating code or calling an interpretive subroutine, a translator must determine the content of the source-language text to be translated. Unlike generation and interpretation, which are processes whose goal is synthesis, the determination of source-language content is analytic. Lexical analysis is required to separate the source-language text into the elements of which the language is composed. Syntactic analysis is required to ascertain the structural relationships among those elements. These analyses of the source-language text are independent, at least in principle, of later stages of translation. True, it may be convenient to combine syntactic and semantic analysis in a compiler, but this is a practical convenience rather than a theoretical necessity. Lexical and syntactic analysis can be effected independently of whether generation or interpretation is to follow, and independently of the choice of target language or of host language. The extent and nature of the initial processing do depend, however, on the source language of the program text being analyzed. Both the type of language and the extent to which its format is fixed influence the analyses.

Before discussing the different requirements which may be imposed, let us agree on a few definitions. The elementary unit of text is the *character*. Printed or displayed, a character normally occupies one column of output (and is sometimes called a "graphic" or a "grapheme"). Examples of characters are shown in Fig. 6.1(a). The input of a character may require a single key stroke on card punch or computer terminal, but sometimes more than one stroke is required. For example, the upper and lower case versions of the same letter are distinguished by the presence or absence of certain shifts. Overstruck characters are typically produced by combining two distinct components and an intervening backspace. The term *stroke* will be used for these elements which can be combined into characters. The last character of Fig. 6.1(a) is an overstruck character produced by three

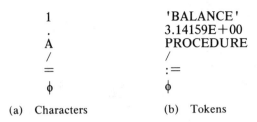

(a)   Characters   (b)   Tokens

Figure 6.1   Example Language Elements

strokes. Sometimes the strokes are converted into the requisite character by hardware, such as the multiple punch feature of a card punch, but more often a program is used. The characters in turn are grouped into *tokens*, the smallest language units which convey meaning. Figure 6.1(b) shows some samples of tokens. The word "symbol" is often used as a synonym for "token", and occasionally for "character" or even "stroke". For this reason we shall not attempt to define "symbol" precisely.

The task of lexical analysis, then, is to subdivide the source-language text into tokens and to identify the *type* of each token, whether identifier, constant, operator, etc. The task of syntactic analysis is to determine how groups of tokens are interrelated.

For an assembler language, the syntactic analysis is usually simple. Keyword parameters must be distinguished from positional, the structure of address expressions must be elucidated, generation-time variables must be distinguished from execution-time variables. By and large, however, the syntax of assembler language is constrained to be simple; interline syntax is particularly restricted. Lexical analysis is made easier in many assemblers by using a fixed format which dictates that only certain types of token are permitted in certain locations.

An interpreter for a language with many control structures, an extensive hierarchy of one-character operators, but allowing only one-character operands, would need a lexical analyzer hardly more intricate than a table lookup routine. Its syntax analyzer, however, would need to handle both complicated expressions and extensive interstatement syntax.

An APL interpreter, on the other hand, requires more lexical analysis and less syntactic analysis. The paucity of control structures simplifies the interstatement syntax; the positional hierarchy of operators (see Section 6.2.2) displays the syntactic structure in a form which permits almost direct execution. The "vi fi" property of APL (see Section 6.3.3) and the use of overstruck characters impose greater demands on the lexical analyzer.

Compilers for languages like PL/I or Pascal normally require a moderate amount of lexical analysis followed by substantial syntactic analysis.

Although the requirements of various translators differ in extent, the nature of the lexical and syntactic analysis is much the same for all. For that reason, the initial source language processing is discussed here for translators in general rather than separately for each type of translator. We discuss syntactic analysis first, in Section 6.2, because of its central importance to translation and for two other reasons. (1) Concepts and techniques of syntactic analysis can be applied to lexical analysis. (2) Some of the requirements on lexical analysis are imposed by syntactic analysis. Then, in Section 6.3, we examine lexical analysis. Finally, the management of symbol tables, so important as a tool not only in initial source-language processing but also in later stages of translation, is reviewed in Section 6.4.

6.2   SYNTACTIC ANALYSIS

In this section we assume that lexical analysis of the source-language text has already been performed. The task at hand therefore is to determine the syntactic structure of a string of tokens. For this part of the translation process, unlike many others, a substantial body of highly developed theory guides our efforts. This theory is a formal mathematical development proceeding from axioms about languages, including computer languages, toward theorems which describe the properties of the languages and of algorithms for analyzing the languages syntactically. Our view in this book is less that of the pure mathematician who values the theorems for their intrinsic interest than it is that of the applied mathematician who uses the theorems to guide the engineering effort of implementing translators. Although the methods to be described are based on theorems, our most immediate debt to the theory will be the use of formalisms for the specification of syntax and the determination of syntactic structure.

6.2.1   *Grammars and Parse Trees*

Systematic generation of code or performance of actions, given arbitrary source-language text, is greatly facilitated by a precise description of how the tokens of the language may be combined into program text. The standard formalism for providing such a description is a *grammar* for the language.

A grammar actually defines a language by specifying which symbols are used in writing the language and which strings of symbols are permitted in the language. Instead of enumerating the acceptable strings, which are typically infinite in number, the grammar comprises four elements. One is the collection of symbols which are used in writing strings in the language. These symbols are called *terminal* symbols. Another element is a collection of *nonterminal* symbols used not in writing the language but in describing it. Each of these two nonempty collections, called a *vocabulary*, is finite and includes no symbol in common with the other. Thus a grammar might have the terminal vocabulary $\{0,1\}$ and the nonterminal vocabulary $\{a,b,s\}$. A third element of the grammar is a finite (and nonempty) set of rules. The nature of the rules depends on the type of grammar. Programming languages are usually described by grammars of the type called *context-free*, and the remainder of this description is correct only for such grammars. Each rule specifies the replacement of a single nonterminal symbol by a finite (and nonempty) string of symbols, each of which may be either terminal or nonterminal. The replacement specified by a rule is optional rather than mandatory. Thus one possible rule might specify that if the nonterminal symbol a appears in a string, it may be replaced by the string '11a'. The fourth element of a grammar is the designation of one of the nonterminal symbols as the initial string from which others are generated by successive application of rules. Because this distinguished symbol is called the *start* symbol or *sentence* symbol, the letter 's' is often used, as in the following grammar.

1. $s = a\ b.$
2. $a = $ "1" "1".
3. $a = $ "1" "1" $a.$
4. $b = $ "0".
5. $b = $ "0" $b.$

In representing a grammar, it is customary to use the notation called *Backus-Naur form* (BNF). Unfortunately, there are many variants of BNF in common use and the differences among them often tend to confuse readers. We have adopted instead a related notation whose use has been cogently recommended by Wirth [1977]. In recognition of its proponent, we shall refer to it as *WSN*, for Wirth Syntax Notation. Each rule of the grammar is written in WSN as a nonterminal symbol followed by an equal sign, then by the string of symbols which replace the nonterminal, and finally by a period. Terminal symbols are enclosed by a pair of quotation marks to differentiate them from nonterminal symbols. The distinguished nonterminal symbol is restricted by some authors from appearing in any replacement string to the right of an equal sign. One consequence of this restriction is the implicit designation of the distinguished nonterminal. Rather than impose any restriction, however, we designate the distinguished nonterminal explicitly, by always using it to begin the first rule. The numbers written at the left are not part of the grammar; they are affixed for ease of reference.

The language defined by a grammar includes all strings and only those strings which are composed exclusively of terminal symbols and are produced from the start symbol by a finite sequence of applications of rules of the grammar. The strings in the language defined by the foregoing grammar all consist of a positive even number of ones followed by a positive number of zeros. The string '110' is therefore in the language (and is in fact the shortest such string), whereas the string '0011' is not in the language. Although each string in this language is of finite length, the number of distinct strings in the language is infinite.

The string '1111000' can be produced from 's' by application of rule 1, yielding '*ab*', then rule 3, yielding '11*ab*', then rule 5, yielding '11*a*0*b*', and finally rules 5 (again), 4, and 2. The sequence of rules 1, 5, 5, 4, 3, 2 also serves, as do several others. Each such sequence is called a *derivation* of the string '1111000'. For the string and grammar of this example, all derivations reflect the same structure, represented in Fig. 6.2 as a tree. Each node corresponds to a symbol. The root node is the start symbol. Each nonterminal symbol node has as its descendants the symbols which replace it under application of a rule of the grammar. Each leaf node is a terminal symbol. The terminals from left to right constitute the string whose syntactic structure is represented by the tree.

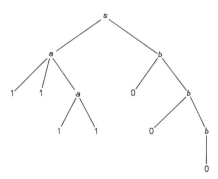

Figure 6.2   Derivation Tree for 1111000

Before looking at further examples of grammars, we present the remaining conventions of WSN. The vertical stroke indicates alternation, as in the use of

$letordig \ = \ letter \ | \ digit.$

instead of the pair

$letordig \ = \ letter.$
$letordig \ = \ digit.$

The alternation symbol obviates repeated writing of the left-hand non-terminal and the equal sign; it increases economy of expression, but does not augment the power of WSN. Another such facility is provided by the pair of symbols for repetition. A symbol string enclosed in curly brackets can be repeated any finite number of times, including zero. Thus an identifier might be defined by

$identifier \ = \ letter \ \{letordigit\}.$

instead of

$identifier \ = \ letter \ | \ identifier \ letordig.$

Although the second form makes the recursiveness of the definition explicit, the first is often more easily grasped. A symbol string enclosed in square brackets may optionally be included or omitted. An example is

$ifstmt \ = \ \text{"IF"} \ condition \ \text{"THEN"} \ stmt \ [\text{"ELSE"} \ stmt].$

in lieu of

$ifstmt \ = \ \text{"IF"} \ condition \ \text{"THEN"} \ stmt \ |$
$\qquad\qquad \text{"IF"} \ condition \ \text{"THEN"} \ stmt \ \text{"ELSE"} \ stmt.$

Parentheses may be used for grouping, as in

$iostmt \ = \ (\text{"READ"} \ | \ \text{"WRITE"}) \ \text{"("} \ identifier \ \text{")"}.$

Observe the distinction between the two pairs of parentheses. The parentheses of the first pair are not enclosed in quotation marks. They are therefore the grouping symbols of WSN, and indicate that either "READ" or "WRITE" may serve as the first symbol of the replacement string. The parentheses of the second pair do have enclosing quotation marks. Each of them is therefore a terminal symbol which appears in the replacement string. A final convention of WSN provides that if a terminal symbol enclosed in quotation marks is itself a quotation mark, it is written twice.

We look now at three examples of the formal specification of the syntax of programming languages or portions of languages. The first example, presented in Fig. 6.3, is limited to arithmetic expressions built from the identifiers X, Y, and Z by addition, multiplication, and grouping operators. The first rule defines an expression either as a term, or else as an expression followed by a plus sign and then by a term. The second alternative would by itself constitute a circular definition. Because of the first alternative, however, the second is in fact not circular. Substituting *term* for *expression* in the second alternative shows that an expression can denote the sum of two terms. Substituting the resulting *term* "+" *term* for *expression* in the second alternative yields *term* "+" *term* "+" *term* as a further possibility. We are thus led to the alternative specification of the first rule as

   expression = *term* {"+" *term*}.

The second rule defines a term similarly as a product of factors. The third rule defines a factor either as one of the three identifiers or as an expression enclosed in parentheses. This last choice completes the circularity of the three rules as a group, and it may appear difficult to see where to begin. Nevertheless, by starting with the distinguished nonterminal *expression*, it is in fact possible to derive an expression. Proof is offered by the parse tree, shown in Fig. 6.4, for the language string '(X+Y)∗Z+X'.

The second example is the specification of a programming minilanguage. The grammar is presented in Fig. 6.5, and Fig. 6.6 shows a minilanguage program defined by the grammar. There are eight rules, of which the last uses ellipsis (technically not part of WSN) to obviate writing 23 of the terminal symbols. The first rule defines a program as a sequence of statements joined by semicolons, much as the first rule of Fig. 6.3 defines an expression as a sequence of terms joined by plus signs. There is, however, an important difference in the formulations of the two recursive alternatives

   expression = *expression* "+" *term*.
   program = *statement* ";" *program*.

In the former, the repeated nonterminal *expression* appears as the leftmost symbol of the replacement string. In the latter, the repeated nonterminal *program* appears as the rightmost symbol of the replacement string. As we shall see, the distinction bears importantly on the choice of parsing method.

   expression = *term* | *expression* "+" *term*.
   term = *factor* | *term* "∗" *factor*.
   factor = "X" | "Y" | "Z" | "(" *expression* ")".

Figure 6.3 A Syntax for Expressions

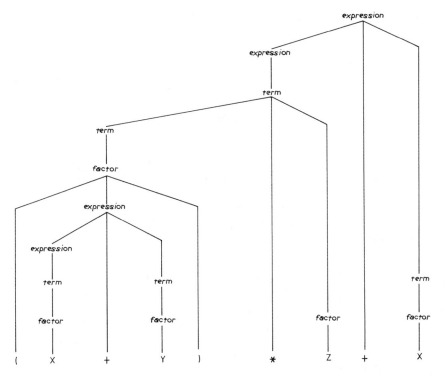

Figure 6.4 Parse Tree for $(X+Y)*Z+X$

Moreover, the meaning of language strings is affected by the order of the nonterminal symbols if the joining terminal represents a nonassociative operator, such as subtraction.

The third example is a more complete programming language, the small subset of Pascal defined in Fig. 6.7. The two sets of rules in the figure together constitute a grammar which fully defines the language subset. The

```
     program = statement | statement ";" program.
   statement = assignment | input/output | conditional | iterative.
  assignment = identifier "←" identifier.
input/output = ("READ" | "WRITE") "(" identifier ")".
 conditional = "IF" condition "THEN" statement "ELSE" statement.
   iterative = "WHILE" condition "DO" statement.
   condition = identifier ("<" | "≤" | "≥" | ">") identifier.
  identifier = "A" | "B" | .. | "Z".
```

Figure 6.5 Grammar for a Minilanguage

READ (N);
READ (X);
WHILE X ≥ N DO READ (X);
READ (Y);
WHILE Y ≥ N DO READ (Y);
IF X < Y THEN A ← Y ELSE A ← X;
WRITE (A)

Figure 6.6   A Minilanguage Program

partition into two sets reflects a typical division of labor between syntactic and lexical analysis. Figure 6.7(a) is a grammar whose terminal symbols are either specific tokens, such as ":=" and "WHILE", or classes of tokens which represent identifiers or relations. The rules of Fig. 6.7(b) define those two classes, and are easily embodied in a lexical analyzer. The lexical rules do not constitute a grammar, because there is no unique distinguished nonterminal.

We have distinguished IDENTIFIER and RELATION typographically from the other terminal and nonterminal symbols. In the full grammar IDENTIFIER and RELATION are nonterminals, whereas in the smaller grammar of Fig. 6.7(a) they are terminals. To indicate their dual role we call them *semiterminals*.

A grammar may be used for either of two purposes. One is to produce strings in the language by the process of *generation*. The single nonterminal symbol is thought of as producing the string of symbols which replaces it. Because of this productive role, rules of the grammar are commonly termed *productions*. The other purpose for a grammar is to determine whether a given string is in the language and, if so, what its structure is. The acceptance or rejection of the string as a member of the language is called *recognition*. The determination of its structure, if it is in the language, is called *parsing*. Even if a source-language program incorporates syntactic errors, mere recognition of that fact is not nearly as helpful to the programmer as is parsing to determine how much of the program is correct and where the errors lie. For that reason, recognition alone is not attempted during program translation. Parsing is always undertaken instead. The process can be thought of as a reconstruction of the derivation tree given only the leaf nodes and the grammar. In this process, the rules of the grammar may be applied in the direction from replacement string to single nonterminal symbol. Because a rule so used reduces the string to a single symbol, we shall (following Wegner [1968]) term it in this context a *reduction* rather than a production.

$$
\begin{aligned}
program &= \text{``VAR''} \; decllist \; \text{``;''} \; cmpdstmt \; \text{``.''} . \\
decllist &= declaration \mid declaration \; \text{``;''} \; decllist . \\
declaration &= \text{IDENTIFIER} \; \text{``:''} \; type . \\
type &= \text{``BOOLEAN''} \mid \text{``CHAR''} \mid \text{``INTEGER''} \mid \text{``REAL''} . \\
cmpdstmt &= \text{``BEGIN''} \; stmtlist \; \text{``END''} . \\
stmtlist &= stmt \mid stmt \; \text{``;''} \; stmtlist . \\
stmt &= simplstmt \mid structstmt . \\
simplstmt &= assignstmt \mid iostmt . \\
assignstmt &= \text{IDENTIFIER} \; \text{``:=''} \; expression . \\
expression &= expression \; \text{``+''} \; term \mid term . \\
term &= term \; \text{``*''} \; factor \mid factor . \\
factor &= \text{``(''} \; expression \; \text{``)''} \mid \text{IDENTIFIER} . \\
iostmt &= (\text{``READ''} \mid \text{``WRITE''}) \; \text{``(''} \; \text{IDENTIFIER} \; \text{``)''} . \\
structstmt &= cmpdstmt \mid ifstmt \mid whilestmt . \\
ifstmt &= \text{``IF''} \; condition \; \text{``THEN''} \; stmt \; [\text{``ELSE''} \; stmt] . \\
whilestmt &= \text{``WHILE''} \; condition \; \text{``DO''} \; stmt . \\
condition &= expression \; \text{RELATION} \; expression .
\end{aligned}
$$

(a) Syntactic rules

$$
\begin{aligned}
\text{IDENTIFIER} &= letter \; \{letter \mid digit\} . \\
letter &= \text{``A''} \mid \text{``B''} \mid .. \mid \text{``Z''} . \\
digit &= \text{``0''} \mid \text{``1''} \mid .. \mid \text{``9''} . \\
\text{RELATION} &= \text{``<''} \mid \text{``} \leq \text{''} \mid \text{``=''} \mid \text{``} \neq \text{''} \mid \text{``} \geq \text{''} \mid \text{``>''} .
\end{aligned}
$$

(b) Lexical rules

Figure 6.7 Two-Part Grammar for Pascal Subset

A programming language parser can usually rely on a lexical analyzer to reduce character strings to identifiers, constants, reserved words, and operator symbols. The task of parsing is to apply a grammar pretty much like that of Fig. 6.7(a) to a source-language program and determine the tree which represents its syntactic structure. Even though not every parser describes the tree directly, the output of any parser must at least reflect it indirectly.

A vast body of knowledge has been developed about parsing programs; the literature is replete with parsing methods. They can be divided into two major classes, whose names indicate the direction followed in constructing the parse tree. *Top-down* parsing starts from the distinguished symbol at the root, which is customarily found (in computer science if not in nature) at the top, and proceeds downward to the string of terminals at the leaves. It applies productions of the grammar, substituting strings for single nonterminals. Application of these productions yields intermediate strings composed of both nonterminals and terminals. At each stage, these strings are compared with the known goal (the string of terminals to be parsed), to select the production to be applied next. *Bottom-up* parsing, on the other hand, starts from the terminals at the leaves and proceeds upward to the root. It applies reductions of the grammar, substituting single nonterminals for strings. The intermediate strings are compared at each stage with the terminals of the original string, to select the reduction to be applied next.

Our primary purpose in this book is not to provide detailed treatment of the major top-down and bottom-up parsing methods. We are concerned rather with exploring the role which parsing plays in the translation process, with understanding, for example, how to harness a parser for service in a compiler. This endeavor does, however, demand familiarity with at least one parsing method. We have chosen to examine two: recursive descent, a top-down method; and operator precedence, a bottom-up method. A grammar for any reasonable programming language is either suitable for recursive descent, or can be rather easily modified to become suitable. Although the algorithm may be slow, it is particularly easy to program, and the translator writer in a hurry can always fall back on recursive descent. Operator precedence can not be applied to all grammars, but it is especially applicable to evaluating expressions even if the rest of the language is not suitable. It illustrates perhaps better than does recursive descent the role of theory in parser design.

The choice of operator precedence and recursive descent to illustrate parsing methods is not intended to suggest that they are necessarily superior to other methods. A great variety of parsing techniques exist; the two presented here do permit the casual writer of translators to program an effective parser. Further study of parsing methods is highly desirable for anyone planning to undertake a production compiler.

In examining the two parsing methods, we shall concentrate here upon the determination of syntactic structure rather than upon its representation. The choice of representation is important, however, to the subsequent stages of translation, and will be considered more fully in Chapter 7.

6.2.2 *Expressions and Precedence*

Before defining operator precedence formally, we review informally some intuitive notions about precedence. The simplest context in which to do this is the evaluation of arithmetic expressions, and we begin with a few definitions.

An *operator* in a programming language can be characterized informally as a token which specifies an operation of function evaluation. An *operand* is a token which specifies a value, either literally (as a constant) or indirectly (as an identifier). An *expression* is a sequence of operands, operators, and perhaps grouping indicators (often parentheses), formed according to certain syntactic rules. With each expression is associated a value which is determined by the values of its operands, the functions specified by its operators, and the sequence in which the latter are applied to values of their arguments. Note that a function can have as an argument either an operand or an expression, and that an operand may be either a constant or an identifier.

The number of arguments required by a function is called its *degree*. Addition is a function of degree 2, hence termed *binary* or *dyadic*. The absolute value function is of degree 1, hence termed *unary* or *monadic*. It is common to apply these terms, by extension, to the operators which represent the functions. We thus speak of the addition operator as being binary.

Because programming language text is almost invariably one-dimensional, there are three ways to place a binary operator relative to its arguments. Each leads to a notational convention whose name reflects the placement of the operator. In *prefix* notation the operator precedes both arguments, in *postfix* notation it follows both arguments, and in *infix* notation it appears between its arguments. Using one-character source-language tokens for clarity, we can represent the subtraction of B from A as follows.

    prefix $-AB$
    infix $A-B$
    postfix $AB-$

If the operator is unary, it precedes its argument in prefix notation and follows its argument in postfix notation. In infix notation, a symmetric choice is available; convention decrees that a unary infix operator precede its argument. Prefix and postfix notations are often called *Polish* notations, after the logician Jan Łukasiewicz, who introduced the former.

Prefix notation has the advantage of corresponding most closely to traditional mathematics, where the result of applying function f to arguments a and b is typically written $f(a,b)$, and where functional composition is written as in $f(h(x))$. The Polish notations accommodate more than two arguments, which infix does not. Infix has nevertheless been adopted for virtually all programming languages, because it is so very familiar. If more than two arguments are needed, the language can either (as in APL) disguise several arguments as one, or else (as in PL/I) permit excursions into prefix notation. We limit the present discussion to unary and binary operators, because the principal arithmetic and logical operators have degree two or less.

It is necessary, of course, to distinguish whether an operator is unary or binary. Sometimes the distinction is purely lexical. The PL/I token $*$ (when it serves as an operator) is always binary. For other tokens, such as | in APL or $-$ in PL/I, the distinction must be made syntactically. This is fairly easily done from the infix notation of source language. If the operator has a left argument, it is binary; if not, it is unary. Although this determination requires syntactic analysis, the degree of analysis is so slight that it can be easily performed as an adjunct to lexical analysis. If an operator is preceded by a left parenthesis or by another operator, it is unary; otherwise it is binary.

Expressions such as those defined by the grammar of Fig. 6.3 can be evaluated in a single left-to-right scan, with the use of two stacks. An operator stack holds the arithmetic and grouping operators; an operand stack holds identifier values and intermediate results. During the scan, each time an identifier is encountered, its value is pushed onto the operand stack. Each time a left parenthesis is encountered, it is pushed onto the operator stack. Each time an addition operator is encountered, it is pushed onto the operator stack. Before the operator is pushed, however, the topmost token on the operator stack is examined. If that token is a $+$ or $*$, then the operation which it represents is performed before the stacking occurs. This operation is performed upon the topmost two values on the operand stack. They are popped, and are replaced by the value which results from performing the operation. The operator token which indicated the operation is then popped before the incoming addition operator token is stacked.

Similar processing is performed for each multiplication operator encountered, except that only a $*$ already on top of the operator stack has its operation performed and symbol popped before the incoming operator is stacked. Whenever a right parenthesis is encountered, the topmost token on the operator stack has its operation performed and is popped in turn, the action being repeated until a left parenthesis is found. The two matching parentheses are then discarded. This evaluation process, which might be performed in an interpreter, is very efficient. Twelve successive stages in the evaluation of $(X+Y)*Z+X$ are shown in Fig. 6.8(a). The values of X, Y, and Z are taken to be 1.5, 2.5, and 2, respectively.

What governs the order in which the operators are applied? It is really the priority or *precedence* of the different occurrences of operators. This precedence has two aspects, *inherent* and *positional*. In the language we

Stack of operators	Current token	Stack of values	Stack of tokens	Code generated for operator
empty	(	empty	empty	
(	X	empty	empty	
(	+	1.5	X	
+ (	Y	1.5	X	
+ (	)	2.5 1.5	Y X	
empty	*	4	TEMP1	LOAD X ADD Y STORE TEMP1
*	Z	4	TEMP1	
*	+	2 4	Z TEMP1	
empty	+	8	TEMP2	LOAD TEMP1 MULT Z STORE TEMP2
+	X	8	TEMP2	
+	none	1.5 8	X TEMP2	
empty	none	9.5	TEMP3	LOAD TEMP2 ADD X STORE TEMP3

(a) Evaluation   (b) Code generation

Figure 6.8   Syntactic Analysis of Expression (X+Y) * Z+X

are now parsing, multiplication has inherent precedence over addition because in either X+Y * Z or X * Y+Z the multiplication is to be performed first. Two occurrences of the same operator, on the other hand, are to be applied in the positional left-to-right order. Both the inherent and the positional precedence are reflected in the grammar of Fig. 6.3. In fact, the precedence rules were selected first, and the grammar built to suit.

The precedence rules embodied in the grammar can be represented conveniently by a *precedence function F*, which assigns to each operator a numerical precedence. The precedence of the left parenthesis is lower than that of any operator. A precedence lower yet than that of the left parenthesis is assigned to a dummy operator token '$', which can be thought of as adjoined to the front of the string to be parsed. Another dummy token '#' is appended to the rear of the string. For the grammar of Fig. 6.3 suitable values of F would be 3 for multiplication, 2 for addition, 1 for the left parenthesis, and 0 for the '$' token.

The precedence function is readily embodied in the straightforward algorithm for expression evaluation presented in Fig. 6.9. Two stacks are used, one for operators and one for operands. The dummy token '$' is stacked automatically at the outset; it is not physically present in the input string, unlike the '#' end marker. Left parentheses and operands are always stacked. A right parenthesis is never stacked; it causes the matching left parenthesis to be discarded, after first directing the intervening operator(s) to be applied. An operator is stacked only after operators of higher precedence at the top of the stack have been applied. Upon termination, the value of the expression remains the sole element on the operand stack.

A slight modification results not in evaluating the expression, but in generating code to perform the evaluation. Such would be the function of a compiler. Instead of stacking values of operands, the compiler stacks their tokens. On encountering an operator of degree k, it generates code which embodies the topmost k operand tokens. New tokens are created to represent temporary results. Figure 6.8(b) shows instructions, in the assembler language of Section 2.2, which could be generated in this fashion.

Operators having equal inherent precedence are assigned a positional precedence by the algorithm. For associative operators, it might appear immaterial whether the precedence decreases from left to right or from right to left. The two resulting directions of evaluation are shown in Fig. 6.10 for integer addition, and yield the same result. Note, however, that the two parse trees differ. The addition of floating-point numbers is not associative; the parser and the programmer should agree on the desired sequence. In deriving a parse tree rather than only evaluating an expression, it is important to conform to the grammar, even for associative operators.

For nonassociative operators, the algorithm of Fig. 6.9 assigns positional precedence which decreases from left to right. This is correct for operators such as subtraction in PL/I, but not for others such as exponentiation (see Fig. 6.10). The use of *two* precedence functions provides a simple cure. One function (F) is applied to operators already on the stack; the other (G)

procedure *EVAL* **real**
    boolean *more* {more operators are to be applied}
    opstack ← **empty** {operator stack}
    valstack ← **empty** {value stack}
    PUSH '$' on *opstack*
    read *token* from *input*
    do forever
        case *token* **of**
            value: *PUSH* value of *token* on *valstack*
                        read *token* from *input*
            '(':   *PUSH token* on *opstack*
                        read *token* from *input*
            operator: *more* ← **true**
                        while *more* **do**
                              if F (*opstack*[top]) < F (*token*)
                                    then *PUSH token* on *opstack*
                                          more ← **false**
                                          read *token* from *input*
                                else *APPLY*
            ')':   *more* ← **true**
                        while *more* **do**
                              if *opstack*[top] = '('
                                    then *POP opstack*
                                          more ← **false**
                                          read *token* from *input*
                                else *APPLY*
            '#':   **while** *opstack*[top] ≠ '$' **do** *APPLY* **od**
                        return *valstack*[top]

procedure *APPLY*
    POP opstack to *operator*
    k ← degree of *operator*
    POP k values from *valstack* to *value* [1..k]
    apply *operator* to *value* [1..k] yielding *result*
    PUSH result on *valstack*

Figure 6.9   Evaluation of Infix Expression

is applied to those not yet stacked. If such *double precedence* functions are used it is necessary to make the corresponding change in the program of Fig. 6.9. The condition

$$F \ (opstack[\text{top}]) \ < \ F \ (token)$$

is replaced instead by

$$F \ (opstack[\text{top}]) \ < \ G \ (token).$$

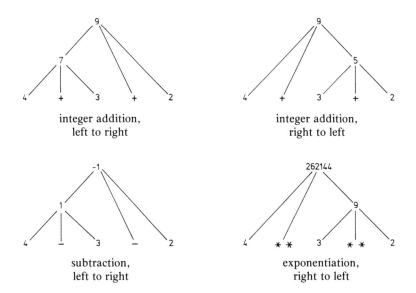

integer addition,
left to right

integer addition,
right to left

subtraction,
left to right

exponentiation,
right to left

Figure 6.10   Positional Precedence for Associative and Nonassociative Operators

The following double precedence functions are adequate for addition, sub-traction, multiplication, division, and exponentiation in PL/I.

	$	(	+	−	*	/	**
F	0	1	2	2	3	3	4
G			2	2	3	3	5

It might be observed here that APL does away very neatly with all of these problems. There is no inherent precedence among operators, except for parentheses, and positional precedence increases from left to right for all operators.

6.2.3   *Operator Precedence Parsing*

Let us now return to the algorithm for parsing expressions. Examine the parse tree of Fig. 6.4. No fewer than 14 reductions are represented, yet the structural information important to translation is entirely contained in the order of performance of only three of them. The reduction of *expression* "+" *term* to *expression* at the left side of the tree occurs before *term* " * " *factor* can be reduced to *term*. This second reduction must occur before the remaining reduction of *expression* "+" *term* to *expression*. It is not important even to what nonterminal symbol those reductions are made, nor to what nonterminals the identifiers are reduced. It is necessary only to know that 'X+Y' is reduced to some nonterminal, which we can designate *temp1*, that '*temp1* * Z' is subsequently reduced to a nonterminal, say *temp2*, and that '*temp2*+X' is finally reduced to a nonterminal. A wholly adequate parse tree, therefore, is that of Fig. 6.11, which depicts only 8 reductions. The different nonterminals, no longer differentiated, are all represented as *n*.

To see how such a simplified parse might be produced, assume that we can tell, by inspection only of terminal symbols (which we continue to differentiate from each other) when it is time to apply a reduction. Conditions which justify this assumption will be described shortly. A single left-to-right scan of the source text suffices, in conjunction with the use of a single stack that holds both terminal and nonterminal symbols. Each symbol of source text is examined and compared with the stack contents, and one of two actions taken. One action is to *shift* by pushing the incoming symbol onto the stack and proceeding to examine the next source symbol. The other action is to *reduce* one or more topmost stack symbols, replacing them on the stack by the nonterminal symbol, and continuing by comparing the new stack content with the same source symbol. A parser which uses these actions is called a *shift/reduce* parser. The desired sequence of decisions for parsing (X+Y) * Z+X is presented in Fig. 6.12, where "reduce *k*" signifies the reduction of the *k* topmost stack symbols. The stack is shown at each stage with its top at the right.

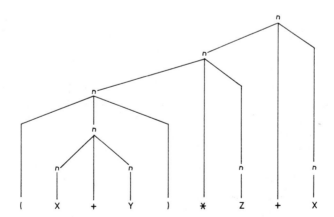

Figure 6.11 Simplified Parse Tree for (X+Y) * Z+X

Stack content	Current symbol	Remaining string	Shift/reduce decision
empty	(	X+Y)*Z+X	shift
(	X	+Y)*Z+X	shift
(X	+	Y)*Z+X	reduce 1
(n	+	Y)*Z+X	shift
(n+	Y	)*Z+X	shift
(n+Y	)	*Z+X	reduce 1
(n+n	)	*Z+X	reduce 3
(n	)	*Z+X	shift
(n)	*	Z+X	reduce 3
n	*	Z+X	shift
n*	Z	+X	shift
n*Z	+	X	reduce 1
n*n	+	X	reduce 3
n	+	X	shift
n+	X	empty	shift
n+X	none	empty	reduce 1
n+n	none	empty	reduce 3
n	none	empty	

Figure 6.12   Parsing Sequence for $(X+Y)*Z+X$

The decision whether to shift or reduce is governed by comparison of the topmost terminal on the stack with the source-text terminal currently being examined. For example, if the current symbol is ')' the choice is always to reduce unless the topmost terminal is '('. If the current symbol is '+', then an identifier or ')' as topmost terminal calls for reduction whereas '(' calls for shifting. We have already encountered a very similar algorithm in Fig. 6.9. If the decision is to reduce, it must be determined further how many symbols are to be reduced. The conditions which permit this determination, as well as the prior shift/reduce decision, will now be investigated by returning to the underlying grammar.

An *operator grammar* is one in which no rule has the form $a = .. b c .. ,$ where b and c are both nonterminals. It can be shown that this restriction guarantees that at no stage in the generation or parsing of any string in the language can any intermediate string contain two adjacent nonterminal symbols. The terminology is presumably due to equating "operator" with "terminal". Although this is an oversimplification, the standard designation "operator grammar" cannot well be avoided. The grammars of Figs. 6.3, 6.5, and 6.7(a) are all operator grammars.

Between any two terminals of an operator grammar, one or more of three important *precedence relations* may hold. Let L and R be any two terminals of an operator grammar. It is convenient to think of them as the left and right members of a pair of successive terminals either in the source text or in the text produced by applying reductions to the source text. The relations $<$, $=$, and $>$ can be defined informally as follows, where a, b, and c are arbitrary nonterminals, which may or may not be distinct.

(1) The relation L $<$ R holds if there exist a rule a = .. L c .. and a derivation from c of a string whose leftmost terminal is R. The relation is diagrammed in Fig. 6.13(a). We wish to reduce R and succeeding symbols* to c before reducing L c.

(2) The relation L $=$ R holds if there exists a rule a = .. L R .. or a = .. L b R ... The relation is diagrammed in Fig. 6.13(b). We wish to reduce L R (or L b R) and surrounding symbols.

(3) The relation L $>$ R holds if there exist a rule a = .. b R .. and a derivation from b of a string whose rightmost terminal is L. The relation is diagrammed in Fig. 6.13(c). We wish to reduce L and preceding symbols* to b before reducing b R.

Let us apply the foregoing definitions to the grammar of Fig. 6.3, which is readily seen to be an operator grammar. From the rule *expression* = *expression* "+" *term* and the derivation (by a single rule) of *term* "*" *factor* from *term*, it follows that "+" $<$ "*". The rule *factor* = "(" *expression* ")" ensures by itself that "(" $=$ ")". Because it is the only rule

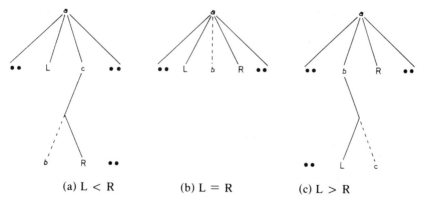

(a) L $<$ R   (b) L $=$ R   (c) L $>$ R

Figure 6.13   Relations in an Operator Grammar

*Under case (1), if the string derived from c begins with the nonterminal b, we wish to reduce b R and succeeding symbols. Similarly, under case (3), if the string derived from b ends with the nonterminal c, we wish to reduce L c and preceding symbols.

with two terminals on its right-hand side, no other pair of terminals can stand in the precedence relation $=$. From that same rule and the further derivation of *expression* " + " *term* from *expression*, it is seen that " + " > ")".

The use of the arithmetic relation symbols in " + " < " * " reflects the fact that " + " has lower precedence than " * " in this grammar. Do not be misled by the choice of symbols, however, into believing that L > R implies R < L, or conversely. In particular, it does *not* hold in this grammar for " + " and ")". To avoid such confusion, many books use <, $\doteq$, and > instead.

If it is the case for an operator grammar that an arbitrary ordered pair of terminals stands in at most one of the three precedence relations, then the grammar is an *operator precedence grammar*. The grammar of Fig. 6.3 is such a grammar; the precedence relation (if any) in which each pair of terminals stands is shown in the *precedence matrix* of Fig. 6.14. Blank entries in the table indicate that the sequence L R (or L *b* R) cannot occur in a legal string or during the reduction of a legal string.

The application of the relations tabulated in Fig. 6.14 to the parse given in Fig. 6.12 can now be illustrated. If the topmost terminal stands in the relation < or the relation $=$ to the current symbol, then the current symbol is shifted onto the stack. If the topmost terminal stands in the relation > to the current symbol, then one or more stack symbols are reduced. The relations which hold between successive pairs of terminals on the stack determine how many symbols are to be reduced. Suppose, for example,

		R						
		+	*	(	)	X	Y	Z
	+	>	<	<	>	<	<	<
	*	>	>	<	>	<	<	<
	(	<	<	<	=	<	<	<
L	)	>	>		>			
	X	>	>		>			
	Y	>	>		>			
	Z	>	>		>			

Figure 6.14   Precedence Matrix for Grammar of Fig. 6.3

that there are five terminals on the stack, $t5$ at the top, preceded by $t4$ through $t1$, and that the current token is $t6$. Let the following relations hold between successive terminals.

$$t5 > t6$$
$$t4 = t5$$
$$t3 = t4$$
$$t2 < t3$$
$$t1 < t2$$

The notation

$$t1 < t2 < t3 = t4 = t5 > t6$$

summarizes the relations in a particularly convenient form. The symbols to be reduced include all terminals starting from the top of the stack and continuing until the first $<$ is encountered. These are precisely the terminals enclosed by the $<$ $>$ pair, which can be thought of as bracketing the string to be reduced. In the example, terminals $t3$, $t4$, and $t5$ are in that string. Moreover, any nonterminals adjacent to any of those terminals are also included. Thus the string to be reduced includes all nonterminal and terminal symbols between $t2$ and $t6$. Figure 6.15 shows how the relations are used at five successive stages in the parse, both to make the shift/reduce decision and to determine how many symbols need to be reduced. Each relation is written beneath the position between its left and right arguments. The last step in Fig. 6.15 illustrates the need for adjoining the dummy terminal "$" which stands in the relation $<$ to all other terminals.

The syntactic structure information which is developed by the operator precedence parser must be used as it is developed, because by the end of the parse nothing is left except a single nonterminal. Although it is possible to build the parse tree explicitly, it is usually more convenient to perform instead some of the actions which depend on the syntactic structure. In a compiler, for example, the ensuing semantic processing, although conceptually distinct from syntactic analysis, is often performed in conjunction with parsing. To accomplish this, the parser may invoke a so-called *semantic routine* whenever it performs a reduction. What action would these routines take for the simple grammar of Fig. 6.3? When an identifier is reduced to n, the identifier (in a generator) or its value (in an interpreter) is pushed onto an operand stack. When $n+n$ is reduced to n, an interpreter pops the topmost two operand values, adds them, and pushes the sum on the stack. Such interpretation might well be performed by an assembler evaluating an address expression. A generator uses the topmost two operand stack entries in producing code to perform the addition and replaces them

stack & current symbol	$	(n +		Y
terminal symbols	$	(+		Y
relations		< <		<
decision	shift			Y

stack & current symbol	$	(n + Y		)
terminal symbols	$	(+ Y		)
relations		< < <		>
decision	reduce		Y	

stack & current symbol	$	(n + n		)
terminal symbols	$	(+		)
relations		< <		>
decision	reduce		n + n	

stack & current symbol	$	(n		)
terminal symbols	$	(		)
relations		<		=
decision	shift			)

stack & current symbol	$	(n)		*
terminal symbols	$	( )		*
relations		< =		>
decision	reduce		(n)	

Figure 6.15   Details of Operator Precedence Parsing

with a reference to the temporary variable which represents their sum. This code is often not yet ready to be executed, but rather is in one of the intermediate forms described in Section 7.2.1. Similar actions are performed when $n * n$ is reduced to n. The easiest reduction of all is that of (n) to n; no action is required.

So far we have considered operator precedence parsing only for expressions. The techniques can be applied to richer languages as well. The mini-language grammar of Fig. 6.5 is also an operator precedence grammar; its precedence matrix is shown in Fig. 6.16 with the choices of L arrayed along the left and those of R across the top. Verifying the operator precedence property by hand is exceptionally tedious, even for such a small grammar. Fortunately, the process is readily mechanized.

For a big grammar, the precedence matrix can be inconveniently large. A more compact representation of the relations between terminals can be given by a pair of precedence functions F and G so constructed that

	;	←	READ	WRITE	(	)	IF	THEN	ELSE	WHILE	DO	<	≤	≥	>	A..Z
;	<	<	<	<			<			<						<
←	>							>	>							<
READ					=											
WRITE					=											
(						=										<
)	>							>	>							
IF		<	<	<		<		=		<						<
THEN		<	<	<		<			=	<						<
ELSE	>	<	<	<		<	>	>		<						<
WHILE											=					<
DO	>	<	<	<		<	>	>		<						<
<															>	<
≤															>	<
≥															>	<
>															>	<
A..Z	>	>				>		>	>		>	>	>	>	>	

Figure 6.16 Precedence Matrix for the Minilanguage Grammar

F (L) $<$ G (R) if L $<$ R and similarly for the other two precedence relations. Unfortunately, there are precedence matrices for which suitable double precedence functions do not exist. For most programming languages representable by operator precedence grammars, however, the construction of double precedence functions is possible.

The operator grammar for the subset of Pascal defined in Fig. 6.7 does not have the operator precedence property. In particular, the relations ";" $<$ ";" and ";" $>$ ";" both hold. This does not mean, however, that operator precedence parsing is totally inapplicable if the grammar as a whole is not an operator precedence grammar. One approach is to use operator precedence to parse a subset which does have the operator precedence property (e.g. expressions in the Pascal grammar), and to use a different method for the rest of the grammar. Another approach is to supplement an operator precedence parser with special routines to resolve the cases in which more than one precedence relation holds. A third approach is to subdivide the grammar into multiple smaller grammars each of which is an operator precedence grammar. Yet a fourth approach is to rewrite the given grammar as an operator precedence grammar which generates the same language. Although there is no guarantee that any of these approaches is applicable in a particular situation, often one of them can indeed be used to enable parsing by this simple and efficient method.

6.2.4 *Recursive Descent Parsing*

A straightforward top-down parsing method is that of *recursive descent.* The analysis descends from the start symbol at the root of the parse tree to the program text whose tokens lie at the leaves. Each terminal symbol is recognized by the lexical scanner. Each nonterminal symbol is recognized by a procedure which attempts to recognize the symbols in the right-hand side of a production associated with that nonterminal. Because nonterminals can appear in the right-hand sides of each other's productions, the procedures for recognizing nonterminals are recursive.

A stack of symbols is not maintained explicitly; the information is implicit in the stack of activation records for the procedure calls. The procedures need no local variables and can communicate without parameters by means of a single global variable. Local variables may well prove convenient, however, for holding attributes of symbols.

In designing the procedures for a recursive descent analyzer, it is often helpful to express the rules of the grammar by means of *syntax diagrams.* Consider the grammar of Pascal in Fig. 6.7(a). The distinguished symbol is *program* and the first procedure to be invoked has as its object the recognition of *program*. The procedure looks in turn for the terminal "VAR", a nonterminal *decllist*, the terminal ";", a nonterminal *cmpdstmt,* and finally the terminal ".". This is symbolized by the following syntax diagram, which can be written directly from the right-hand side of the production for *program*. Rectangular boxes are used for nonterminals and rounded boxes for terminals.

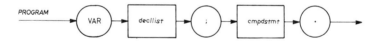

The syntax diagram for *decllist* can also be written directly from its production.

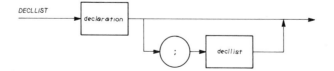

The alternation (symbolized by "|" in WSN) is represented as a choice of paths in the syntax diagram.

The recursive recognition of *decllist* can be portrayed more graphically by directing the flow back to the start of the diagram. This modification yields the following syntax diagram.

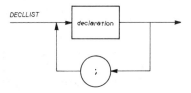

The recursive nature of the production can be made more evident in WSN, too. The rule can be rewritten to match the second syntax diagram directly.

decllist = *declaration* {";" *declaration*}.

A problem should be evident at this point. Does the semicolon which follows an instance of *declaration* presage another instance of *declaration* or an instance of *cmpdstmt*? Substitution of the syntax diagram for *decllist* in place of the box enclosing *decllist* in the syntax diagram for *program* illustrates the problem.

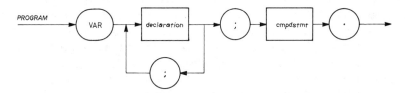

The direction of flow is nondeterministic. Two approaches to the problem suggest themselves. One is to guess at a direction and record the point in the analysis at which the guess is made. If the analysis fails at a later stage, it is assumed that the guess was incorrect, and backtracking is employed to restart from the decision point in a different direction. This tack can always be taken, but may result in often repeating parts of the analysis. The time required to parse a program in this manner can grow as rapidly as exponentially with the length of the program. The designation "recursive descent" is normally withheld from backtrack parsers.

A more satisfactory approach, which is usually possible with programming languages, is to rewrite the grammar to avoid choices among nonterminals. Because *cmpdstmt* always has "BEGIN" as its first token whereas *declaration* never does, the following revision offers a deterministic choice which obviates the need to backtrack.

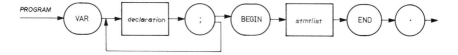

After a semicolon is recognized, the next terminal is scanned to determine whether it is "BEGIN". If not, it is presumably the first terminal of a declaration. This means that in attempting to recognize a declaration which follows a semicolon it must be assumed that its first terminal has already been found. If a single procedure is to recognize a declaration, whether preceded by "VAR" or by a semicolon, then that assumption should be made independently of whether the call to the procedure follows the recognition of "VAR" or of a semicolon. For uniformity, then, *all* of the recognition procedures expect upon entry that the one global variable *token* holds the first terminal symbol of the unrecognized portion of the source program. Similarly, they also ensure that, prior to exit, the next terminal symbol is placed in *token* for use in subsequent processing.

Any production of the grammar can be recast as a procedure to recognize the single nonterminal on its left-hand side. The recognition procedure for *declaration* is shown in Fig. 6.17. We do not need to know here what the procedure *ERROR* does. It may perform any action from merely printing an error message to terminating the parse. The procedure *SCANNER* finds the next terminal symbol of the string being parsed and assigns it as the value of the identifier named as the parameter.

Even simpler than the translation of a production into a recognition procedure is the translation of a syntax diagram into a recognition procedure. Each rectangular box becomes a call to another procedure to recognize the enclosed nonterminal; each rounded box becomes a test for the enclosed terminal. The recognition procedure based on the most recent syntax diagram for *program* is shown in Fig. 6.18. Because that procedure

procedure *DECLARATION*
    if *token* ≠ IDENTIFIER **then** *ERROR*
    SCANNER (*token*)
    if *token* ≠ ':' **then** *ERROR*
    SCANNER (*token*)
    TYPE

Figure 6.17 Procedure to Recognize *declaration*

procedure *PROGRAM*
  if *token* ≠ 'VAR' **then** *ERROR*
  SCANNER (*token*)
  repeat
    DECLARATION
    if *token* ≠ ';' **then** *ERROR*
    SCANNER (*token*)
  until *token* = 'BEGIN'
  SCANNER (*token*)
  STMTLIST
  if *token* ≠ 'END' **then** *ERROR*
  SCANNER (*token*)
  if *token* ≠ '.' **then** *ERROR*
  SCANNER (*token*)
  if *token* ≠ **empty then** *ERROR*

Figure 6.18 Procedure to Recognize *program*

is the first recognition procedure to be invoked in the recursive descent, provision must be made for reading the first token into *token*. Either *PROGRAM* must begin exceptionally with a call of *SCANNER* or its invocation must be preceded by such a call. The latter convention is adopted here.

The productions for *stmt, simplstmt,* and *structstmt* appear to present a choice among several nonterminals. The grammar can be written, however, to recast the choice among the terminals IDENTIFIER, "READ", "WRITE", "BEGIN", "IF", and "WHILE". Even if IDENTIFIER were not a terminal of the grammar, the choice would be deterministic. To avoid non-determinism it is necessary only that $n-1$ of n choices be introduced by a terminal. If none of those terminals is recognized, the nth direction is chosen. It is required, of course, that none of the $n-1$ terminals can be derived, as the first token, from the nonterminal which introduces the nth choice.

One of the attractions of recursive descent is that the grammar need not be highly constrained, as for operator precedence. There is, however, one important restriction, illustrated by the production for *expression* in Fig. 6.7(a). An attempt to create a syntax diagram leads to the following impasse.

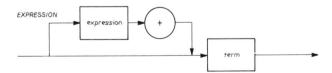

Substitution of the entire diagram for the box enclosing *expression* leads to an infinite regression of diagrams. Replacement of the box by an arrow to the beginning leads nowhere. The problem is caused by the leftmost symbol on the right-hand side of the production being identical to the nonterminal on the left-hand side. This occurrence is known as *direct left recursion*, and renders recursive descent unworkable. Even more insidious is *general left recursion*, in which the application of a sequence of productions may eventually, not just immediately, yield a string whose leftmost symbol is identical to the original nonterminal. It is possible to test a grammar for general left recursion, but difficult to eliminate it. Direct left recursion, on the other hand, is tractable. One attack is to write productions using right recursion rather than left recursion. An example is our choice of

decllist = *declaration* | *declaration* ";" *decllist.*

rather than the equivalent

decllist = *declaration* | *decllist* ";" *declaration.*

in writing the grammar of Fig. 6.7(a). The substitution of right recursion for left is not always possible, however, because it changes the meaning of nonassociative operators. An alternative attack is to express the repetition directly, as in

expression = *term* {"+" *term*}.
     term = *factor* {"∗" *factor*}.

which lead easily to recognition procedures.

We must not lose sight of the purpose of the syntactic analysis. How can semantic routines be combined with recognition by recursive descent? As in discussing operator precedence we postpone the details of semantic processing to Chapter 7; here we examine the parsing of expressions only. The procedure for recognizing *term* might be written as *TERM* in Fig. 6.19. A call to a semantic routine would be inserted within the loop after the call to *FACTOR*. That semantic routine would pop the topmost two operand stack entries and replace them by a single entry, as described in Section 6.2.3 with respect to operator precedence parsing in either an interpreter or a generator.

procedure *TERM*
    FACTOR
    while *token* = '∗' **do**
        SCANNER (*token*)
        FACTOR

Figure 6.19   Procedure to Recognize *term*

6.3 LEXICAL ANALYSIS

6.3.1 *Classification of Tokens*

The primary task of lexical analysis is to assemble characters into tokens and to determine which category of terminal symbol of the grammar each token belongs to. The terminals are often classified for this purpose into *lexical types*. The major types are words, constants, and operators, each of which can be further divided into subtypes. A word may be a *reserved* word (e.g. 'VAR' in Pascal), a *keyword* (e.g. 'SUM' in PL/I), or an identifier. A constant may be numeric or nonnumeric and there are often finer distinctions within each of these subtypes. Operators include, among others, arithmetic operators, grouping symbols such as parentheses, and the punctuation marks used to separate operands in lists.

The lexical analyzer usually determines at least to which major lexical type each token belongs and, except sometimes for words, to which subtype. It usually reports not only type information but also the identity of the token, by passing to the syntax analyzer either the token itself or a pointer into a table. Perhaps there is one table for words, another for numeric constants, a third for character-string constants, and yet a fourth for operators. Perhaps a single table is used instead, with entries of uniform length independent of the variable lengths of the source-language tokens which the entries represent. Details of token storage are discussed in Section 7.2.2.

The determination that 'VAR' is a reserved name in Pascal can be performed by either the scanner or the parser. One of them, to be sure, must check each word against a table of reserved words. The over-all requirements of initial source-language analysis are pretty much fixed for a given language. Because the boundary between lexical and syntactic analysis is not firm, however, the division of labor between parser and scanner is to some extent arbitrary.

In identifying and classifying tokens, the scanner needs to isolate each token from its neighbors. The beginning and end of each token must be recognizable. The degree to which the format of the source-language text is fixed affects substantially how easy it is to isolate tokens. If the positions of tokens are fixed (e.g. the label in IBM 360-370 assembler language), the beginning of each token can be found without testing characters. Similarly, if their length is fixed (e.g. identifiers in unextended BASIC), the end of each token can be identified without such testing. Sometimes one or more tokens (usually, but not necessarily, one character long) are defined to be *delimiters*, which mark the extent of variable-length tokens.

Many assembler languages use the comma to delimit multiple operands in an operand field which has a fixed beginning. With a format which is wholly fixed it is possible to decide in advance of lexical analysis where to find each token. If there is some format freedom but sufficient delimiters are provided, relatively little preprocessing is required to isolate the tokens.

In a free-format language, however, it is usually necessary to perform the isolation of tokens concurrently with their identification. Thus in analyzing the PL/I fragment '3.14 ∗ DIAM' the rules for construction of constants would both delimit '3.14' before the asterisk and identify it as a constant. Here a token serves as a delimiter, although its primary purpose is to represent an operation. In many languages the space is used as a delimiter; in fact, where one space is permitted, multiple spaces usually have the same effect.

Very many languages have provision for comments. These must be discarded prior to syntactic analysis. The ease with which comments can be recognized varies inversely with the freedom allowed the programmer in inserting them. In line-oriented source languages a specified character in a specified position (e.g. 'C' in column 1 for Fortran) flags the entire line as a comment. This is so easily tested that the reading routine used by the scanner can spare the latter the trouble of examining the line at all. Sometimes a reserved character in an arbitrary position flags the remainder of the line as a comment. The reserved character and the end-of-line can then be considered a pair of comment delimiters which, together with the enclosed comment, are to be discarded. This is a special case of the specified pair of tokens (e.g. '/∗' and '∗/' in PL/I) which delimit the comment. The use of a reserved character (e.g. the "lamp" symbol in APL) makes comment recognition simpler than if multipurpose characters are used in the comment delimiter. Tokens within a comment are usually completely ignored; they may even be permitted to include characters not admitted in the programming language. Specified characters are sometimes used at the start of a token to identify its lexical type. An example is the '@' used in Chapter 2 to mark literals.

6.3.2 Scanning Methods

Because there is no firm division between lexical and syntactic analysis, one way to scan source text is to include scanning as part of the parsing. This is accomplished by using a grammar whose terminal symbols are the characters themselves. Recursive descent provides a natural vehicle for this technique. In the grammar of Fig. 6.7, for example, the semiterminal symbols of part (a) can be treated as nonterminals, and the rules of part

(b) converted into nonterminal recognition procedures. The recognition of reserved words and other multicharacter terminals (e.g. ':=') would be performed not by calling a separate *SCANNER* to obtain a token for testing, but by successive calls to a character-fetching procedure to obtain a character for testing.

Substantial effort may be needed to transform the entire grammar into a form suitable for recursive descent without backtracking. The cost of backtracking in the token identification portion only is not too severe, however, because it is confined to regions of the tree near the leaves and cannot result in undoing as much analysis as can backtracking to points nearer the root. Consequently, the use of recursive descent to perform the complete analysis from character string to parse tree is quite practical.

If the grammar which describes the lexical analysis is simple enough, a particularly efficient scanner can be designed. (The reader familiar with formal languages and their acceptors will observe that the grammar must be *regular*; the recognizer is a finite-state automaton.) We begin by describing the scanning process by means of *state* diagrams. Unlike the syntax diagrams, in which the recognition of symbols is associated with nodes, state diagrams employ arcs to represent the recognition of characters, and reserve the nodes to represent states of the analysis. For example, the recognition of an unsigned integer is represented by the following state diagram.

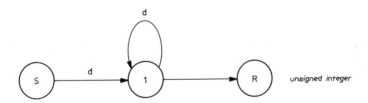

The scanner begins operation in start state S. Upon recognizing a digit (denoted "*d*" to avoid writing "0"|"1"|..|"9") the scanner makes a transition to state 1. Each further digit recognized leaves the scanner in state 1; the first non-digit encountered causes a transition to the recognition state R. In that state the scanner has recognized an unsigned integer and already has read the next character, which may begin another token. Alternatively, that character may be a non-token delimiter. The label on an arc names the characters whose encounter causes the transition corresponding to the arc. The absence of a label is a synonym for "any other character".

The state diagram

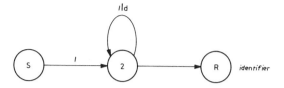

depicts the recognition of an identifier, with "*l*" representing an alphabetic letter and "|" used, as in WSN, for alternation. The two state diagrams can be merged, because there is only one start state and one recognition state.

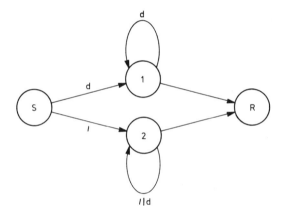

Attainment of state R indicates, as before, that a token was recognized and the next character read. It no longer identifies the token. This information is recoverable from knowledge of whether the state preceding state R was state 1 or state 2. A simple program to perform the transitions and keep track of the previous state is easily written. It uses a *state-transition table* to represent the state diagram. The table which corresponds to the four-state diagram just presented appears as Fig. 6.20. Each row designates a state; each column designates a lexical *class* of characters. (In the table, "other" means neither digit nor letter.) The table entry in position (i,k) is the state to which a character of class k causes a transition from state i.

The scanning program is given in Fig. 6.21. Each invocation of *GET-CHAR* delivers the next character to the first parameter and that character's lexical class to the second. The variables *char* and *class*, which are used as actual parameters, are made global to preserve their contents from one execution of *SCAN* to the next, and to permit them to be initialized by

Lexical class

	d	l	other
S	1	2	
1	1	R	R
2	2	2	R
R			

State (applies to the rows S, 1, 2, R)

Figure 6.20   State-Transition Table

invoking *GETCHAR* prior to the first execution of *SCAN*. The loop is always executed at least once because we so draw the state diagrams as to prohibit transitions from state S directly to state R. The token is assembled one character at a time. Its type is the simple function *TYPE* of *prevstate*. This scanner, which recognizes one token, is an example of a table-driven program, in which the flow is controlled by an explicit table (here *statetable*, which represents the lexical rules).

The transition table of Fig. 6.20 is missing some entries. Because the scanner terminates in state R, that state is never succeeded by another. Row R of the table is therefore superfluous and is customarily omitted. When a character of class "other" is encountered in state S, the succeeding state is not specified by the state diagram, hence is omitted from the table. Two interpretations are possible. One is that such a character is not permitted as the initial character of a token in the language and that the corresponding table position should be marked as an error. The other is that the state diagram is only a partial specification of the lexical rules and that another diagram defines the tokens initiated by a different initial

```
procedure SCAN (token, type)
    {char and class are global}
    token ← empty
    prevstate ← start
    currstate ← statetable [prevstate, class]
    while currstate ≠ recognized do
        token ← token, char {catenation}
        GETCHAR (char, class)
        prevstate ← currstate
        currstate ← statetable [prevstate, class]
    type ← TYPE (prevstate)
```

Figure 6.21   Table-Driven Scanner

character. Analysis of that diagram will provide the missing entry, and may well require expansion of the table.

Adopting the second interpretation, we complete our specification in Fig. 6.22. Part (a) displays the state diagram corresponding to the following rules for recognizing unsigned numbers.

$$
\begin{aligned}
\textit{unsignedreal} \;=\;& \textit{unsignedinteger fraction} \\
\mid\;& \textit{unsignedinteger scalefactor} \\
\mid\;& \textit{unsignedinteger fraction scalefactor.} \\
\textit{unsignedinteger} \;=\;& \textit{digit \{digit\}.} \\
\textit{fraction} \;=\;& \text{“.” } \textit{unsignedinteger.} \\
\textit{scalefactor} \;=\;& \text{“E” } [\textit{sign}] \textit{ unsignedinteger.} \\
\textit{sign} \;=\;& \text{“+” } | \text{ “$-$”.}
\end{aligned}
$$

The diagram previously shown for unsigned integers is incorporated. Error transitions, such as from state 3 for any character other than a decimal digit, are not shown. The state diagram for recognition of identifiers is redrawn as part (b). Part (c) shows how comments introduced by '/∗' and terminated by '∗/', as in PL/I, are ignored. Part (d) completes the specification by defining all initial characters other than '/', letters, or digits to be one-character tokens of special symbols.

6.3.3 Character Recognition

The identification of each character is in principle trivial. A simple table lookup determines the lexical class of each character, and both the character and its class are passed to the scanner. The character is used in assembling the token; the lexical class, in directing the analysis. The state diagrams must be studied carefully to ensure that the lexical classes are properly defined. For the rules described in Fig. 6.22, for example, the 26 letters do not all fall in the same class because of the special role which 'E' plays in representing real numbers. Similarly, five of the operator characters (period, plus sign, minus sign, asterisk, and slash) fall into four classes distinct from that of the other non-digit, non-letter characters.

Efficiency of operation is sometimes enhanced by incorporating in the character recognizer some simple functions whose removal from the scanner would greatly decrease the frequency with which the scanner calls the character recognizer. One such function is the discarding of comments. Another is the discarding of nonsignificant blanks. The latter is particularly easily programmed if the scanner informs the character recognizer with each call whether blanks are significant in the current context.

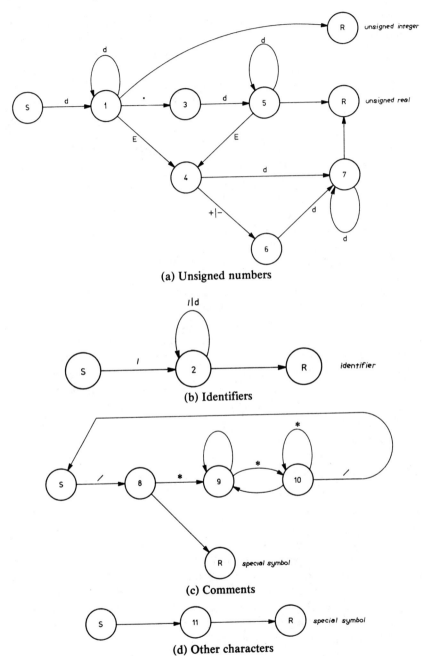

(a) Unsigned numbers

(b) Identifiers

(c) Comments

(d) Other characters

Figure 6.22 State Diagrams of Lexical Rules

The real challenge in character recognition occurs when the input stream is highly encoded, as is common when unbuffered terminals are used. The identity of many characters depends not on a single stroke, but on multiple strokes which are often not adjacent and may well be far separated from one another. Examples of such strokes are the backspace and shifts into and out of upper case. The strokes used to indicate erasure of a character, of a partial line, or of an entire line, must be interpreted correctly. If shifts are used, the character recognizer can store the value of the most recent shift and interrogate the appropriate table to interpret each incoming character accordingly. Some of the work may be accomplished in the control program charged with the responsibility of communicating with terminals. If not, it devolves on the translator.

The *visual fidelity* ("vi fi") property of APL input ("what you see goes in") mandates the use of a buffer by the character recognizer. The order in which APL characters, or even elements of overstruck characters, are transmitted is defined to be immaterial to the system. The APL character 'ϕ' for example, is composed by overstriking 'o', which is the upper case character selected by the key marked 'O', upon '|', which is the upper case character selected by the key marked 'M'. The two strokes to be overstruck may appear in the input in either order, and may even be widely separated. Thus the effect of 'fuMbbdAfBbbuOdf', where "f" and "b" represent forward and backward spaces, "u" and "d" represent up and down locking shifts, and the upper case letters represent the strokes transmitted by the keys so marked, is precisely the same as that of the more conventional 'AuObMdB'. The character string represented by either sequence of strokes is 'AϕB'. The decoding process is kept manageable by limiting the vi fi to rearrangements within one line of input.

6.3.4 Lexical Ambiguity

Lexical Ambiguity occurs when the application of only lexical rules fails to identify a token uniquely. The English words "putting" and "does" are examples of this familiar occurrence in natural language. In programming languages, one example is a character which can represent either a unary or a binary operator. The minus sign is such a character in many languages, and in APL a substantial number of characters share that property. Another sort of example arises in Fortran, where all blanks except those within Hollerith constants (i.e. character strings), are non-significant and therefore ignored. Thus the text fragment 'DO33I' represents one token in the assignment statement 'DO33I = 7' but three tokens in the loop control statement 'DO 33 I = 7, 11'. Similarly the fragment '25.E' must be split in the context '25.EQ' but not in the context '25.E4'.

There are three principal approaches to the problem of lexical ambiguity. One is for the scanner to report multiple interpretations to the parser, which then selects whichever one can be correctly parsed. This permits the scanner to be written as a separate pass, with attendant storage economies. Then the intermediate text of tokens and their syntactic types must be encoded to indicate alternate choices. If a separate pass is not made, the calling sequence used by the parser to call the scanner becomes considerably more complicated for all calls, although the ambiguities are relatively infrequent.

A second approach is for the scanner to examine the context of the ambiguous fragment. Although this endows the scanner, technically speaking, with syntactic powers, a very limited examination of lexical classes often suffices. The unary/binary ambiguity is resolved by retaining information about the previous token. If it was a left parenthesis or an operator, then the ambiguous operator is unary; otherwise it is binary. An alternative interpretation, of course, is that the unary and binary operators are represented by the same unambiguous token. There is then no lexical ambiguity, and the parser determines which operator is represented. The '25.E' ambiguity can be resolved by indulging in three characters of lookahead after the '5', rather than the usual one character. If 'Q' is found the decimal point belongs to '.EQ.' whereas a digit is part of a real-number constant.

The third approach is for the scanner to make only one lexical analysis at a time, but to work in close cooperation with the parser. The latter can reject a lexical analysis which is inconsistent with the parse and call upon the former to try again. An extension of this idea is to permit the scanner to call the parser to aid it in disambiguating a fragment. This form of cooperation is particularly suited to implementation by coroutines.

6.4 SYMBOL TABLE MANAGEMENT

The degree to which the meaning of a token is known to the translator depends upon the type of token. The meaning of a constant is simply its value, which is evident from inspection of the constant. For this reason, constants are sometimes said to be "self-defining". The meaning of an operator is defined by the language, and is normally implicit in the design of the translator. A name, on the other hand, may have a predefined meaning or it may have a meaning assigned by the programmer. A token such as "IF" in Pascal has a meaning which is fully as fixed as that of an operator. It is not available for use as an identifier and is therefore said to be a *reserved* word. Other words, which are permitted to be used as identifiers in a programming language—or as labels in an assembler language—have meanings defined by the programmer. Upon encountering such a symbol, the translator must be able to refer to its meaning. A *symbol table* is used to hold the meanings associated with user-defined symbols. Normal lexical analysis does not distinguish reserved words from others. To make this distinction, we can keep reserved words in a separate table which is interrogated before the regular symbol table. Alternatively, a single table can be used, in which reserved words are entered automatically, and flagged as such, before translation begins.

The meaning of a symbol is expressed by means of its attributes. These may be as few in number as one, such as the location of an assembler-language label, or there may be very many. Among possible attributes are source-text line number, type, number of dimensions, length of each dimension, internal tree structure, and storage class. The first reference to a symbol serves as an explicit or implicit declaration and inserts the symbol into the table. Either that access inserts the attributes, or a small number (often only one) of subsequent accesses do. Most accesses retrieve attributes. Usually the symbol is not deleted. Retrievals require a search for the designated symbol; in practice, insertions also require such a search.

Because of these frequent searches, effective symbol table management is crucial to efficient translation, whether in an assembler, macro processor, linker, interpreter, or compiler. The chief differences among the translators are the number of attributes and the potential for block structure. In the following sections we review briefly the appropriateness of several elementary data structures for use in representing symbol tables, particularly emphasizing the use of hashing functions. We conclude by explaining how to handle block structure.

6.4.1 *Data Structures for Symbol Tables*

The simplest structure which one might consider for representing a symbol table is an unsorted linear array. Search is serial and requires $O(n)$ time if there are n symbols in the array. A symbol to be inserted if not found is simply appended to the end of the array at an insignificant extra cost. Although the unsorted array with serial scan is very easy to implement, it uses much time if n is large.

A marked improvement is obtained by replacing the serial scan by a binary search, which takes only $O(\log n)$ time. Binary search requires that the elements of the array be sorted. If an element is to be inserted, it cannot be simply appended. Half of the elements, on the average, must be displaced one position to make room for the insertion, which therefore takes $O(n)$ time.

In binary search, each element has two possible successors in the search, one if the element compares higher than the search argument, and one if lower. There is thus a tree structure implicit in the table. It is possible to make this tree structure explicit, and to optimize and balance the tree. A primary gain is that insertion time can be reduced to $O(\log n)$. Because insertion is so much less frequent than retrieval, this is not a substantial gain. Although tree-structured symbol tables are indeed used in translators, we shall not take the space here to describe them.

An alternative to searching a data structure is to compute the address of the search argument. The process of computing the symbol's address from the symbol itself is known as *hashing*. If the address can indeed be computed directly, the mean time for search or for insertion is independent of n and is in fact $O(1)$. Figure 6.23 summarizes the orders of magnitude of search time and insertion time for the foregoing approaches.

Because of the relatively low frequency of insertion, search time predominates. In comparing the time requirements of the different table organizations, it is important to realize that the order of magnitude notation suppresses multiplicative constants. The importance of the unstated coefficients is illustrated by the fact that the linear expression n has a smaller value than the logarithmic expression $11 \log_2 n$ for n as large as 64. The availability of table lookup instructions in the computer to be used may indeed make a serial scan faster than a binary search.

Further gains in speed are possible if the symbols to be used are known, and their frequencies of occurrence can be estimated. This occurs, for example, with assembler-language operation codes. A simple technique is to order the symbols by decreasing frequency of occurrence and to scan serially. Although worst-case search time is still $O(n)$, the coefficient can be markedly reduced if a few symbols occur with high probability. It is also possible to use frequency information in balancing a tree probabilistically.

	Search	Insertion
Unsorted array	$O(n)$	$O(1)$
Sorted array	$O(\log n)$	$O(n)$
Tree	$O(\log n)$	$O(\log n)$
Hashing	$O(1)$	$O(1)$

Figure 6.23 Order of Magnitude Time Requirements

For unknown symbols, however, hashing is often the most effective approach to reducing search time for large n. In computing the address of a symbol from the symbol it is fruitful to consider the properties of addresses and those of symbols. The table comprises a fixed, known set A of addresses. No two symbols occupy the same address. The set of addresses is compact, i.e. there are no gaps. In fact, we normally use main storage for speed and consecutive addresses for simplicity and storage economy. Although the set S of possible symbols is known, being defined by the language to be translated, the set S' of actual symbols which enter a given translation is neither fixed nor known in advance. The symbols are required, however, to be distinct, except in a language with block structure, whose effect upon symbol table management is discussed in Section 6.4.4. The actual symbol set S' is rarely compact, and it is typically very much smaller than the set S of all possible symbols.

Hashing is the application of a *key transformation* $T: S \rightarrow A$ which maps each symbol $s \in S$ into an address $a \in A$. We are interested in the behavior of T not so much for the large, known set S of all possible symbols as for the small, unknown set S' of actual symbols. The actual symbols which are mapped into the same address a constitute an equivalence class C_a of symbols. We can define the equivalence class formally, given $a \in A$, as $C_a = \{s \in S' \mid T(s) = a\}$. A particular equivalence class may be empty, or it may contain one symbol, or it may contain several symbols. If it contains more than one, a *collision* is said to have occurred, because only one symbol can occupy a given address. Means must then be provided for distinguishing among the symbols in the equivalence class, and other addresses must be found to hold all but the first symbol destined for the computed address. If the equivalence class is large, considerable extra effort is required. The occurrence of large equivalence classes is known as *clustering*.

An ideal choice of hashing function T would ensure that its restriction $T': S' \rightarrow A$ would have the following three properties. (1) It maps S' onto most of A (provided S' is not much smaller than A), to avoid wasting space in the symbol table. For convenience, we shall describe such a hashing function as *compact*. (2) It has a unique inverse, meaning that only one symbol is mapped into a given address, thus eliminating collisions. (3) It is simple, hence fast to compute. Unfortunately, T' is unknown because S' is unknown, and we are free to choose only T, not T'. Moreover, we cannot in general attain all three of the desired properties simultaneously. We can, however, achieve any pair. We must elect simplicity, or our $O(1)$ search time will in fact be slower than the $O(\log n)$ time of a competing symbol table organization. We can guarantee freedom from collisions among the unknown symbols S' only by so doing for the larger set S. This would require a symbol table as large as S, usually not a practical possibility. The normal choice, therefore, is to design a hashing function which is simple and compact.

A disadvantage is that we must plan for collisions. We design a hashing function for S and hope that it works well for whatever S' we encounter in practice. A convenient standard of comparison for the behavior of T' is the generation of addresses drawn from all of A at random, with replacement. It is easily shown for this case that the table size (number of addresses) must substantially exceed the number of symbols in S' to hold the number of collisions down to a reasonable level. A rule of thumb which usually works well in practice is to make the table large enough that symbols will occupy not more than 80% of the addresses. We consider in Section 6.4.3 some techniques for handling the collisions which do occur. First, however, we describe some hashing functions appropriate for symbols.

6.4.2   *Hashing Functions for Symbols*

Programmers often refer to related objects by using a group of symbols which differ in as little as a single character position. Any hashing function which does not depend on that character position will map the entire group into a single address. To avoid such clustering, a suitable hashing function must therefore depend on all characters of the symbol.

The symbol is usually alphanumeric, and in some languages can be very long compared to a machine word. Symbol table addresses are numeric, and most computers (and languages) provide a richer assortment of operations on numeric quantities than on character strings. An important component in hashing symbols is therefore to treat the symbol string as though it were purely numeric, usually by considering the bits of its representation to constitute a binary numeral. This is accomplished almost trivially in assembler languages, with ease in PL/I (by means of UNSPEC), and with differing degrees of difficulty in other languages.

One very simple hashing function divides the symbol by the table size and uses the remainder as a zero-origin address within the table. Poor choice of the divisor, however, can result in substantial clustering. Suppose, for example, that a 512-word table is used, and that addressing is binary. Then the remainder after division of the symbol by 512 is just the original low-order 9 bits of the symbol. The address depends only on the low-order character and on part of its neighbor. This is bad enough in general; for left-justified short symbols, which necessarily have spaces as the low-order characters, it is simply terrible. A much better choice of divisor is a prime number. We can either use a prime slightly smaller than the table size, say 509, or we can make the table size itself a prime, perhaps 509 or 521.

Another hashing function, particularly suitable for long symbols, is known as *folding*. The symbol is split into pieces of a few characters each, and the pieces are added together. Addition overflow is ignored; it can also be suppressed by using exclusive **or** (modulo 2 addition) if that operation is available.

A third type of function depends on multiplication. One variation is to multiply the symbol by an appropriate constant and take the leading bits of the least significant half of the product. Another is the *mid-square* method, in which the n-bit symbol is squared. The middle n bits of the $2n$-bit product are selected as the address, because they depend on every bit of the symbol.

In some computers, the encodings of characters which are permitted in symbols is highly redundant. For example, alphanumeric characters are represented in the IBM 360-370 by 8 bits of which the first two are invariably 11. Another form of redundancy is that variable-length symbols are often represented as fixed-length strings having a fixed character (the space) in all unused positions. A refinement which can be applied to many hashing functions is to ignore redundant bits or redundant characters. If symbols are of varying length, a method appropriate to the length can be chosen at the cost of time to test the length and of space to hold code for more than one method. Another way to invest some extra time and space is to use two or more of the foregoing hashing functions in combination. Thus a transformation might be preceded by folding to produce a one-word operand, or followed by division to yield addresses in the range of the table size.

6.4.3   *Overflow Techniques*

If an attempt is made to insert a symbol where there is one already, *overflow* is said to have occurred and space must be found elsewhere. This can always be done, provided that the table size is as large as the number of symbols to be inserted.

One approach is to reduce the frequency of collisions by providing at each table address room for not merely one symbol (and its attributes), but rather a *bucket* which can hold more than one symbol. Application of the hashing function is followed by a serial scan within the bucket. If the bucket size is b, then the first b members of an equivalence class to be inserted will fit in the bucket; overflow does not occur unless $b+1$ members of an equivalence class are to be inserted. It is not necessary that the number of addresses $|A|$ computed by the hashing function be as large as the number of symbols $|S'|$. The requirement is rather $b|A| \geq |S'|$. There is little point, however, in using buckets if the frequency of overflow is not reduced. Consequently, the use of buckets normally entails the provision of some extra storage. Nevertheless, buckets do not eliminate overflow; they only reduce its frequency. Some other method of handling overflow must be used in conjunction with buckets.

A second approach to overflow is *open addressing*, also known as "scatter storage". If the address computed by the hashing function is occupied by a symbol other than the search argument, another address is computed somehow and the search continues from there. If that new address is occupied, a third address is computed and the search continues until it finds the argument, an empty address, or an address which has already been examined. If the last case arises during an insertion attempt, the table is considered to be full, even if empty unexamined addresses remain. It is always possible to choose an open addressing strategy which guarantees that this will not occur unless the table is full. Three ways of probing the table after a collision at address a are the following. In *linear* probing, the address examined on the ith attempt is $a + ri$ (modulo the table size), where r is some integer constant. If $r = 1$, as is common, then the entire table is probed before failure is reported. The recomputation is fast, in most cases requiring only the addition of r and a test that the new address is within the range of the table. If, however, collisions occur at successive addresses, further collisions are induced by displaced symbols and the resulting congestion can slow down considerably the execution of the symbol table routines. This effect is mitigated by *quadratic* probing, in which the address examined on the ith attempt is $a + si + ti^2$ (modulo the table size). If the table size is prime, quadratic probing will examine half the table before reporting failure. If the constants $s + t$ and $2t$ are stored, the recomputation requires one multiplication and two additions. The last example of open addressing is to *rehash* the original address, using it as the argument of a hashing function. This second function is usually somewhat different from the function used to transform the symbol because their arguments are of different lengths.

A third approach to overflow is related to open addressing, but seeks to eliminate the repeated computation of the same probe address each time a search is made for the same symbol. Once the probe address has been determined, by whatever means, it is stored as a pointer along with the previous symbol in a search *chain*. The price of saving the recomputation time is the provision of storage for all the pointers. A disadvantage of chained overflow is that means are required to prevent chains from becoming tangled when two chains intersect at one address. We shall not treat that problem here.

The foregoing techniques all place overflow symbols at addresses which might otherwise legitimately be occupied by other symbols, thus inducing collisions where none were present. A fourth approach to overflow avoids this problem by using for overflow symbols a table area distinct from the primary symbol table. If collisions are not too frequent, a wholly satisfactory organization of the overflow table is as a linear list which is scanned serially. If the overflow table is expected to be large, time can be saved by appending newly inserted symbols at the end and using one pointer field in each entry to chain together the members of each equivalence class.

6.4.4   *Block Structure in Symbol Tables*

In a language with block structure, two or more distinct objects may have the same name. Each of the two objects must nevertheless have its own symbol table entry, because its attributes are not shared by its namesakes. Finding the entry which corresponds to the occurrence of a symbol within a given program block requires a conceptual search of the environment, starting from that block and proceeding outward through enclosing blocks until a declaration of the symbol is first encountered. There are three principal approaches to implementing this conceptual search of the environment as an actual search of the symbol table. One is to include the block number as an attribute; a second is to replace nonunique names of distinct objects by unique names; the third is to group together in the symbol table all entries for symbols declared in the same block. We examine each approach in turn.

If the block number is used as an attribute, there will be duplicate symbols whose entries can be distinguished only by examining the block number. This approach diminishes the already low appeal of an unsorted linear table, unless it is very short, because of the necessity to scan the entire table to ensure finding the symbol instance associated with the innermost block of the environment. Search by hashing can be readily performed at the cost of a pointer field in each entry, used to link entries for the same symbol in different blocks. Because the duplicated symbols are not necessarily inserted in the table in nesting sequence, merely linking them into a chain in the order of insertion is insufficient for rapid searching. In fact, a chain of pointers is less advantageous than a set of pointers which captures the static nesting structure of the program. Each entry for a symbol should point rather to the closest entry for the same symbol in an enclosing block. These pointers are directed upward toward the root of the tree which describes the static nesting. To yield the desired linkage pattern, the pointers can be reset whenever a symbol is inserted or a block is closed.

If a sorted linear table is used, entries for duplicate symbols will necessarily be consecutive. If a given symbol occurs k times, at most k extra probes will be required (or $k-1$ if the last entry for each symbol is marked as such). The disadvantage that search time is $O(\log n)$ must still be accepted.

The second approach to block structure is to replace duplicated symbols by distinct symbols. Uniqueness of symbols can be ensured if each duplicated symbol is qualified by the block number. The qualification is most readily accomplished by catenating the block number to the symbol. This approach requires multiple searches, each for a different version of the symbol. When a symbol is first encountered, there is no way of knowing whether it will be duplicated in blocks to be entered later. The name qualification must therefore be applied to all symbols.

Our third approach to implementing block structure in the symbol table is to group entries by block and keep track of which portion of the table corresponds to which block. Figure 6.24 shows the block structure and declarations for two different versions of a program. The blocks are numbered in the sequence in which their openings are encountered. In Fig. 6.24(a), declarations are restricted to precede any other text within their block. Once a block is entered, all declarations in every block which encloses it have already been encountered. Because that restriction considerably simplifies symbol table construction, we begin by assuming declarations to be so restricted. Later we shall consider unrestricted declarations, as in Fig. 6.24(b).

Given the restriction on placement of declarations, we can build a dynamically changing symbol table with the use of two arrays. One array, *table*, holds symbol and attribute entries, appended to the array as they are encountered and removed from the end of the array as the block in which they are declared is closed. The other array, *level*, holds pointers to those entries in the first array which begin a new block. Figure 6.25 shows four stages in the life of such a symbol table while the program of Fig. 6.24(a) is being scanned. The index values for each array element are shown at the left. Symbol attributes have been omitted; they could be placed either together with the symbols or else in an array of the same length in correspondence with *table*. For ease in interpreting the figure, the block number appears in parentheses next to the symbol. It need not actually be stored in *table*.

Stage (a) holds after the declarations of block 1 have been examined. After scanning has proceeded beyond the declarations of block 3, the sym-

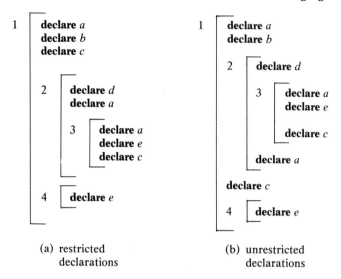

| (a) restricted | (b) unrestricted |
| declarations | declarations |

Figure 6.24 Block Structure in Source Text

bol table attains stage (b). The pointers 1, 4, 6 in the second array indicate the first symbol declared in each of blocks 1, 2, and 3, which constitute block 3's environment. After the closure of block 3 has been scanned, but before the closure of block 2, stage (c) holds. The symbols declared in block 3 have been removed from the symbol array, and the pointer to the first of them has been removed from the pointer array. Stage (d) holds after scanning has advanced beyond the closure of block 2, the opening of block 4, and the last declaration. The second pointer, 4, points to the first declaration not of the second block in text order but rather of the block nested at the second level. Whereas the second-level block at stages (b)

	table	level	table	level	table	level	table	level
8.			c (3)					
7.			e (3)					
6.			a (3)					
5.			a (2)		a (2)			
4.			d (2)		d (2)		e (4)	
3.	c (1)		c (1)	6	c (1)		c (1)	
2.	b (1)		b (1)	4	b (1)	4	b (1)	4
1.	a (1)	1	a (1)	1	a (1)	1	a (1)	1
	(a) in block 1		(b) in block 3		(c) in block 2		(d) in block 4	

Figure 6.25 Dynamic Symbol Table

and (c) was block 2, now block 4 holds that position. The pointer array is thus a compilation-time analog of the execution-time display. Instead of pointing to activation records of the different blocks, it points to their symbol table entries.

Because the foregoing dynamic symbol table grows and shrinks according to a LIFO discipline, it is sometimes called a *stack symbol table*. Such a designation is not wholly accurate, however, because the pointers allow access to positions other than the top. Once the text has been completely scanned, the dynamic symbol table no longer exists. Its use is restricted, therefore, to one-pass compilation. We shall soon present an alternative organization suitable for multiple-pass translation. First, however, we examine the management of a dynamic symbol table.

The table building process is facilitated by the provision of two pointers, one to the next available position in each of the two arrays. Let the index of the first unused element in the symbol array *table* be *tabletop* and that of the first unused element in the pointer array *level* be *leveltop*. Both pointers are initialized to 1 before scanning begins. When a declaration is encountered, the appropriate entry is placed in *table* [*tabletop*] and *tabletop* is incremented by 1. Entry to a new block causes the execution of

$$level\ [leveltop] \leftarrow tabletop$$
$$leveltop \leftarrow leveltop + 1$$

Exit from a block undoes the foregoing action by executing

$$leveltop \leftarrow leveltop - 1$$
$$tabletop \leftarrow level\ [leveltop]$$

Linear search begins at *table* [*tabletop* − 1], precluding the need to delete entries for old blocks, and proceeds toward the first element. The first entry encountered for the desired symbol is the one corresponding to the environment of the current block. Search time is still $O(n)$.

Binary search for a symbol requires the symbols to be ordered according to the collating sequence. Because the table is ordered instead by blocks, the desired search order is embodied in a second table of pointers. This table, shown in Fig. 6.26 for stages (a) and (b) in the preceding program scan, is defined by *alpha*[*i*] = *k*, where *table*[*k*] is the *i*th symbol in collating order. Search proceeds by repeatedly bisecting *alpha*, comparing values not of pointers in *alpha*, but of the corresponding symbols in *table*. If duplicate entries are encountered in *table*, the one with the highest pointer value in *alpha* is the desired one. Search thus requires $O(\log n)$ time, but with the constant of proportionality increased by the necessity to make the accesses indirectly. Encounter of a new identifier requires $O(n)$ time to insert the pointer in *alpha*. Block

	alpha	table	level			alpha	table	level
					8.	7	c (3)	
					7.	4	e (3)	
					6.	8	a (3)	
					5.	3	a (2)	
					4.	2	d (2)	
3.	3	c (1)			3.	6	c (1)	6
2.	2	b (1)			2.	5	b (1)	4
1.	1	a (1)	1		1.	1	a (1)	1
	(a) in block 1					(b) in block 3		

Figure 6.26   Block Structure with Binary Search

closure also requires $O(n)$ time to purge *alpha* of pointers not lower than the new value of *tabletop*.

The rapid search provided by hashing is still available with a block-structured table. As for binary search, an auxiliary table of pointers is required, because the position of entries in the symbol table is dictated by the block structure rather than by the value of the hashing function. Instead of open addressing to handle collisions, explicit pointers are used to link symbols in the same equivalence class, including duplicates of the same symbol. Each chain begins with the most recently inserted symbol, thus guaranteeing that the first occurrence of a symbol on an equivalence class chain is the one in the current environment. Let the hashing function transform the symbol *a* to 3, *b* to 5, *c* also to 5, *d* to 6, and *e* to 1. The complete symbol table is shown in Fig. 6.27 for two stages during the scan. Each element in the array *place* is accessed by hashing a symbol and points to whichever symbol in the associated equivalence class was most recently inserted into *table*. The pointer field in each entry of *table* links the symbol to the preceding entry in the same equivalence class. In both *place* and *table*, 0 serves as a null pointer.

Searching requires one application of the key transformation to access *place*, one stage of indirection to reach *table*, and a linear scan of the equivalence class. For a reasonable key transformation this is still $O(1)$ time. Insertion of a new symbol requires simple chain maintenance with no scan, and block opening requires no special action. Block closure, on the other hand, is complicated by the necessity of resetting the chain head pointers in *place*. Access to the correct entries in *place* requires application of the key transformation to each symbol deleted. The time requirement for this relatively infrequent operation is therefore $O(n)$.

The dynamic symbol table organizations we have considered limit the

place	table	level
8.		c (3) 3	
7.		e (3) 0	
6.	4	a (3) 5	
5.	8	a (2) 1	
4.	0	d (2) 0	
3.	6	c (1) 2	6
2.	0	b (1) 0	4
1.	7	a (1) 0	1

(a) in block 3

place	table	level
6.	4		
5.	3	a (2) 1	
4.	0	d (2) 0	
3.	5	c (1) 2	
2.	0	b (1) 0	4
1.	0	a (1) 0	1

(b) in block 2

Figure 6.27 Block Structure with Hashing

compiler to a single pass, because table entries are deleted as soon as the scanner has finished examining the corresponding block. For multipass compilation, all the symbols must remain available after scanning is complete. Because symbols are not deleted when block closure is encountered, there may be symbols from more than one block at a given nesting level. The pointer array *level* therefore becomes incapable of distinguishing among the various blocks, and must be replaced by a fuller specification of the complete block structure. The array *block* designates for each block both the first (*lo*) and the last (*hi*) symbol table entries associated with the block, and specifies the immediately enclosing block (*enc*). The number of entries in *block* is equal not to the maximum nesting level but to the total number of blocks. The complete symbol table for our example program is shown in Fig. 6.28 as it stands at the conclusion of scanning. Pointers for binary searching or for hashing are omitted.

Linear search of the static block-structured symbol table is straightforward. For a reference in block i, search begins at $table[hi[i]]$ and proceeds downward through $table[lo[i]]$, whereupon i is replaced by $enc[i]$ and

	table	block		
9.	e (4)			
8.	c (3)			
7.	e (3)			
6.	a (3)	lo	hi	enc
5.	a (2)			
4.	d (2)	9	9	1
3.	c (1)	6	8	2
2.	b (1)	4	5	1
1.	a (1)	1	3	0

Figure 6.28 Static Symbol Table

the search continues. Each probe now requires two comparisons, one of the desired symbol with the entry and one of the index with $lo[i]$. The construction of *block* is nearly trivial, and of course no action is needed when block closure is encountered.

Binary search and hashing are both less efficient than with a dynamic table, because the first occurrence of the desired symbol may lie in a block outside the environment being considered, and there is no way to verify its eligibility without a further search of *block*. For this reason, use of the block number as an attribute is advisable if either binary search or hashing is contemplated with a static symbol table.

Our symbol table construction methods have thus far assumed that declarations precede embedded blocks. If this restriction is removed, as in Fig. 6.24(b), declarations for one block may be encountered before the scan of the surrounding block is complete. If symbols are appended to *table* as they are encountered, the entries for a block will no longer be contiguous, nor will nesting order be related to table order.

Matters are easily set aright. Because the proper grouping of table entries is not known until block closure is scanned, symbols are appended to the table only at that time. The blocks are therefore represented in the table in the order of their closures, not, as heretofore, in the order of their openings. Each symbol waits, between its declaration and the block closure, in a stack. The symbol is pushed onto the stack when its declaration is encountered and popped from the stack when its block closure is encountered. Elements of the array *block* are created as before in the order of block openings. Not until a block is closed, however, does its entry in the array *block* point to the array *table*. Prior to that time, one of its fields (we have chosen hi) specifies how many of its declarations have been stacked. Figure 6.29 illustrates four stages in the table construction process for the program of Fig. 6.24(b).

At stage (a), three blocks have been entered, and five entries stacked, but no block closed, as indicated by the value 0 in each field lo. After the declaration of c in block 3 is encountered, it is stacked and the hi field of $block[3]$ incremented to 3, the number of its entries on the stack. When closure of block 3 is encountered, that field is used to control popping the 3 entries from the stack and appending them to the symbol table. During that process $lo[3]$ and $hi[3]$ are set to 1 and 3, the lowest and highest indices of the corresponding entries in *table*. By stage (b) the foregoing action has been completed and a second declaration encountered in block 2, whose closure has been encountered by stage (c), as has the last declaration of block 1. Before the closure of block 1, block 4 with its lone declaration is opened. Stage (d) shows the completed table.

	table	block lo hi enc			stack
5.					e (3)
4.					a (3)
3.		0	2	2	d (2)
2.		0	1	1	b (1)
1.		0	2	0	a (1)

(a) after **declare** e (3)

table	block lo hi enc			stack
				a (2)
a (3)	1	3	2	d (2)
e (3)	0	2	1	b (1)
c (3)	0	2	0	a (1)

(b) after **declare** a (2)

	table	block lo hi enc			stack
9.					
8.					
7.					
6.					
5.	d (2)				
4.	a (2)				
3.	a (3)	1	3	2	c (1)
2.	e (3)	4	5	1	b (1)
1.	c (3)	0	3	0	a (1)

(c) after **declare** c (1)

table	block lo hi enc			stack
a (1)				
b (1)				
c (1)				
e (4)				
d (2)				
a (2)	6	6	1	
a (3)	1	3	2	
e (3)	4	5	1	
c (3)	7	9	0	

(d) after block 1 closure

Figure 6.29   Symbol Table Construction for Program with Deferred Declarations

Thus far we have assumed that a symbol is entered in the table only when its declaration is encountered. It is often convenient, and in one-pass translation mandatory, to enter a symbol in the table as soon as the first reference to it is encountered. But the association of a symbol with its block is not always possible if symbol reference is permitted to precede symbol declaration. In PL/I, for example, GOTO L may be a jump to a label yet to be encountered in the current block, to a label already encountered in the current block or an enclosing block, or to a label in an enclosing block but not yet encountered.

The foregoing ambiguity can always be resolved by multiple passes in a compiler, or by an extra scan of the full text by an interpreter. If processing without extra passes is desired, the ambiguity can be prohibited by restricting the source language. An obvious restriction is to require declaration to precede reference. This is good practice anyhow with respect to variables and procedures, but many programmers find it unduly restrictive for labels. An alternative restriction on the use of labels is to prohibit the "unusual return", a jump to a label in an enclosing block. This restriction has the further merit of simplifying the execution-time management of the activation-record stack.

FOR FURTHER STUDY

Several good introductions to grammars and parsing for programming languages have been written. One of the easiest to read, but fairly long, is Chapter 3 of Lee [1974]. A good, brief presentation is Chapter 13 of Rohl [1975]. Intermediate in length are Chapter 8 of Ullman [1976] and Chapters 4 and 5 of Aho and Ullman [1977]. Two interesting short communications on the representation of syntax are Knuth [1964] and Wirth [1977].

Operator precedence parsing is due to Floyd [1963], who gives a method for constructing double precedence functions, if they exist, from an operator precedence grammar. One of the fullest and most readable expositions of operator precedence parsing is given in Section 5.3 of Aho and Ullman [1977]. Another good treatment is that in Section 6.1 of Gries [1971]. Those two sources give algorithms for computing the precedence relations for an operator grammar. Hopgood [1969] offers a brief treatment in Sections 7.3–7.4.

Recursive descent parsing was apparently first used by Lucas [1961]. The method is clearly explained in Gries [1971, sect. 4.3] and Aho and Ullman [1977, sect. 5.4]. Its use in a compiler is reviewed in McKeeman [1974a, sect. 1.A.2]. The more general topic of syntax-directed top-down parsing is considered in Cheatham and Sattley [1964], and at greater length in Lewis, Rosenkrantz, and Stearns [1976, ch. 8].

One of the most attractive methods of syntactic analysis, not covered in this book, is LR parsing, due to Knuth [1965]. It is described well in Aho and Johnson [1974] and Chapter 6 of Aho and Ullman [1977].

Lexical scanning is explored by Cocke and Schwartz [1970, ch. 3], Gries [1971, ch. 3], Rohl [1975, ch. 3], and Aho and Ullman [1977, ch. 3], all of whom relate it explicitly to state transitions. The treatment in Hopgood [1969, ch. 6] is briefer. Unlike the others, however, it includes character recognition and line reconstruction.

Symbol tables in the context of translators are presented briefly by Wegner [1968, sect. 2.2], and more fully by Hopgood [1969, ch. 4], Gries [1971, ch. 9–10], and Aho and Ullman [1977, ch. 9]. Tree-structured tables are emphasized in Severance [1974] and in Horowitz and Sahni [1976, ch. 9]. Maurer and Lewis [1975] offer a good survey of hashing. Block structure in symbol tables is discussed in Gries [1971, sect. 9.5], Aho and Ullman [1977, sect. 9.3], and, for one-pass compilers only, McKeeman [1974b].

EXERCISES

6.1 Can one recognize without parsing? Can one parse without recognizing?

6.2 Consider the grammar of Fig. 6.3 and the derivation of Fig. 6.4. In how many different orders can the reductions be applied? Is any other derivation tree obtainable? Does the string parsed exhibit syntactic ambiguity?

6.3 Consider the string

IF X<Y THEN IF X>Z THEN A:=B ELSE A:=C

and the Pascal subset grammar of Fig. 6.7.
a) Display all possible parse trees of the string as *stmt*.
b) State for each parse the value, if any, assigned to A under each of the four possible pairs of values of the two conditions. Assume that B has value 0 and C has value 1.
c) Now let the new terminal "FI" be appended to the right end of the replacement substring for *ifstmt*. For each parse, rewrite the string (using "FI") to reflect unambiguously the corresponding structure.

6.4 Programming language text was described in Section 6.2.2 as one-dimensional, yet it surely looks two-dimensional. Explain.

6.5 Construct an example of the ambiguity which can arise in postfix notation if a given token can represent either a unary or a binary operator.

6.6 Trace the execution of the program of Fig. 6.9, as modified in the text for double precedence, in evaluating $5+6*(7-2**(12/4)**2)+1$.

6.7 Devise one-pass algorithms to evaluate a prefix expression
a) scanning right-to-left;
b) scanning left-to-right.

6.8 Extend the double precedence table of Section 6.2.2 to include *all* unary and binary operators of PL/I. You may assume that it can be determined in advance whether an occurrence of any operator token is unary or binary.

6.9 Extend the grammar of Fig. 6.3 to include subtraction ("−") and exponentiation (" ** "). Give to subtraction the same precedence as to addition, and to exponentiation a higher precedence than to multiplication. Ensure, for these nonassociative operators, that subtractions are performed left to right and exponentiations right to left.

6.10 Construct a grammar which imposes the required positional hierarchy in evaluating APL expressions composed of one-letter identifiers, the eight unary and binary operators +, −, ×, and ÷, and parentheses. Assume that tokens for unary operators have already been distinguished from binary.

6.11 Execute manually an operator precedence parse of each of the following strings, using the grammar of Fig. 6.3. Show for each parse at least the degree of detail given in Fig. 6.12, plus a parse tree in which each nonterminal is marked with the number of the corresponding decision to reduce.

a) $X * (Y+Z)$
b) $X+Y) * Z$
c) $X+(Y * (Z+X)) * (X+Y * Z)$
d) $Y * ((X+Y * Z)+X)$
e) $(X * (Y+Z)+Z$

6.12 Extend the precedence matrix of Fig. 6.14 to incorporate explicitly the dummy tokens which mark the beginning and end of the string.

6.13 Write a set of recursive descent parsing routines for the grammar constructed in Exercise 6.9.

6.14 The PL/I fragment

    IF A THEN IF B THEN C=1; ELSE C=2;

is unambiguous; the second THEN matches the ELSE. Yet a grammar such as that of Fig. 6.7 is ambiguous with respect to a nested conditional statement. How could a recursive descent parser specified by that ambiguous grammar nevertheless be made to parse such constructions correctly? Give a brief answer.

6.15 Suppose that you are building, for a compiler, a parser which combines operator precedence parsing of expressions with recursive descent parsing of the language as a whole (but excluding lexical analysis). Explain how the required programs can be made to work together.

6.16 Draw a state diagram for the lexical analysis of quoted strings in PL/I.

6.17 Construct the state transition table which corresponds to the state diagrams of Fig. 6.22.

6.18 Amend the state diagram of Fig. 6.22(a) by adding arcs, and states as necessary, to represent the detection of errors in recognizing an unsigned real number.

6.19 A symbol table having the eleven addresses 0–10 is managed with the use of hashing and open addressing. The hashing function in use maps each identifier to its length in characters. The following identifiers are presented for insertion in the order shown: SEGMENT, SECTOR, RADIUS, PI, PERIM, DIAMETER, CIRCUMF, CHORD, CENTER, AREA, and ARC.
Both for linear probing (with $r=2$) and for quadratic probing (with $s=2$ and $t=2$) show the symbol table and state the number of probes which have been made

a) after the first 8 symbols have been presented;

b) after all 11 symbols have been presented.

For each symbol, count the initial insertion attempt (with $i=0$) as one probe.

6.20 One way to build a symbol table for a language with block structure is to distinguish duplicate names by qualifying each occurrence with the block number. Is it sufficient to qualify each name with its nesting level instead of with the block number? Explain.

Chapter 7

COMPILATION

7.1 FUNCTION

Generative translation from a language which is not machine-oriented into a more easily executed form (e.g. object code for a specific computer) is called *compilation*, and the programs which perform this translation are called *compilers*. From one point of view, compilation is just an extension of macro processing, with the source language generalized beyond the machine orientation of most macro-processor input. Yet the differences between typical macro-assembler languages and most programming languages are not merely quantitative. The qualitative differences are such that compilers are generally not constructed in the same manner as macro assemblers. To examine compilation further, we begin by dissecting a typical compilation and then examining some of the language features which impose functional requirements on the compiler.

7.1.1 *Overview of Compilation*

The process of compilation can be performed as a sequence of six major steps. Although two or more of these steps can be implemented together in a particular compiler, they are conceptually distinct and subject to a sequential order imposed by logic. In that order, they are the following.

Lexical analysis
Syntactic analysis
Semantic processing
Storage allocation
Target code generation
Assembly

Lexical analysis in general has been treated in Section 6.3. A concomitant of lexical analysis in a compiler is the construction of a symbol table for user-determined identifiers and of a storage facility for constants. Numeric constants can be handled much as in an assembler's literal table or as in processing immediate operands; string constants, which can have widely different lengths, need different care.

Syntactic analysis has been discussed briefly in Section 6.2. As mentioned there, lexical analysis may be either performed as a subroutine of the syntactic analysis or combined with it in some manner. Because of the length of programs which may be compiled, it is usually not practical to develop the complete parse tree before continuing the compilation. For this reason, semantic processing is normally undertaken whenever the parser has recognized a language construct. Thus it is common for both lexical analysis and semantic processing routines to be called by the parser. Operator precedence and recursive descent parsers are among those most commonly used in compilers. Among other important parsing methods are those called "simple precedence", "bounded context", "LL(1)", and "LR(1)". Rather than discussing them here, however, we refer the reader to more specialized works.

Semantic processing, also called "semantic analysis" or "semantic interpretation", has two facets. One is "interpretation" (in the conventional sense of the word, not as opposed to "generation"), the determination of the meaning of the language constructs recognized by the syntactic analysis. The other is the representation of that meaning in a form intermediate between the source language and the target language, and called *intermediate code*. Like source language, intermediate code is independent of the details of the target machine. Like the target language, however, it reflects the types of operations available in a target machine. It is often fruitful to think of intermediate code as being composed of calls of macros which can be defined for the target machine language.

Storage allocation includes both the determination of storage requirements and the specification of algorithms to perform addressing calculations at execution time. Storage must be provided not only for the variables defined in the source program and for the constants (literals) which appear in it, but also for several kinds of parameters and for temporary results in expression evaluation and type conversion. Addressing calculations range from trivial, as in accessing a local scalar variable, to moderately complex, as in accessing an element of an array declared in an enclosing block and having dynamically specified bounds.

Target code generation is the translation from intermediate code to a machine-dependent representation, often similar to assembler language. Symbolic names are typically retained in symbolic form. Code generation can be likened to macro expansion for which the prototypes match calls in intermediate code and the skeletons are defined for the target machine.

With certain forms of intermediate code, this generation step is in fact just pure macro processing without nesting.

Assembly is the final translation to the output form. If, as is common, that form is object code for some machine, then the assembly step is very similar to Pass 2 of a two-pass assembler. The output may even be machine code, as in a load-and-go compiler. The boundary between the code generation and assembly steps is not firm; the task entrusted to the pair of them can be divided in various ways. The more complex the code generation, the simpler the assembly.

The first three steps, lexical analysis, syntactic analysis, and semantic processing, are analytic and machine-independent. The last three steps, storage allocation, code generation, and assembly, are synthetic and machine-dependent. The intermediate code stands at the interface between the machine-independent and the machine-dependent steps.

An important process in many compilers is the investment of effort to increase the efficiency of the compiled code. This *code optimization* is performed once per compilation and enjoyed once per execution. The anticipated number of executions per compilation is the major determinant of how much optimization should be undertaken. Some optimization (e.g. elimination of common subexpressions) is machine-independent; other optimization (e.g. elimination of redundant store instructions) is machine-dependent. If optimization is performed, the six principal steps are augmented by one or two more. Machine-independent optimization is often performed in a separate step, usually after semantic processing. Machine-dependent optimization can be undertaken as a separate final step, but is more often combined with code generation or even with machine-independent optimization.

7.1.2 *Source-Language Features*

A large number of features of programming languages contribute to the greater difficulty of compilation as compared with assembly. A catalog of many of these features follows.

The declaration of an identifier may be implicit in its use rather than provided explicitly. Examples include labels, undeclared variables, and names of built-in files and functions. Determining what an implicitly declared identifier represents may be relatively easy, as for labels, or relatively difficult, as in determining whether SUM in PL/I is the built-in function or a variable. If an explicit declaration is deferred to a point beyond the first use of the identifier, semantic processing may be rendered more difficult.

Elementary variables with different attributes can be organized into tree-structured aggregates, such as group items in COBOL, records in Pascal, or structures in PL/I. The compiler may be required to compute addresses of leaves, or of groups of leaves, which correspond to fully- or partly-qualified names in the source language. The compiler must also be able to decompose into its constituent parts an operation performed BY NAME (PL/I) or CORRESPONDING (COBOL).

Address computation for array elements or cross-sections is also required. This is straightforward if the array dimensions are bound at compilation time, but not if the language permits dynamic arrays. In that event the compiler must generate code which will compute the required addresses by use of values which are not available until execution time.

Interrupt function modules require code to test for the conditions which cause the interrupts, as well as for immediate invocation of and eventual return from the modules.

The use of recursive procedures requires the compiler to provide at translation time for the production at execution time of an indeterminate number of copies of the activation record for the procedure. It is particularly important not merely that the data areas be distinct, but also that the appropriate different values of link fields be generated for each copy, to permit proper stack management.

The existence of multiple data types, even in the absence of user-defined types as in Pascal, requires type checking, type conversion, or some of each. If types are specified at compilation time, the compiler can perform checking; otherwise it must generate code to perform execution-time checking. Type conversion, except of constants, must be deferred to execution time.

Facilities for formatting input and output are often very extensive. To generate code from such specifications as those of EDIT-directed input/output in PL/I, the compiler must translate from a large, nonalgorithmic sublanguage.

The use of pointer variables to qualify references to identifiers, as in PL/I, requires the compiler both to establish pointers which will hold the correct execution-time addresses and to provide for indirect addressing at execution time. The availability of explicit-base addressing in the target machine greatly simplifies this task.

The variety of storage classes, especially in PL/I, mandates a variety of schemes for accessing storage. A particularly intriguing class is that of the **own** variable (Algol) or STATIC INTERNAL variable (PL/I). The variable must remain addressable, with its value intact, even when the only block which can access it is inactive and therefore not represented by an activation record.

The existence of block structure imposes further burdens. Multiple uses of an identifier may refer to the same entity or to different ones, depending on the static nesting of the blocks in which the identifiers are declared. Storage for identifiers local to a block, unless they are STATIC or **own**, must be allocated upon each entry to the block and freed upon each exit.

Call by name is another feature which, if provided, greatly complicates the task of the compiler, for the reasons discussed in Section 3.5.3. That section describes briefly the use of thunks to implement call by name.

The last language feature in this catalog occurs in PL/I. Because labels may be passed as parameters, a GOTO may transfer from within a procedure to a label in another block which does not enclose it statically and to which the static chain therefore does not lead.

These and other complicating features of programming languages help explain why compilers for rich languages are complex programs. Nevertheless, the basic process of compilation is readily understandable. Although this chapter can hardly hope to convey all of the material in whole books on compiler design, it does explain methods for handling some of the foregoing language features.

7.1.3 Compilers v. Assemblers

The many source-language features described in the preceding section result in a number of salient differences between compilers and assemblers. On any one item the distinction may not be clear-cut. Moreover, it may be difficult to distinguish a simple compiler from a powerful macro assembler. Nevertheless, the differences are usually substantial enough that there remains a qualitative distinction between assemblers and compilers.

Generally, a compiler performs a one-to-many translation, generating many target-language statements from a single source-language statement, whereas an assembler performs a one-to-one translation. There are exceptions, of course. A declaration statement does not result in the generation of any target code (unless it incorporates refinements such as PL/I's INITIAL attribute), and the simple assignment A ← B may well be translated into a single target statement. An assembler will generate no machine code to correspond to most assembler instructions, but may generate substantial amounts of code from a single CONST instruction. Moreover, a macro assembler will generate many lines from a one-line call. Nevertheless, the characterization of compilers as one-to-many and of assemblers as one-to-one is reasonably accurate.

An assembler is relatively little concerned with dependence among statements. Except for symbol definition and, on some machines, storage alignment, the translation of one statement is independent of that of other statements. This is not true of the compiler, where there is much greater mutual dependence among source-language statements. Declaration statements are explicitly related to statements which refer to the entities declared, and I/O statements are often explicitly dependent upon format statements. Implicit dependence occurs in loops and other control structures. Another form of implicit dependence is dictated by the target machine rather than by the source language. This is the interstatement competition for such resources as the registers which are to be designated in the code generated from several statements.

An assembler usually faces much simpler initial source-language processing than does a compiler. This is due in part to the reduced mutual dependence of statements, but also to the simpler forms of individual statements. It is true that an assembler may have to face address expressions and macro calls, both of which can be rather complex. These are rarely as intricate, however, as the statements which may be faced by a compiler.

A compiler usually encounters many more kinds of operands than does an assembler. Not only are there integer, real, boolean, and character types, but there are complex (in the mathematical sense), label, entry-name, multidimensional array, and tree-structured operands. Even for the types which the two may have in common, the compiler must perform type checking and conversion, whereas the assembler leaves this burden to the programmer.

Another difference is in error handling. Because compiler-language programs embody greater redundancy than do assembler-language programs, the compiler is often called upon to perform more detailed checking, to issue elaborate and informative diagnostic messages, and often also to attempt repairs. The modern debugging compiler is a far cry from the sole message "parse failed" of one of the early compilers. Although assemblers are generally no longer that laconic either, assemblers usually perform less extensive error handling than do compilers.

A final difference is that the compiler, unlike the assembler, is concerned with the flow of control at execution time. The assembler-language programmer provides his own subroutine linkages, perhaps through use of macro instructions. The assembler really need not distinguish a loop-closing branch from a subroutine call. The compiler, particularly for a block-structured language, may face tasks as complex as allocating storage for the activation records of recursive procedures or evaluating arguments called by name.

7.1.4   *Target-Language Choice*

The target language of a compiler may be either object (or machine) code, almost ready to be interpreted by computer hardware, or else in another form which requires further translation. Three organizations of the over-all translation process are shown in Fig. 7.1. Organization (a) is that of the traditional compiler, which generates either object code ready for relocation (and perhaps linking) or else machine code ready for loading. It is this organization which is implemented in the six steps described in Section 7.1.1.

If the last of those six steps, assembly, is omitted from the compiler, organization (b) results. Here a separate assembler program performs the final stages of translation. This organization is attractive when the compiler must be built in a hurry, because the assembler is presumably already

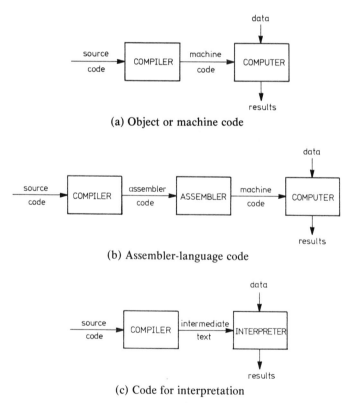

(a) Object or machine code

(b) Assembler-language code

(c) Code for interpretation

Figure 7.1   Translation Process for Different Compiler Target Languages

available. The translation is less efficient than in (a), however, because the assembler is not specialized to the restricted form of code produced by the compiler. Moreover, it builds a new symbol table instead of using the one already built by the compiler. Furthermore, the two-stage translation process requires either extra time to load the assembler after the compilation is complete, or space to hold the assembler in main storage during the compilation.

Organization (c) demands even less of the compiler, but requires an interpreter to translate the compiled program further. Unlike organizations (a) and (b), where the target-language specification is imposed on the compiler designer, in (c) the compiler and interpreter are designed together and the intermediate language can be specified to suit. In several situations, the relative simplicity of the compiler compensates for the speed loss of the interpreter. One occurs for programs with a high ratio of compilations to executions. For programs under development this ratio may approach unity, and for "one-shot" programs it may be nearly as great. Another arises for programs with short execution times. A third situation holds when the hardware incorporates features designed to facilitate interpretation of the compiler output. In other words, if the machine architecture and corresponding machine language are designed to execute intermediate code, then organization (c) may be a very efficient approach. An example is provided by the descriptors and stack mechanism of the Burroughs B5000 and its successors, which are highly suited to the direct execution of programs in postfix notation (described in Section 7.2.1).

7.2 IMPLEMENTATION STRUCTURES

In a compiler, the algorithms and the data representations are interdependent, just as they are for any other program. In developing a particular compiler, the choice of control and data structures must proceed hand in hand with refinement of the algorithms. In compiler description, however, we are not bound by this interdependence and choose to defer our study of the processing algorithms until after examination of three structural issues. These are (1) how to represent the intermediate code, (2) how to store programmer-specified entities, and (3) how to organize the compiler itself.

7.2.1 *Representations of Intermediate Code*

Postfix. Polish postfix notation is particularly attractive for the computer representation of arithmetic expressions. A minor advantage is the space saving due to the property that parentheses are never required. For example, the 7-token infix expression $(X+Y)*Z$ is represented by the 5-token postfix expression $XY+Z*$. The principal advantage of postfix representation over infix is that single-pass left-to-right evaluation requires only one stack. An operator stack is not needed, because operators are applied as soon as they are encountered.

The one required stack holds only values, and is initially empty. Each time an operand is encountered, its value is pushed onto the stack. Each time an operator of degree i is encountered, the top i values are popped, the operator is applied to them, and the resulting value is stacked. At the conclusion of the scan, the stack will contain precisely one value, that of the expression scanned. This evaluation process, which might be performed in an interpreter, is very efficient. A slight modification results not in evaluating the expression, but in performing the code generation required in a compiler.

Other programming-language constructs, too, can be readily represented in postfix notation. The assignment statement $A \leftarrow B$ becomes $A\ B \leftarrow$ and the branch GOTO L1 becomes L1 GOTO. In generating code for either of these constructs, the entries are popped from the stack, but nothing is pushed onto the stack afterwards, as is done for expressions. The details of code generation, for other representations as well as for postfix, are considered in Section 7.3.

Compound, alternative, and iterative control structures are also easily represented in postfix. Compound statements (e.g. those grouped within a **begin-end** pair) require no special handling. Postfix representations of the individual statements are just catenated in sequence. Alternation and iteration, however, implicitly specify jumping to points in the source text which are not necessarily labeled. Means are therefore required of representing jumps which are specified by the compiler rather than directly by the programmer. If the symbols of the postfix text are numbered serially from the beginning, then these numbers can be used as jump destinations. An unconditional jump might have the syntax

<destination> JUMP

where <destination> is the serial number of the text symbol, a label, to which the branch is made. The source-language operator GOTO is distinct from JUMP because the operand of the former is a pointer to a symbol table entry, not the serial number of a text symbol. Conditional jumps might have operators JPOS, JNEG, JZERO, and the like, with syntax

expression <destination> Jconditional.

If the jump condition is satisfied, then the next text symbol to scan after the jump is the one specified; otherwise, normal processing continues. In either event, *expression* and <destination> are popped from the stack and nothing is pushed back on.

To see how alternation can be expressed in postfix notation without requiring any backup in the left-to-right scan of the postfix text, consider the following statement.

IF *cond* THEN *stmt1* ELSE *stmt2*

The postfix form of the statement is

cond <dest2> JFALSE *stmt1* <destout> JUMP *stmt2*

where <dest2> is the serial number of the first symbol of *stmt2* and <destout> is the number of the first symbol which follows the text shown. For example, the PL/I statement pair

```
IF A<B THEN C = B+D*4;
         ELSE C = A+D*4;
```

might be translated into

37	38	39	40	41	42	43	44	45	46	47	48	49	50	51	52	53	54	55	56	57
A	B	−	51	JPZ	C	B	D	4	*	+	←	58	JUMP	C	A	D	4	*	+	←

where the serial number of each symbol appears directly above the symbol and JPZ is a jump on accumulator positive or zero.

Quadruples. A convenient way to represent the execution of a binary operator is to list four items: the operator, its two operands, and the destination of the result. Intermediate code is often represented by means of such *quadruples*. If we list the four items in the order described, then the assignment D ← B*B − 4*A*C could be translated into the following sequence of quadruples.

*	B	B	T1
*	4	A	T2
*	T2	C	T3
−	T1	T3	D

The temporary variables T1, T2, and T3 are used to represent the results of applying each operator. On a single-accumulator machine, T2 could be held in the accumulator, but T1 and T3 would correspond to temporary storage locations.

Unary operators can be represented by leaving one operand position empty. Jumps can be represented by using the first operand position for the expression to be tested, if any, and the result position for the destination, which is given as the serial number of a quadruple. Except as otherwise directed by jumps, quadruples are executed in serial order.

If 10 quadruples using 4 temporary variables had already been generated when the PL/I statement pair

$$\text{IF } A{<}B \text{ THEN } C = B{+}D{*}4;$$
$$\text{ELSE } C = A{+}D{*}4;$$

was encountered, then the generated quadruples might be the following.

11.	—	A	B	T5
12.	JPZ	T5		16
13.	*	D	4	T6
14.	+	B	T6	C
15.	JUMP			18
16.	*	D	4	T7
17.	+	A	T7	C

Quadruples have the advantage of corresponding more closely to machine language than does postfix (except for stack machines). Their chief disadvantage is the number of temporary variables which must be described. This problem is attacked by the next representation to be discussed.

Triples. If the result field is omitted from a quadruple, a *triple* results. When reference must be made to a result, the number of the triple which produced it is used instead. Not only do many temporary variable names vanish from the symbol table, but nearly one-fourth of the space for the intermediate code is saved. The intermediate code for the same pair of PL/I statements as before can now be written as follows.

11.	—	A	B
12.	JPZ	(11)	(17)
13.	*	D	4
14.	+	B	(13)
15.	←	(14)	C
16.	JUMP		(20)
17.	*	D	4
18.	+	A	(17)
19.	←	(18)	C

Note the requirement to distinguish syntactically between a triple number, e.g. "(13)", and a constant, e.g. "4". Thus triple 13 specifies the multiplication of D by the literal constant 4, whereas triple 14 specifies the addition of B and the result produced by the execution of triple 13. In the conditional jump triple 12, the second field refers to a result, that of executing triple 11, but the third refers to a destination.

Indirect Triples. A given triple, such as (13) or (17) in the foregoing example, can occur many times in one program. This is particularly true if subscripts are used, because identical subscripting calculations are frequently written more than once, as in X[I] ← X[I] + Z[I]. Multiple occurrences of a given triple can be replaced by multiple references to a single occurrence. The result is an *indirect triple*, referred to by its serial number in a list of all distinct triples. The order of execution of the triples is specified in a separate sequence vector. Our example can be rewritten in indirect triples as follows.

	distinct triples				sequence
11.	—	A	B	11.	11
12.	JPZ	(11)	17	12.	12
13.	*	D	4	13.	13
14.	+	B	(13)	14.	14
15.	←	(14)	C	15.	15
16.	JUMP		20	16.	16
17.	+	A	(13)	17.	13
18.	←	(17)	C	18.	17
				19.	18

Note that jump destinations. are no longer given as triple numbers, but rather as indices to the sequence vector.

For this short example, the use of indirect triples costs space, rather than saves it. For a longer program, the opposite is more often true. Indirect triples offer another advantage if code optimization is to be performed. The resulting deletion of redundant triples or re-ordering of remaining triples can be performed in the sequence vector, obviating the rearrangement of the much larger list of triples.

7.2.2 *Storage of Tokens*

The lexical analyzer and symbol table manager together determine which source-language identifiers name the same entity. In subsequent processing, it is important for the compiler to know that two occurrences of an identifier do name the same variable or the same label, but it is immaterial what the source-language name is. The replacement of each identifier token by a pointer to the identifier's entry in the symbol table imposes therefore no limitation on the compiler's ability to translate. Except in languages with severe restrictions on identifier length, a substantial space saving may result. There is also some time saving because it is quicker to operate on a short pointer than on a long identifier.

Another benefit is that variable-length identifier tokens have been replaced by uniform-length tokens. Great simplification can be obtained by providing tokens of uniform length not just for identifiers but for all token types. The resulting elements are called *uniform tokens* or *uniform symbols*. Each consists of two fields, a type code and an index. The index specifies a location in whichever table is appropriate to the type. There may be, for example, a table of identifiers, a table of constants, a table of reserved words, and a table of operators. The type code may be just a code, or it may be the address of the associated table. Some tokens, such as one-character operators, may indeed be replaced by uniform symbols longer than the original tokens. Nevertheless, the replacement of identifiers and constants, especially long character strings, usually does reduce the size of the program to be compiled. Far more important is the ability to test, copy, and stack tokens of uniform length. Another advantage in many computers is the replacement of characters and character strings by numbers. The latter are often more easily and more rapidly compared than the former, and they are surely much more convenient to use as indices into tables of tokens or of addresses of processing routines.

What kinds of tables are required for the uniform symbols to point to? Identifiers and their attributes are kept in a symbol table, as already discussed. If the source language has block structure, a block-structured symbol table, as described in Section 6.4.4, is required. Reserved words may be placed in the symbol table prior to compilation, or they may be kept in a separate table. The latter choice usually simplifies the parsing at the cost of complicating the scanning. Because the meaning of reserved words is predefined, it is possible to omit their attributes from the table. In fact, the table itself can be discarded if all reserved words are identified in initial processing before later stages of translation are undertaken. The same is true of special symbols, such as operators. Syntactic analysis and semantic processing can proceed quite comfortably given only the information that a token is the ith reserved word or the kth special symbol.

The handling of constants is somewhat more involved. Character-string constants are characterized by length which can be highly variable. To avoid the waste inherent in allocating table entries big enough to hold the longest possible string, a different approach is customary. All character-string constants are stored consecutively in a *string space*. Because their lengths are not fixed, each must be given a length specification. One method is to incorporate a length field in the uniform symbol, but this field lengthens unnecessarily the uniform symbols for other token types and may complicate their processing. Another method is to insert partition codes between successive entries in the string space, but this requires continual testing during string retrieval. Probably most satisfactory is to place the length of a string in a fixed-length field just before the start of the string. The index in the uniform symbol then points to this field rather than to the first character of the adjacent string.

Numeric constants, like literals in assembler language, must ultimately be converted to machine representation. If this is done upon initial encounter, then a table of fixed-length entries can be used for each type of numeric constant. If constant generation is to be deferred until other code is generated, the variable length of the source-language representations suggests the use of the string space. In that event, however, it may be necessary at least to determine in advance the type of each constant, to ensure the generation of code for the execution-time type conversions required by the language definition.

7.2.3 Compiler Organization

The different translator organizations described in Section 2.3.2 for assemblers apply also to compilers. The text-in-core organization is appropriate if the amount of compiler program also in core is kept reasonably small. This can be accomplished by subdividing the compiler into *phases*, each of which performs a small part of the total function. There might, for example, be separate phases for scanning, parsing expressions, parsing other constructs, converting constants to internal representation, determining when temporary variables can be reused, eliminating redundant STORE/LOAD pairs from intermediate code, handling storage allocation for dynamic arrays, etc. Some compilers have been written with dozens of phases.

The pure translator-in-core organization implies a one-pass compiler. A single pass really suffices to perform compilation if the source language is not too rich and if appropriate compiler design decisions are taken. For example, variables should be declared prior to use. The grammar and parser should be of a type which obviates backtracking. The compiler can embody a one-pass assembler, or the designer can simply decree that the target code will be executed by an interpreter or assembled by a separate assembler.

A variant of the foregoing organizations makes multiple passes over the program, each one requiring the presence not of the entire compiler, but of a major portion. A typical two-pass organization is to perform the machine-independent functions in Pass 1 and the machine-dependent functions in Pass 2. Additional passes might be used to perform separately any of the six major processing steps described in Section 7.1.1 (except perhaps semantic processing), to perform machine-independent optimization of the intermediate code, or to perform machine-dependent optimization of the preassembly or postassembly code. The principal advantage of multiple passes is reduction in the main storage space required for the compiler. If a macro facility is provided for generating source text to be compiled, it is usually most easily implemented in an extra pass at the beginning.

The all-in-core organization requires more space for a full compiler than for a mere assembler, or else limits the source program size more severely. This organization is indeed used, however, particularly in compilers designed for debugging small programs. At the cost of over-all translation time, space can often be saved by compiling to intermediate code which is then executed interpretively.

The *neither-in-core* organization should perhaps be named, too. It may be the case that the program is long, the language rich, and the space limited. If so, the program for each pass will have to be brought into main storage in pieces, overlaying pieces loaded earlier. If a paging system is used, paging traffic produced by the compiler can be reduced by carefully laying out the compiler code in pages with a high degree of locality of reference. This process is more easily described, of course, than performed. *Any* program will run more efficiently on a paging system if most references from within a page are to the same page. It is therefore also attractive to have the compiler attempt to produce target code with this property.

7.3 BASIC IMPLEMENTATION PROCESSES

The six basic steps of compilation have already been enumerated: lexical analysis, syntactic analysis, semantic processing, storage allocation, target code generation, and final assembly. The first two of these, although particularly important to compilers, are encountered in all translators and have already been discussed. Much more could be said, particularly about parsing methods, and the reader should bear in mind that many methods are used other than the two which have been presented. A knowledge of these two alone provides sufficient background, however, for understanding the relation of semantic processing to syntactic analysis, regardless of the choice of parsing method.

The last of the six basic steps, final assembly, is very close to the task performed by a conventional assembler. There are differences, of course, the major one being that the symbol table has already been built. Program-defined symbols are entered during lexical or syntactic analysis; compiler-produced symbols may be entered during semantic processing. If the target code generation includes running a location counter, then final assembly can be limited to the equivalent of Pass 2 of a standard two-pass assembler. The description in Chapter 2 is therefore applicable to compilers as well as to assemblers. The remainder of this section will focus on the three steps which are specific to compilers.

7.3.1 *Semantic Processing*

The parsing algorithms described in Chapter 6 do not merely recognize a string in the programming language, even though no derivation tree is produced explicitly. The algorithms do in fact also parse the string; the derivation tree is implicit in the order in which rules of the grammar are applied. If target code is ultimately to be produced, however, an explicit representation of the tree is indeed required; this is embodied in the intermediate code. The task of semantic processing is to produce this explicit linear representation of the derivation tree, associating with it the semantic information content of the original program. That semantic information resides originally in the tokens which constitute the program text. Semantic processing associates the appropriate semantic information with each non-terminal as it is recognized and thus develops the semantic information required in the intermediate code.

To illustrate semantic processing we first show how semantic routines are associated with rules of the grammar in both bottom-up and top-down parsing of expressions, and then consider the semantics of other programming language constructs. Quadruples will be used throughout as the intermediate form. Except for an occasional problem, the generation of postfix or of triples is similar.

We begin with the expression $(X+Y)*Z$ and the grammar of Fig. 7.2. This operator precedence grammar differs from that of Fig. 6.3 only in having IDENT as a terminal, rather than a choice among three specific identifiers. The lexical scanner will recognize each of X, Y, and Z as an instance of IDENT.

An operator precedence parse, similar to that of Fig. 6.12, is shown in the first three columns of Fig. 7.3. Here the parenthesized number following the word "reduce" is the number of the grammar rule in Fig. 7.2 to be applied as a reduction. The intermediate code quadruples

+	X	Y	T1
*	T1	Z	T2

are to be produced during the bottom-up parsing. The first quadruple should be generated when $n+n$ is reduced to n. This can be accomplished by a semantic routine which is called when reduction 1 of the grammar is applied. Unfortunately, the syntax stack has no information about which identifiers are involved. It is hardly adequate to generate

$$+ \qquad n \qquad n \qquad n$$

each time reduction 1 is applied. Identifier information must therefore be associated with entries on the syntax stack. Fortunately, the lexical analyzer provides not only the lexical type of each identifier, but also its name or a pointer to the corresponding symbol table entry. If this information is associated first with IDENT and subsequently with the successive non-terminals to which IDENT is reduced, a quadruple can be generated which refers to the specific identifier. This semantic information is shown in the fourth column of Fig. 7.3, held on a semantics stack which grows and shrinks in synchronism with the syntax stack. Here the identifier itself is used for clarity. In a practical implementation this might be replaced either by the address of the symbol table entry or by the address of the storage location, if the allocation has already been made.

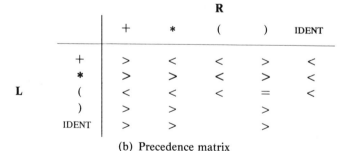

	1.	*expression*	$=$	*expression* "+" *term*.
	2.	*expression*	$=$	*term*.
	3.	*term*	$=$	*term* " * " *factor*.
	4.	*term*	$=$	*factor*.
	5.	*factor*	$=$	"(" *expression* ")".
	6.	*factor*	$=$	IDENT.

(a) Rules

		R				
		+	*	(	)	IDENT
L	+	>	<	<	>	<
	*	>	>	<	>	<
	(	<	<	<	=	<
	)	>	>		>	
	IDENT	>	>		>	

(b) Precedence matrix

Figure 7.2   Grammar for Expressions

Syntax stack	Current symbol	Shift/Reduce decision	Semantics stack	Semantic routine
empty	(	shift	empty	0
(	IDENT	shift	null	7
(IDENT	+	reduce (6)	null X	*none*
(n	+	shift	null X	0
(n +	IDENT	shift	null X null	7
(n + IDENT	)	reduce (6)	null X null Y	*none*
(n + n	)	reduce (1)	null X null Y	1
(n	)	shift	null T1	0
(n)	*	reduce (5)	null T1 null	5
n	*	shift	T1	0
n *	IDENT	shift	T1 null	7
n * IDENT		reduce (6)	T1 null Z	*none*
n * n		reduce (3)	T1 null Z	3
n			T2	

Figure 7.3 Parse of $(X+Y)*Z$ with Semantic Actions

In writing the semantic routines, we assume the existence of three
auxiliary procedures. *QUAD* (a,b,c,d) writes a quadruple with the four
parameters as its fields. It also increments by unity the global variable
quadno, which holds the number of the next quadruple to be generated.
POP (*stack, vbl*) copies the top element of *stack* to *vbl* and pops the stack.
PUSH (*stack, vbl*) pushes a copy of *vbl* onto *stack*.

We can now write the semantic routine to be associated with reduction
1 as

$i \leftarrow i+1$
POP (*semantics, opd2*)
POP (*semantics, opd1*)
POP (*semantics, opd1*)
PUSH (*semantics*, 'Ti')
QUAD ('+',*opd1,opd2*,'Ti')

in which the second call of *POP* is required to skip over the null semantic
entry which corresponds to the terminal + on the syntax stack. The incrementation of i, which is global to the semantic routine, ensures the
generation of distinct temporary variable names. A similar semantic
routine is provided for reduction 3 (multiplication).

Means are still required for ensuring that the correct identifier information is indeed on the semantics stack when the quadruples are generated.
Every time a symbol is shifted onto the syntax stack, the required item is
shifted (pushed) onto the semantics stack. For identifiers, the identifier

name is pushed; for all other symbols, a null item is pushed. The semantic action for reductions 2, 4, and 6 is merely to continue to associate the same identifier name with the topmost syntax stack element. For those reductions no semantic routines need be provided. Reduction 5, which replaces (n) by n, does not result in any change of identifier, but the null entries which correspond to the two parentheses must be discarded. The semantic routine therefore includes three pops and one push. Figure 7.3 is completed by a fifth column, which gives the number of the semantic routine to be called. Numbers between 1 and 6 correspond to the rules of the grammar in Fig. 7.2(a), routine 0 stacks a null entry, and routine 7 stacks the identifier name. Of the eight semantic routines, only routines 1 and 3 generate intermediate code.

There may be yet more stacks for different kinds of semantic information. The type of each variable or expression is an obvious candidate. Although the syntax and semantics stacks are conceptually distinct, they may be implemented as a single stack whose entries have multiple fields. If a two-stack implementation is retained, however, some simplification is possible in the semantic routines which have been described. If the semantics stack is pushed only for identifiers, there will never be any null entries on it. Then the semantic routines for reductions 1 and 3 will not need the second pop, and a semantic routine for reduction 5 will not be required at all.

In top-down parsing by recursive descent, no explicit syntax stack is created; the stack of activation records serves instead. Figure 7.4 presents three recursive descent routines for parsing (without semantic processing) the grammar of Fig. 7.2.

Semantic processing is most readily performed by incorporating into each routine the semantic action appropriate to the nonterminal which the routine recognizes. This requires that the semantic information associated with the nonterminal be produced by that routine. Several kinds of semantic information may be required, and it is convenient to provide a parameter for the transmission of each. We shall concern ourselves here only with the name of each variable. This permits us to recast each recognition routine as a procedure with a single parameter in which to place the name of the original or temporary variable associated with the nonterminal which has been recognized. Local variables are used within each routine to hold the names delivered by the recognition procedures which it calls. The procedure *SCANNER* is modified accordingly, and now has two parameters. To the first it delivers, as before, the actual token it has found. To the second parameter it delivers, but only if the token is an identifier, the name of the identifier. The three recognition routines have been recast

```
procedure EXPRESSION
    TERM
    while token = '+' do
        SCANNER (token)
        TERM

procedure TERM
    FACTOR
    while token = '*' do
        SCANNER (token)
        FACTOR

procedure FACTOR
    case token of
        IDENT:
        '(':    SCANNER (token)
                EXPRESSION
                if token ≠ ')' then ERROR
        other:  ERROR
    SCANNER (token)
```

Figure 7.4   Recognition Routines for Grammar of Fig. 7.2

in Fig. 7.5 as one-parameter procedures with semantic processing included. Their use would be invoked by a sequence such as

```
i ← 1
SCANNER(token, idname)
EXPRESSION (name)
```

in which the counter i ensures, as before, that different intermediate results have unique names, and *name* is a character variable which will eventually hold the name associated with the expression being parsed.

A brief examination of procedure *TERM* will help to explain how the semantic processing is accomplished. The call to *FACTOR* delivers the name of the factor to local variable *opd1*. That execution of *FACTOR* concluded with a lookahead call of *SCANNER*, which made the next terminal available for examination in the global variable *token*. If that terminal is not an asterisk, then no intermediate code is generated and the name of the factor is delivered as the name of the term. If, on the other hand, that terminal is an asterisk, then a call of *SCANNER* prepares another call of *FACTOR*, and the name of the next factor is placed in the local variable *opd2*. Intermediate code is now generated and the search for more factors continues. Each time, the first operand of the quadruple is given the name of the previously created temporary variable. The name of the last temporary variable is delivered as the name of the term.

```
procedure EXPRESSION (exprname)
    char exprname
    char opd1,opd2
    begin
        TERM (opd1)
        while token = '+' do
            SCANNER (token,idname)
            TERM (opd2)
            QUAD ('+',opd1,opd2,'Ti')
            opd1 ← 'Ti'
            i ← i+1
        exprname ← opd1
    end

procedure TERM (termname)
    char termname
    char opd1,opd2
    begin
        FACTOR (opd1)
        while token = '*' do
            SCANNER (token,idname)
            FACTOR (opd2)
            QUAD ('*',opd1,opd2,'Ti')
            opd1 ← 'Ti'
            i ← i+1
        termname ← opd1
    end

procedure FACTOR (factname)
    char factname
    begin
        case token of
            IDENT: factname ← idname
            '(':    SCANNER (token,idname)
                    EXPRESSION (factname)
                    if token ≠ ')' then ERROR
            other: ERROR
        SCANNER (token,idname)
    end
```

Figure 7.5   Recognition Routines with Semantic Processing

We now look beyond the realm of expression evaluation and ask what semantic processing is required by other programming language constructs. An assignment to an unsubscripted variable results in very simple generation. In reducing

$stmt$ = IDENT ":=" $expression$.

where the name of the identifier is in *opd1* and that of the expression is in *opd2*, it is sufficient to execute *QUAD* (':=',*opd2*,,*opd1*). Thus A := (X * Y)+Z might yield

*	X	Y	T1
+	T1	Z	T2
:=	T2		A

where it is hoped that subsequent optimization would replace the last two quadruples by a single one which delivers the sum to A directly. A more attractive action would be simply to insert the name of the identifier in place of the temporary variable in the destination field of the last quadruple generated for *expression*.

The declaration of an identifier usually does not result in the generation of intermediate code. It does cause semantic information to be stored by the compiler for later use. The identifier's type is entered in the symbol table. If the identifier is an array name, the number of dimensions is entered in the symbol table and the bounds for each dimension, if supplied, are saved for later use in performing address calculations.

A source-language declaration statement may incorporate the specification of an initial value, as with PL/I's INITIAL attribute. The compiler can treat the INITIAL specification as it would an assignment statement and generate the code to perform the assignment at execution time. If, however, the variable is of storage class STATIC or is declared in the outermost block, execution-time efficiency can be enhanced by generating the specified value during compilation. This may be accomplished either by flagging the symbol table entry and noting the value or by entering the value into the table of constants, along with a pointer to the symbol table entry. The pointer is used to place the generated constant in the storage associated with the identifier rather than in the literal pool.

Branches involving labels and GOTO statements can be processed in a manner which need not distinguish forward from backward references. With each label there is associated in the symbol table the number of the first quadruple in the intermediate code for the statement which follows that label. When the GOTO is recognized, a quadruple is generated which specifies not the target *quadruple* (whose number is not known if the branch is forward) but rather the target *label*. This jump to label quadruple might be generated by the call *QUAD* ('JLABEL',,,*labelname*), where *labelname* contains the name of the label. The quadruple number associated with the label is entered in the symbol table when the label definition is encountered during parsing. When all labels have been processed, it is an easy matter to substitute quadruple numbers or storage addresses and to generate code with jumps to numeric addresses.

The use of JLABEL as an intermediate step can be bypassed by handling forward and backward branches differently. For a backward branch the symbol table yields the quadruple number, and the call *QUAD* ('JUMP',,, *labelname.number*) suffices. For a forward branch, the quadruple JUMP ,,,0 is generated and the number of the quadruple is placed with the label in the symbol table. If that label already pointed to a quadruple, the quadruple numbers are chained. When the label definition is eventually encountered, the chain is followed and the jump destination fields are replaced by the number of the quadruple now known to correspond to the label. This chain-following action is similar to that of one-pass assemblers.

Conditional statements involve a bit more work. A convenient form in which to represent their syntax is the following.

1.	*ifstmt = ifclause stmt.*
2.	*ifstmt = truepart stmt.*
3.	*truepart = ifclause stmt* "ELSE".
4.	*ifclause =* "IF" *condition* "THEN".

The PL/I text

```
IF A<B THEN C = B+D*4;
        ELSE C = A+D*4;
```

should cause quadruples such as the following to be generated, where JFALSE is a jump on result false.

11.	<	A	B	T5
12.	JFALSE	T5		16
13.	*	D	4	T6
14.	+	B	T6	C
15.	JUMP			18
16.	*	D	4	T7
17.	+	A	T7	C

Parsing of *condition* results in the generation of quadruple 11. Reduction 4 is then applied, and it must generate a quadruple with a jump forward to an undetermined destination quadruple. The semantic routine for reduction 4 generates a JFALSE quadruple with no destination address, and saves the address of the generated quadruple as semantic information associated with the nonterminal *ifclause*.

Quadruples 13 and 14 are then generated during the recognition of C = B+D * 4; as *stmt*, and reduction 3 is applied next because of the presence of ELSE. The associated semantic routine must insert the address 16 in the destination field of quadruple 12, whose number was earlier placed in association with *ifclause*. Before doing so, it must generate the unconditional jump forward as quadruple 15, albeit without a destination, and thereby advance *quadno*.

Quadruples 16 and 17 are subsequently generated during the recognition of C = A+D*4; as *stmt*, and reduction 2 is applied next. The only semantic action required at this time is to enter the destination address in quadruple 15. Processing of the conditional statement is then complete. If, instead of the source text presented, the ELSE clause were missing, reduction 1 would be made instead of reductions 3 and 2, and similar semantic action performed.

The four semantic routines are shown in Fig. 7.6. The stack *semantics* is to be understood here as only that portion of the semantic information pertaining to destination quadruple numbers. The quadruples are stored in the two-dimensional array *quadruple*, whose first index is the quadruple number and whose second index selects one of the four fields. Patching the destination field of a previously generated quadruple is not convenient if that quadruple has been written to an external file. In that event, the semantic routine makes a record of the modification, which is applied after the quadruple is next read in. In routine (d), the operand Ti is the tempo-

> *POP (semantics, origin)*
> *quadruple [origin,4]* ← *quadno*
>
> (a) *ifstmt* = *ifclause stmt.*
>
> *POP (semantics, origin)*
> quadruple [*origin, 4*] ← *quadno*
>
> (b) *ifstmt* = *truepart stmt.*
>
> *POP (semantics, origin)*
> *PUSH (semantics, quadno)*
> *QUAD ('JUMP',,,)*
> *quadruple [origin, 4]* ← *quadno*
>
> (c) *truepart* = *ifclause stmt* "ELSE".
>
> *PUSH (semantics, quadno)*
> *QUAD ('JFALSE','Ti',,)*
>
> (d) *ifclause* = "IF" *condition* "THEN".

Figure 7.6   Semantic Routines for Conditional Statements

rary variable which holds the result of evaluating *condition*. This is satisfactory for the Pascal subset defined in Fig. 6.7, but is not correct if *condition* can be a simple boolean variable rather than a relational expression. The necessary modification is requested in an exercise.

The syntax which we have been using here for conditional statements is ambiguous, as is that of Fig. 6.7. Two distinct parse subtrees for the same language construct are shown in Fig. 7.7, in which the four rules already introduced are complemented by the rule *stmt = ifstmt*. The example is an instance of the well-known problem of matching each "ELSE" with the correct "THEN" in Pascal, PL/I, and similar languages. The correct interpretation of the syntactically ambiguous conditional statement is the one shown in the upper portion of Fig. 7.7. Each "ELSE" is to match the nearest preceding unmatched "THEN".

How can we ensure that the correct semantic interpretation is made? One approach is to rewrite the grammar to remove the ambiguity and admit only the desired interpretation. This is difficult to do in general, and usually results in the introduction of many more rules and nonterminals.

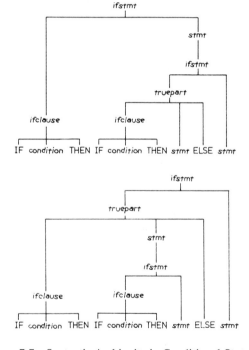

Figure 7.7 Syntactic Ambiguity in Conditional Statement

An alternative is to write the parser to accept only the desired semantic interpretation. Consider the problem of applying a shift/reduce parser to conditional statements in which an "ELSE" clause is optional. Suppose that the incoming terminal is "ELSE", the topmost stack terminal is **"THEN"**, and there is another "THEN" lower on the stack. The conventional grammar does not specify which of the two occurrences of "THEN" is to be matched. No matter. The correct semantic interpretation for most languages results from the simple solution of always shifting "ELSE" onto the stack. The key approach is not to worry excessively about the grammar, but rather to design the parser to do what is wanted. Consider next a recursive descent parser for the same language. The procedure which recognizes *ifstmt* begins by finding "IF" *condition* "THEN" *statement*. Instead of returning from this point, it proceeds to check whether the next terminal is **"ELSE"**. If so, the "ELSE" clause is also recognized as part of *ifstmt*. Thus each "ELSE" will be matched with the proper "THEN".

As a final example, consider the semantic processing associated with an iterative control structure. The statement WHILE $A+B<C$ DO $A :=$ $A * A+B$ should yield the following quadruples.

24.	$+$	A	B	T12
25.	$<$	T12	C	T13
26.	JFALSE	T13		30
27.	$*$	A	A	T14
28.	$+$	T14	B	A
29.	JUMP			24

A convenient form of syntax is

> *whilestmt* $=$ *whilepart stmt*.
> *whilepart* $=$ "WHILE" *condition* "DO".

For the example text, quadruples 24 and 25 are generated for *condition* after the number 24 has been retained during the recognition of *whilepart*. Further semantic actions in recognizing the latter include the generation of quadruple 26 (with the forward destination reference missing) and retention of its quadruple number, too. During recognition of *whilestmt*, quadruples 27 and 28 are generated for *stmt* and quadruple 29 is generated to close the loop. Finally, the forward reference is inserted in quadruple 26. The two processing routines are shown in Fig. 7.8. We assume that *STMT* leaves the stack *semantics* as it found it. Iterative structures using **repeat-until** are handled similarly.

```
procedure WHILEPART
    begin
        if token ≠ 'WHILE' then ERROR
        PUSH (semantics,quadno)                     {start of condition}
        SCANNER (token)
        CONDITION                                   {generating more quadruples}
        if token ≠ 'DO' then ERROR
        PUSH (semantics,quadno)                     {forward jump location}
        SCANNER (token)
        QUAD ('JFALSE', 'Ti',,)
    end

procedure WHILESTMT
    integer origin,dest
    begin
        WHILEPART
        STMT                                        {generating more quads}
        POP (semantics,origin)
        POP (semantics,dest)
        QUAD ('JUMP',,,dest)                        {incrementing quadno}
        quadruple [origin,4] ← quadno
    end
```

Figure 7.8   Parsing and Semantic Routines for **while-do**

The indexed loop contains more components than do the simpler iterative structures. The Pascal statement model

"FOR" *ident* ":=" *expr1* "DOWNTO" *expr2* "DO" *stmt*

should lead to the following sorts of quadruples.

$$
\left.
\begin{array}{l}
q+1. \\
\\
r-1.
\end{array}
\right\} \quad \text{quad(s) for } ident \text{ ":=" } expr1
$$

$$
\left.
\begin{array}{l}
r. \\
\\
s-3.
\end{array}
\right\} \quad \text{quad(s) for } expr2
$$

$s-2.$	**JUMP**			s
$s-1.$	$-$	*ident*	@1	*ident*
$s.$	$<$	*ident*	*expr2*	Ti
$s+1.$	**JTRUE**	Ti		$t+1$

$$
\left.
\begin{array}{l}
s+2. \\
\\
t-1.
\end{array}
\right\} \quad \text{quad(s) for } stmt
$$

$t.$	**JUMP**		$s-1$

If the statement syntax is defined by

> *forstmt* = "FOR" *ident* ":=" *forlist* "DO" *stmt*.
> *forlist* = *expression* "DOWNTO" *expression*.

it is virtually impossible to associate semantic actions with each reduction. A suitable definition is given instead by

> *forstmt* = *idxpart* "DO" *stmt*.
> *idxpart* = *forpart* "DOWNTO" *expression*.
> *forpart* = "FOR" *ident* ":=" *expression*.

Semantic actions associated with the second reduction increment i and generate quadruples $s-2$ through $s+1$, and semantic actions associated with the first reduction generate quadruple t. The adjustment of the jump destination addresses is straightforward.

This last example illustrates the importance to semantic processing of having the syntactic analysis performed in a suitable manner. In rewriting a grammar to facilitate semantic processing, care must be taken, however, not to change the language defined by the grammar.

The present section is illustrative rather than exhaustive. Several important programming language constructs have not been considered. A major omission is that of arrays and subscripts, which cause the generation of arithmetic instructions which perform addressing calculations, even in the absence of knowledge at compilation time of the size of an array. Expression lists, which appear not only in subscripting, but also in declarations (as lists of variables) and in input/output statements, have been omitted. The many problems raised by block structure have been ignored. An interesting example is a GOTO naming a label which may be a forward reference (not yet defined) within the same block, a backward reference into an enclosing block, or even a forward reference into an enclosing block.

Not only have these and other features been excluded from our consideration, but so has a major function of compilers, that of error checking. Two forms of checking, in particular, are typically associated with the semantic routines. One is the detection of multiply-defined labels; the other is verification that variables and expressions are of the appropriate type. This verification includes checking arguments of expressions for type compatibility, like ensuring that expressions which control conditional branching are boolean, and verifying that branch destinations are indeed labels.

7.3.2 *Storage Allocation*

Before target code can be generated, the addresses of variables and constants to be accessed at execution time must be determinable (except, of course, for any relocation factor). It is also required that the code generator have a means of producing code which will either incorporate or calculate the necessary addresses. If allocation and access are provided for variables, then constants surely pose no problem. The discussion in this section is therefore presented in terms of variables. Just as a variable has scope, or extent in space, so does it have *life*, or extent in time. Some variables exist only while the block in which they are declared is active. These are called *dynamic variables* and space allocated to them is called *dynamic storage*. Others have life which extends beyond that of the blocks to which they are local. Those are called *static variables* and the space allocated to them is called *static storage*. Use of the terms "static" and "dynamic" in this context must be distinguished from their use to describe the nesting of program blocks in the compilation-time text or of activation records in the execution-time stack.

In addition to the distinction between static and dynamic storage, another distinction is important to the compiler. The attributes of a variable may or may not be known at compilation time. To the extent that allocation of storage is dependent upon unknown attributes (e.g. the size of an array or the type of a variable), the task of the storage allocation step is rendered more difficult. Before considering either dynamic storage or the execution-time specification of attributes, we consider static storage for variables whose attributes are known at compilation time.

Static variables with known attributes. All storage in Fortran, **own** variables in Algol (except arrays whose bounds are formal parameters), and STATIC storage in PL/I can be allocated by the compiler on the basis of complete information. The compiler can scan the symbol table, allocating to each elementary variable the amount of space it requires, and incrementing a counter appropriately. The amount allocated depends both on the architecture of the target machine and on the desired trade-off between space and time requirements of the target code. A boolean variable may be allocated either an entire word (or byte on a byte-addressed machine), or a single bit in a word which it shares with other boolean variables. The former uses more space, but the latter requires extra time for packing and unpacking. A character-string variable will be allocated the number of words or bytes appropriate to its length, with some waste perhaps if a nonintegral number of words is required. If the string is of variable length, two approaches are possible. One is to allocate and free space dynamically as the string expands and shrinks; the other is to allocate the maximum amount at all times. In either event, extra space is required to store at least the current length and perhaps the maximum length, although the latter quantity may be embedded instead in the generated target code. A variable declared as **integer** or FIXED is usually allocated a single word. If a radix point is implied, the generated code must provide for scaling. So-called "variable field length" data, especially decimal numbers (as in the IBM 360-370), are often used. Despite the name, the length of each item is typically fixed, and enough bytes or words are allocated. A variable declared as **real** or FLOAT is allocated a word or double word, as appropriate to the stated precision, for a target machine with floating-point instructions. If the floating-point operations are to be performed by subroutines, a more convenient allocation is usually a pair of words, one for the fraction and one for the exponent.

Some machines, particularly those with byte addressing, impose *alignment* restrictions on the addresses at which a datum may be stored. In the IBM 360, for example, the addresses of double words must be multiples of 8; those of full words, multiples of 4; and those of half words, multiples of 2. If the next address to be allocated is not an appropriate multiple, one or more bytes must be skipped until a suitable address is reached. The attendant storage waste can be eliminated by first allocating all double words, then all full words, etc. This requires multiple scans over the symbol table.

Elementary variables with the same attributes can be collected by the programmer into an array and accessed by the use of a common name qualified by subscripts. A one-dimensional array, or vector, of variables is allocated consecutive units of storage in the amount appropriate to each element. The total required is easily computed as the product of that amount by the number of elements. To access an array element it is necessary to know where the array begins, how long each element is, and which element is desired. The starting or base address B is available from the symbol table, as are the element length N and the lower and upper subscript bounds L and U. The starting address of the ith element is therefore $B + N * (i - L)$. If i is known at compilation time, as in PRESSURE[3], then the address can be calculated in full by the compiler. If i will be the result of evaluating an expression at execution time, as in PRESSURE[J+1], then the compiler can calculate the constant part $B - N * L$ and generate execution-time code to evaluate the subscript expression, multiply it by N, and add it to the constant part, yielding the address of the desired operand.

An arbitrary one-dimensional array is mapped naturally onto main storage, which is itself essentially a vector (with the address as subscript).

A two-dimensional array, or matrix, is not vectorial, and means are required for mapping it onto the vectorial structure of storage. A one-stage mapping is effected by storing the elements consecutively in a prescribed order. The two obvious orders are one row at a time and one column at a time. Let an array of M rows and N columns be declared as $A[1..M, 1..N]$. The sequence in *row-major* order (one row at a time), in which the first index changes least frequently, is

$$A[1,1], A[1,2], \ldots, A[1,N], A[2,1], A[2,2], \ldots, A[2,N], \ldots, A[M,1], A[M,2], \ldots, A[M,N],$$

whereas in *column-major* order it is

$$A[1,1], A[2,1], \ldots, A[M,1], A[1,2], A[2,2], \ldots, A[M,2], \ldots, A[1,N], A[2,N], \ldots, A[M,N].$$

Although standard Fortran uses column-major order, row-major order is more common and will be assumed henceforth.

Let an array of one-word items be declared as $X[L1..U1, L2..U2]$, where the number of rows is $R = U1-(L1-1)$ and the number of columns is $C = U2-(L2-1)$. Then if the starting address is B, the address of $X[i,k]$ is $(i-L1)*C + (k-L2) + B$. The constant part $B-(L2+C*L1)$ is calculated once, at compilation time, and can be stored with the entry for X in the symbol table. The remaining part $(i*C)+k$ will in general be calculated at execution time from the index expression values i and k at the cost of one multiplication and one addition; a second addition is needed to add the constant part of the address.

An alternative to linearizing a two-dimensional array is to store each row separately as a vector. An extra vector of pointers $P[L1..U1]$ holds the starting address for each row. Determination of the address of $X[i,k]$ requires first an access to $P[i]$, the value of which is added to $k-L2$ before the desired matrix element can then be accessed. In this two-stage mapping, an extra storage access replaces the multiplication required for a linearized matrix. This multiplication may be costly on some machines. Another advantage is that not all rows need be in main storage simultaneously. This can be of considerable benefit in solving large linear systems by elimination methods, which typically require only two rows at a time during much of the processing. If the entire array is in main storage, then this allocation method requires extra storage space for the vector of pointers.

Either the linearization or the successive access method is easily generalized to multidimensional arrays. Such arrays are most likely to be used on large machines with fast multiplication, and linearization is probably more common. The execution-time address calculation in two dimensions can be viewed as the evaluation of a first-degree mixed-radix polynomial in

R and C. For n dimensions it generalizes to a polynomial of degree $n-1$ in the mixed radices r_i, which are the lengths of the array in each dimension. The calculation requires $n-1$ multiplications and n additions.

An important function in accessing array elements is to ensure that the values of the subscript expressions lie within the bounds of the array. If they do not, access is attempted to some other area in storage. The result may be the reading of invalid data, the writing of incorrect results, modification of the running program, destruction of another user's program or data, or an attempt to address an area protected against the current program. Whether the consequences are the insidious calculation of nearly correct results or abrupt termination of execution, they are undesirable. Production of intermediate code to check index expressions against the array bounds may or may not be provided. Because bounds checking requires considerable time and space, it is often omitted in compiling programs believed to be correct. In a compiler for debugging, however, it is extremely valuable. In some compilers it is available optionally.

For tree-structured aggregates of elementary variables, storage needs to be allocated only for the elementary variables, which are the leaves of the tree. This is most readily done in leaf order, and is straightforward even if arrays appear either at the leaf level or at higher levels of the tree. The chief complexity introduced by tree-structured variables is due to the use of identifiers to correspond to other nodes than leaves, and to the use of a given identifier for more than one non-root node. These are problems of symbol table design which do not affect the allocation process.

Dynamic variables with known attributes. We turn now to allocation of storage which is dynamic, but still for variables all of whose attributes are known at compilation time. The easiest such dynamic allocation is for those variables which are created upon activation of the block to which they are local and deleted upon exit from the block. Storage for these variables is allocated in the activation record of that block. Even if activation records are stored consecutively, absolute storage addresses cannot be assigned by the compiler because the sequence of activation records on the execution-time stack is not predictable at compilation time. Instead, the compiler assigns to each variable a two-part address (l, d) composed of the block nesting level l and a displacement d within the block. A variable local to the current block is stored in that block's activation record, and can be accessed by use of d alone, provided that the starting location of the current activation record is made available to the program. This can be done by loading the program and activation record together, relocating addresses in the former to correspond to the location of the latter. A disadvantage is the necessity to perform relocation every time a block is invoked. An alternative method is particularly suited to machines with base-register addressing. Each time an activation record is allocated, its starting address is provided as a base for use by the program.

Access to nonlocal identifiers requires indirection. Although there may exist several blocks at a given nesting level l in the static text, at most one of them is in the environment of the current block at any given moment during execution time. Let the current block, at level c, include a reference to a variable at location (e, d) in the enclosing block at level e. Assume a numbering convention which assigns nesting level 1 to the outermost block, and successively higher integers for successively deeper nesting. If the nesting structure is represented at execution time by a static chain, then $c - e$ links in that chain must be followed to determine the starting address of the enclosing block. Because the number $c - e$ is known at compilation time, the compiler can generate code for the current block to access the variable. If the nesting structure is represented at execution time by a display, then the eth element of the display is the desired starting address, and a single stage of indirect addressing, easily generated at compilation time, provides the desired access.

Whether a static chain or a display is used, it must be adjusted on block entry and exit. For the static chain, block entry requires the setting of one static link. That link points either to the previously current block or to another block in the static chain emanating from the previously current block. In either event, code can be generated for the previously current block to supply the required address. Block exit requires no action. Maintenance of a display is more demanding. On block entry, the starting address of the new current block is appended to the end of the display, after deletion of the addresses, if any, of blocks not in the environment of the current block. The reverse process, which is performed on block exit, may require that addresses of blocks which are inaccessible prior to exit be appended after deletion of the current block's address. This can be facilitated by providing a stack of displays, which are address vectors of different lengths. An alternative, and rather convenient arrangement, is to store each display in the activation record which uses it.

Maintenance of a display requires more time or space, or both, than does maintenance of a static chain. Use of a display requires less time and space than does use of a static chain. The choice depends on the complexity required to compile the maintenance and access processes and on the expected relative frequencies of access to nonlocal identifiers and of block entry and exit. A compromise made in at least one Pascal compiler is the use of a static chain together with a pointer to global storage, which usually contains the most frequently accessed nonlocal identifiers. That pointer can be viewed, of course, as a partial display.

Storage for some variables is allocated dynamically not on block entry but under programmer control. This is true of both CONTROLLED and BASED storage in PL/I. Even if the attributes are known, the total storage requirement is not, because the number of allocations of each variable cannot be determined at compilation time. The customary solution is to allocate and free space on top of the activation-record stack as requests are encountered at execution time. Because of the lack of constraints on the order in which allocations are freed, it is not possible to manage that portion of storage purely as a stack.

The allocation method just described is sometimes called *block-level* allocation, because a separate activation record is provided for each block. The convenience of assigning a distinct base register to each block, or at least to each accessible block, is available only if the number of such activation records is not too large. One way to reduce the number of activation records is to provide them only for procedure blocks. Storage associated with the various non-procedure blocks nested within a procedure is allocated within the activation record for the procedure. In the resulting *procedure-level* allocation, the burden of maintaining displays is reduced, as is the number of base registers required. Extra space for blocks at the same level of nesting is not required under this method any more than it is under block-level allocation. A certain amount of bookkeeping is necessary, however, to keep track of the allocations.

Dynamic variables with unknown attributes. Identifier attributes which are not known at compilation time can be handled by compiling a *template* or *descriptor* to be filled in later. One example is the address of a nonlocal identifier. It is by no means necessary to recompute the address for accesses subsequent to the first if a location is reserved in the using activation record to hold the address once computed. Although the time saving is small compared to use of a display, it can be substantial relative to use of a long static chain. The attribute whose lack most seriously affects storage allocation is the specification of array bounds. If the declaration of array size can be postponed until execution time, the array is said to be *dynamic*. What is already known at compilation time is the number of dimensions, hence the nature of the calculation which will be required to access an array element. What is not yet known is the value of each constant which enters the calculation. If the declaration X[L1..U1, L2..U2], which we considered earlier, is processed in the absence of values for the four bounds, then the required constants C and $B - (L2 + C * L1)$, where B is the starting address of the array, and C is the number of columns, $U2 - (L2 - 1)$, cannot be compiled. Moreover, storage for the array cannot be allocated because its size is unknown.

What can be allocated, however, is a descriptor for the array, called a *dope vector*. The dope vector will ultimately hold B and the four bounds, and perhaps also the length of an individual element. Because the length of the dope vector depends on the number of dimensions of the array it describes, the dope vector's own length must be either specified in the dope vector itself or compiled into the address-generating code. The dope vector is filled in when the array bounds are specified at execution time, whether on block entry or even later. The current stack top is used as the address B, and the stack top is redefined to an address beyond B just far enough to allow for an array of the specified size. Thus the size of the activation record depends on the bounds of its dynamic arrays. Another interpretation is that dynamic arrays are stacked above the activation record, rather than within it. Whatever the interpretation, fixed-size items, including all the dope vectors, must precede any variable-size items. Once B and the bounds are known, code generated at compilation time computes at execution time the constants required to determine addresses of subscripted identifiers. These constants are then stored in activation record locations referenced by the code, also generated at compilation time, which performs the address calculations. A convenient place to store these constants is in the dope vector itself, and they may well be placed there instead of the bounds and the starting address. If subscript checking is to be performed, however, the bounds should be kept too. Reference to a dynamic array in an enclosing block is made through its dope vector, which is at a known displacement (i.e. fixed at compilation time) within the activation record for its block.

A typical layout for an activation record is shown in Fig. 7.9. While the block is current, some of the items shown may be held in registers for faster operation. This is particularly true of the instruction counter, environment indicator, and parameters or their addresses.

One item shown has not yet been discussed. Storage must be allocated for the temporary variables ("temporaries") generated into the intermediate code. Their names may be preserved either in the symbol table or in a separate table. In allocating storage for temporaries, it is usually desirable to re-use space once a temporary is no longer needed. To the extent that the use of temporaries is either nested or disjoint, as it is in expression evaluation, locations can be assigned in a execution-time stack. Overlapping

Organizational Information
    instruction counter
    back pointer to previous activation record (dynamic link)
    environment indicator [one of the following]
        back pointer to enclosing activation record (static link)
        pointer to start of current display
        entire current display
    save area [if block issues calls]

Nonlocal Addresses
    pointers to actual parameters [if block is called]
    pointers to values of nonlocal identifiers [optional]

Local Storage Allocated at Compilation Time
    values of local identifiers
    values of temporary variables (work area)
    values of arrays with fixed bounds
    dope vectors for arrays with dynamic bounds

Local Storage Allocated at Execution Time
    arrays with dynamic bounds
    BASED and CONTROLLED variables

Figure 7.9 Typical Content of Activation Record

use of temporaries can occur, however, perhaps as the result of optimization to remove the redundant computation of common subexpressions. In general, it is necessary then to determine at compilation time the *range* of quadruple numbers over which each temporary must be saved. This range may exceed the span from the numerically first to the numerically last quadruple which references the temporary. For example, the entire body of a loop may lie in the range of a temporary which is used in the test at the start of the loop code. Several methods exist for determining the range of temporaries and for assigning the minimum required number of locations.

7.3.3 *Target Code Generation*

The choice of target language generated by a compiler has already been discussed in Section 7.1.4. The present section is restricted almost entirely to the generation of object (or machine) code, but first we review alternatives to generating object code alone. In interpretive execution, a generalized execution-time *service* routine can be provided for each programming-language construct, perhaps for each different operation in the intermediate code. These service routines are used as the interpretive subroutines in executing statements in a relatively high-level target language. The interpretive loop prepares the parameters for the service routines and exercises over-all control. The task of code generation is thus greatly simplified at the cost of reduced speed of execution of the program. This is accomplished by deferring part of the translation until more attributes are bound. For some source-language instructions, this deferral is so appealing that service routines are usually used for them even if the bulk of the program is translated into object code. This is particularly true for input and output statements. The space saving of providing a fixed set of specialized routines called at execution time, instead of generating code for each source-program I/O statement, often outweighs the costs of subroutine linkage.

The advantages of interpretive execution can be captured in part by the use of what is termed *threaded code*. Instead of relying on an interpretive loop to execute the service routines, the compiler generates a list of the addresses of those routines in the sequence in which they are to be called. Each service routine terminates by loading the next address from the list and branching to it. Actual parameters can be inserted in the list after the address of the service routine which uses them. Execution is faster than for pure interpretation, because subroutine linkage is eliminated. The space requirement is typically smaller than for pure generation, because one instance of a routine plus n instances of its address occupy less space than do n instances of the body of the routine.

The generation of object code can be thought of as the expansion of macros defined by the compiler writer and called by the intermediate code. The implementation of code generation in some compilers actually hews rather closely to that model. Code generation is thus conceptually simple, but it can be extremely complicated in practice because of its great dependence on the architecture of the target machine.

The number of central registers may be 0, 1, or many and, if there are many, the function of a given register may be specialized (accumulator, base, index, etc.) or general. If there is only one accumulator, noncommutative arithmetic operations such as subtraction and division must be handled differently from commutative operations. It may even be necessary to remove an operand already being held in the accumulator. Whether there are many registers or only one, it is necessary to keep track at compilation time of what quantities will be in each register at execution time. This information is required in ensuring proper utilization of intermediate results and helpful in such optimizations as elimination of redundant stores and loads. If the target machine uses a stack rather than addressable registers, the code to be generated is quite different.

The instruction set of the target machine may offer choices of code generation patterns, and it may impose constraints which must be circumvented. Instructions to copy data from one storage location to another are standard in machines without an accumulator but they may be provided in others as well. The assignment quadruple $:=,T2,,A$ would then normally cause generation of a storage-to-storage copy instruction. If, however, T2 will be in the accumulator at that point during execution, a store instruction should be generated instead. If the machine has no divide instruction, then a division specified by the intermediate code must cause generation of either in-line code to compute the quotient by other means or a call to a service routine. A similar remark holds for a machine with no multiply instruction.

Relational operators in the intermediate code also raise problems. Many machines do not provide instructions for each of the six common relational operators. If the intermediate code specifies one which is not available, the operator must be synthesized from those which are (e.g. $A=B$ as $A \leq B$ **and** $B \leq A$). On some machines, arithmetic instructions must be used to perform comparisons. If the operands are character strings, serious complications arise if the source-language collating sequence does not match the target-machine encoding sequence. If the operands are arithmetic, different complications may ensue. In evaluating $A < B$ by performing $A - B$ followed by a test for negative result, underflow and even overflow are possible.

The boolean operators available in the source language may not all have counterparts in machine language. In some machines, none is provided and arithmetic instructions must be used. Single-bit logical **and** can be replaced by multiplication, **or** by an addition followed by loading unity if the result is nonzero, and **not** either by subtraction from unity or, if the operand is already in an accumulator, by first subtracting unity from it and then taking the absolute value (if *that* operation is provided). If boolean instructions are available in the machine, the set provided may not be the same as that available in the source language and used in the intermediate code. Although those provided in the machine will normally be capable of generating all 16 boolean functions of two or fewer arguments, the amount of code required may be substantial. The reader is invited to express **xor** (exclusive or) in terms of **and** and **not** alone. It is simpler to encode **xor** arithmetically (absolute value of difference).

If the machine instruction set is rich, the generation of efficient code can capitalize on the added instructions. Immediate addressing can save the storage required to hold the addresses of constants. Negation can be performed with a load negative instruction. The load address (LA) instruction of the IBM 360-370 provides the most efficient addition of a positive integer less than 4096 (provided that both addend and sum are positive integers less than 2^{24}). And so on.

Some of the functions performed in code generation are required, whatever the architecture of the target machine. Typical of this class are type conversion and constant generation. Conversion of operand types will usually be performed by calling conversion routines at execution time. Because storage will need to be allocated for the results of conversion, it is usually more convenient to specify type conversion during production of intermediate code than during generation of target code. The generation of constants by a compiler is no different from their generation by an assembler, except that the translator rather than the programmer must ensure that the pool of constants will be addressable.

The code generation routines are concerned with how operands of machine instructions will be addressed. The computation of addresses of operands in storage is intimately associated with the organization of execution-time storage, and has been discussed in Section 7.3.2. The form which the required addresses take, and the instructions needed to perform indirect addressing, depend on the target machine. Addressing of operands in registers is dependent on the register assignments, which are performed by the code generation routines, and on the target-machine instruction formats.

The generation routines must be appropriate to the form of intermediate code which serves as their input. If postfix notation is used, code generation is similar to the one-pass single-stack evaluation method described at the beginning of Section 7.2.1. A slight modification of that method results not in evaluating an expression, but in generating code to perform the evaluation. Instead of stacking values of operands, the compiler stacks their tokens. On encountering an operator of degree i, it generates code which embodies the topmost i operand tokens. New tokens, created to represent temporary results, are stacked as required. Nonarithmetic operators, such as assignments and jumps, are handled straightforwardly. Figure 7.10 shows instructions, in the assembler language of Section 2.2, which could be generated in this fashion.

The source text is the PL/I conditional statement

```
IF A<B THEN C = B+D*4;
       ELSE C = A+D*4;
```

for which the intermediate postfix code is given in Section 7.2.1. Each line of the figure shows the postfix token being examined, the code (if any) generated as a result of encountering the token, and the stack of tokens (with top to the right) as it stands after the encounter. Note that a line of output code, such as that produced after examination of tokens 51 and 55, is not necessarily generated all at once. An auxiliary table, not shown, saves forward references and causes labels such as LABEL51 to be gen-

	token	code		stack
37.	A			A
38.	B			A B
39.	–	LOAD	A	
		SUB	B	
		STORE	T1	T1
40.	51			T1 51
41.	JPZ	LOAD	T1	
		BRPOS	LABEL51	
		BRZERO	LABEL51	
42.	C			C
43.	B			C B
44.	D			C B D
45.	4			C B D 4
46.	*	LOAD	@4	
		MULT	D	
		STORE	T2	C B T2
47.	+	LOAD	T2	
		ADD	B	
		STORE	T3	C T3
48.	←	LOAD	T3	
		STORE	C	
49.	58			58
50.	JUMP	BR	LABEL58	
51.	C	LABEL51		C
52.	A			C A
53.	D			C A D
54.	4			C A D 4
55.	*	LOAD	@4	
		MULT	D	
		STORE	T4	C A T4
56.	+	LOAD	T4	
		ADD	A	
		STORE	T5	C T5
57.	←	LOAD	T5	
		STORE	C	

Figure 7.10 Code Generation from Postfix

erated. Further improvement of the generated code is clearly possible, for there are several redundant STORE/LOAD pairs. Section 7.4.1 discusses code improvement, and the example in the next paragraph illustrates one way to avoid redundancy in the original generation.

A typical routine for generating from a quadruple the code to perform an addition is shown in Fig. 7.11. A field in the symbol table or list of temporaries stores with each variable a flag *inacc* which has value **true** if that variable will be in the target machine's single accumulator prior to execution of the next instruction to be generated, and **false** otherwise. The accumulator can hold simultaneously the values of two or more variables, if those values are equal, as they are after executing an assignment such as I ← N. A list of the names of all variables whose value will be in the accumulator prior to execution of the next instruction to be generated is held in the global list *accvalue*. The generation routine tests the flags of the addition operands to determine whether either will already be in the accumulator, thus obviating a LOAD instruction. Following code generation, the name of the result is entered on *accvalue* and its flag is set to **true** to indicate that it will be available in the accumulator for the next generation. The names of all other variables are removed from *accvalue* and their flags are set to **false**. Although the flags are designated in the program by qualified names, an actual implementation would probably use a procedure, with the variable's name as parameter, to test or set the flag. Another simplification made in the example is the choice of assembler language as the code to be generated. Actually, machine representations of operation codes and of operand addresses would usually be generated instead.

The generation of code from triples is a bit different, because an intermediate result is referred to not by name, but by the number of the triple which produced it. Descriptions of temporary values do not need to be maintained throughout the compilation, as they are for quadruples, and this is a major reason for the use of triples in intermediate code. Details of code generation from triples will not be discussed here.

If the intermediate code is in such a form that target code can be generated from it in a single pass, then target code generation can be performed directly by the semantic routines, with no need for intermediate code. This increases the bulk and complexity of the semantic routines, but permits one-pass compilation.

By and large, code generation is characterized by the maintenance of much status information, many tests of status, and the consideration of many different cases. It is highly machine dependent and quite complex.

```
procedure ADD(a,b,c)
    char a,b,c
    begin
            if a.inacc then generate 'ADD      ',b
        else if b.inacc then generate 'ADD      ',a
        else            generate 'LOAD     ',a
                        generate 'ADD      ',b
        generate 'STORE ',c
        delete all names from accvalue,
            setting the inacc flag of each to false
        insert c on accvalue
        c.inacc ← true
    end
```

Figure 7.11 Code Generation Routine for Quadruple $(+,a,b,c)$

7.4 EXTENSIONS

The foregoing descriptions of implementation structures and processes have assumed a requirement to perform translation of error-free input and to perform it as simply as possible. The assumption that the source-language program is free of error can never be entirely justified, even if an earlier compilation has failed to detect any errors. Even resubmission of the same program text to the same compiler can be marred by a data transmission error. The requirement to keep translation simple may yield to a requirement to produce efficient target code. The resulting concerns for code optimization and for error handling may be felt at several steps in compilation rather than being associated with a particular step. An examination of those concerns will be followed by a brief indication of how the computer itself can be used as a tool in compiler writing.

7.4.1 *Code Optimization*

The term *code optimization* is a widely used misnomer. There is no agreed standard for defining optimality nor does it appear likely that there is any guarantee of achieving what might be agreed upon as optimal. What is possible, however, is to make *improvements* to the code generated by the implementation processes discussed in Section 7.3. These improvements, which may move, remove, or replace code, usually both speed up execution of the compiled program and reduce its size. Code optimization, as we shall continue to call it because the term has become entrenched, may be applied to both the machine-independent and the machine-dependent aspects of the program.

We first examine machine-independent optimization. In generating code for the PL/I statement pair

```
IF A<B THEN C = B+D*4;
        ELSE C = A+D*4;
```

we saw that the computation of $D * 4$ could be performed once rather than twice, as it can for the pair

```
R = B+D*4;
S = A+D*4;
```

Yet this saving is precluded if the second statement is labeled, as in

```
    R = B+D*4;
L:  S = A+D*4;
```

Why must the common subexpression now be computed twice? Because the flow of control may enter the second statement without having passed through the first, with no guarantee that D holds the same value as it does when control flows through both statements. This observation leads to the concept of a *basic block* of a program. A basic block is a portion of a program with a single entry, a single exit, and no internal branching. The flow of control of a program can be depicted as a directed graph whose nodes are the basic blocks and whose arcs indicate the possible sequences of execution. The basic blocks are not to be confused with the "blocks" which describe the static nesting in a block-structured language.

The classical approach to machine-independent optimization is to divide the program into its basic blocks, perform *local* optimization upon each block, and then perform *global* optimization upon the program as a whole. In performing local optimization, no information is used from outside the block. In practice, perhaps as much as three-fourths of the speed improvement is due to local optimization. Global optimization uses a description of the interblock flow of control to determine in which blocks values are assigned to or read from identifiers and expressions, thereby permitting the elimination of redundant references. Although more and more attention is being directed to optimization of source code, machine-independent optimization is still generally performed on the intermediate code. A major reason for this is that address calculation arithmetic which is implicit in the source code is made explicit in the intermediate code, hence directly accessible to optimization. A partial enumeration of types of machine-independent optimizations is presented next; descriptions of their implementations are omitted.

(1) Code Motion. One example is moving an invariant computation out of a loop. If the assignment X ← Y * Z appears within the body of a loop which does not change the values of Y and Z, then it can be replaced by TEMP ← Y * Z in the initialization and X ← TEMP within the body. This saves time during each iteration. Another example is *hoisting*, which saves space. In

IF *cond* THEN X[I,J] := *expr1* ELSE X[I,J] := *expr2*

the addressing calculation for X[I,J], which would be generated in two locations, can be moved to a position immediately before the test (provided, of course, that evaluation of *cond* leaves I and J unchanged).

(2) Strength Reduction. An arithmetic operation can often be replaced by one of lower "strength". Thus, if N is a small integer, it may be faster to

evaluate X∗∗N by repeated multiplication than to call a service routine for exponentiation. An extreme case is the total elimination of an addition or subtraction of zero or of a multiplication or division by unity. An important benefit of strength reduction is that it often permits further optimizations to be made.

(3) Loop Unrolling. Time can be saved at the expense of space by writing out sequentially a set of operations initially coded iteratively. If the number of iterations is a constant known at compilation time, the result can be straight-line code with no tests or branches. This can be applied, for example, to the reduced form of X ∗∗ N if the integer N is a constant. If the number of iterations is not known at compilation time, it may still be possible to increase the loop size and reduce the number of iterations, hence time for tests and branches.

(4) Constant Propagation. Also known as *folding*, this is the compilation-time computation of values from constants. If no assignments to I intervene between I ← 5 and a subsequent X[I+1], the entire addressing calculation can be performed at compilation time and eliminated from the generated code.

(5) Elimination of Redundant Expressions. The classic example is the common subexpression, such as D∗4 in the first example of the section. Another is the repeated addressing calculation, as in A[I,J] ← 1−B[I,J]. Although the former could have been obviated by a careful programmer, the latter could not.

(6) Elimination of Dead Variables. A *dead* variable is one whose value is not used later in the computation. A loop index may be a dead variable; others may occur as the result of previous optimizations.

(7) Elimination of Useless Variables. A *useless* variable is one whose value is never used. It, too, may result from other optimizations. Not only can any assignment to such a variable be suppressed; even its space allocation can be taken away.

Whereas machine-independent optimization is most conveniently performed on the intermediate code, usually as a separate step before storage allocation, machine-dependent optimization must wait for a later stage in the compilation. Although it may be performed as a separate step following the generation of target code, it is usually combined with the code generation. Two machine-dependent optimizations are the following.

(1) Redundant STORE instructions or STORE/LOAD pairs, such as those of Fig. 4.15, can be eliminated.

(2) If the machine has several registers, the assignment of registers to hold different temporary values, base addresses, and index amounts can be made in a variety of ways. "Optimizing" these assignments can reduce considerably the need to save and restore register contents. It can also permit the use of register-register machine operations in place of the usually slower register-storage operations.

Depending on the precise architecture of the target machine, a host of other optimizations may be available.

7.4.2 *Error Handling*

The compiler cannot reasonably be expected to deal with such errors as the programmer encoding the wrong algorithm. It may or may not be designed to generate code to cope with such execution-time errors as dividing by zero, reading a record from an empty buffer, or using the value of an uninitialized variable. But it must be concerned with errors which are manifested during compilation. It is those errors which are the concern of the present section.

Compilation-time errors can be classified rather broadly and arbitrarily into three groups: lexical, syntactic, and semantic. Lexical errors involve incorrect *tokens*. One example is the unrecognized word, which may be a misspelled identifier or keyword, or perhaps an identifier left over from an earlier version of the program. Another example is the illegal character, often the result of a keying or transmission error. Syntactic errors involve incorrect *structure*. Examples include missing delimiters, mismatched parentheses, missing keywords, and the like. Semantic errors involve incorrect *use* of identifiers and expressions. Among the examples are use of the wrong number of array subscripts or procedure call parameters, mismatched expression types, and the use of undefined values. An instance of the last may not be detectable at compilation time. The unreferenced variable and inaccessible statement, if considered errors, are also semantic.

What can be done about compilation-time errors? Redundancy in the program can be used (1) to *detect* an error, perhaps also to stop, (2) to *recover* from an error and continue compiling, or (3) to *correct* an error by changing the source program. What *should* be done? Detection is mandatory to prevent the generation of garbage without informing the user. Recovery with continued processing is very useful, because it gives the compiler a chance to detect more errors than just the first. Informative messages should be issued, describing both the error and the recovery. The number of runs needed to identify all compiler-detectable errors can thus be substantially reduced. Attempting not merely to continue the compilation, but to revise the source to make it correct may sound attractive. It is rather dangerous, however, except perhaps for lexical errors, for it requires the compiler to divine the programmer's intent.

Provisions for error recovery can permeate the design of a compiler. Although implementation details will not be considered here, space does permit a brief description of approaches. One general consideration is that it is usually more satisfactory to insert tokens into an incorrect program text than to delete tokens, because of the consequent information loss due to the latter.

Lexical errors, if ignored, will lead to subsequent syntactic or semantic errors. Because a symbol table and a keyword list are available, it is often reasonable to attempt to correct misspellings. Thus an unrecognized identifier can be compared with the known ones, and the closest match selected. This requires either a distance measure on words or the use of information describing the frequency of different types of misspellings.

Most of the error recovery performed by compilers is from syntactic errors. If an error is detected during parsing, the compiler can skip to the next keyword or to the end of the statement (if identifiable). This loses semantic information, however, and is therefore less attractive than trying to repair the local context and resume parsing. Probably the most satisfactory technique is to insert terminal symbols. In top-down parsing, the partial parse indicates what type of terminal is acceptable as the next symbol. In bottom-up parsing, the determination of what terminal symbol to insert is more complex. The detailed requirements of error recovery depend on the parsing method and often on the specific grammar.

The most difficult, and perhaps the most numerous, errors encountered in compilation are semantic. The usual approach to recovery is to generate identifiers whose use is semantically correct and to generate assignments of locally suitable values to them. Unfortunately, what appears locally to be a repair may turn out in a larger program context to be a disruption. The consequence may well be the creation of subsequent errors, often in great number. The extra error messages which result can be very aggravating. This problem arises in recovery from syntactic errors as well as semantic. The suppression of extra or duplicated error messages is a challenging task.

7.4.3 *Compiler-Writing Systems*

An important tool for the compiler writer can be the computer itself. Although much of the compiler, particularly the machine-dependent steps, is characterized by *ad hoc* techniques and lack of system, other parts can be described systematically and formally. From such a description, it may be possible to generate the corresponding part of the compiler. The generators are often called *compiler-writing systems*, although the claim implied by that term is a bit extravagant.

Most compiler-writing systems are parser generators. The formal specification of a grammar serves as input, and a parser for the grammar is produced. Scanner generators have also been written. Automated aids have been built to assist in producing semantic routines, but true semantic routine generators are a more elusive goal. A major reason is the difficulty of specifying the semantics of a programming language formally yet succinctly. Current work with so-called "attribute grammars" and other approaches to defining semantics offer hope that compiler-writing systems can be extended further in that direction.

FOR FURTHER STUDY

Overviews of compiler design are presented in the tutorial by Glass [1969], Chapter 11 of Gear [1974], and Chapter 9 of Ullman [1976]. Among the most informative extensive treatments are Part I of McKeeman, Horning, and Wortman [1970], and the books by Hopgood [1969], Cocke and Schwartz [1970], Gries [1971], Rohl [1975], and Aho and Ullman [1977]. Most of the foregoing books cover all the matters discussed in this chapter, as well as lexical and syntactic analysis.

Execution-time storage management is carefully considered by Wegner [1968, ch. 4] and Griffiths [1974a]. Particularly attractive treatments of storage allocation are in Aho and Ullman [1977, ch. 10] and in Hopgood [1969, ch. 9], which includes an analysis of the range of temporary variables.

Good surveys of code generation are those of Hopgood [1969, ch. 8], Waite [1974], and Aho and Ullman [1977, ch. 15]. An interesting technique is described in Elson and Rake [1970]. The use of interpretation is discussed in Gries [1971, ch. 16] and that of threaded code in Bell [1973].

Two attractive general discussions of optimization are Chapter 9 of Rohl [1975] and Chapter 12 of Aho and Ullman [1977]. An important technique of local optimization is described in McKeeman [1965]. The discussion of machine-independent optimization in Allen [1969] includes a clear description of basic blocks. A catalog of optimizations is offered in Allen and Cocke [1972].

Error handling is discussed in general in Aho and Ullman [1977, ch. 11] and for the widely-used PL/C compiler in Conway and Wilcox [1973]. The correction of spelling errors is discussed in Freeman [1964] and Morgan [1970].

Feldman and Gries [1968] present a thorough survey of early work in compiler-writing systems. Briefer surveys are in Chapter 10 of Hopgood [1969] and Chapter 20 of Gries [1971]. In Chapter 8, Cocke and Schwartz [1970] describe the self-compiling compiler, and Part II of McKeeman, Horning, and Wortman [1970] is devoted to the important compiler-writing system XPL. The exposition by Griffiths [1974b], unlike the earlier ones, considers the incorporation of semantics. Two specific systems designed to provide semantic generation are described in Lecarme and Bochmann [1974] and Lorho [1977]. A simple introduction to attribute grammars is given in Jazayeri and Walter [1975]. A more extensive one is presented in Section 5 of Marcotty, Ledgard, and Bochmann [1976].

EXERCISES

7.1   Represent the Pascal statement

      IF X < Y THEN IF X > Z THEN A := B ELSE A := C
           ELSE IF X > Z THEN A := C ELSE A := D

    in intermediate code, using
    a) postfix;
    b) quadruples;
    c) triples;
    d) indirect triples.

7.2   Under what circumstances might it be better not to replace the tokens of a compiler source language by uniform tokens?

7.3   How does the use of a separate table for reserved words complicate scanning and simplify parsing?

7.4   Why is the assembly step of a compiler like Pass 2 alone of a two-pass assembler?

7.5   Why is A := B represented in postfix as A B ASSIGN rather than B A ASSIGN?

7.6   Devise a method for the single-pass generation of postfix intermediate code for backward branches in source language.

7.7   Write the instructions required for the semantic processing of reductions 3 and 5 in Fig. 7.2(a).

7.8 Let the grammar of Fig. 7.2 be extended by the rules

1a. *expression = expression " − " term.*
3a.   *term = term "/" factor.*

a) Modify the programs of Fig. 7.5 to accommodate the extension. You do not need to copy unchanged procedures or unchanged portions of procedures.

b) Verify your design by tracing the translation of $A*(B-C)/(D+E)$. Show the sequence of invocations and returns, the semantic information delivered by each procedure, and the generated quadruples.

7.9 Write the semantic routines for the indexed loop described toward the end of Section 7.3.1. You need not code the parse, but do indicate with which reduction each piece of semantic code is associated.

7.10 Write a semantic routine for processing a **repeat-until** loop.

7.11 Here is one syntactic form of the **case** statement in PL/I.

SELECT (*expr*);
       WHEN (*expr₁*) *stmt₁*
       {WHEN (*exprᵢ*) *stmtᵢ*}
       OTHERWISE *stmtₙ*
END;

The generated code should perform $stmt_i$ for the least i such that $expr = expr_i$. If there is no such i, then it is to perform $stmt_n$.

a) Show all the quadruples which must be generated during recognition of the complete SELECT statement shown.

b) Write semantic routines to generate the quadruples other than those generated during recognition of an instance of *expr* or *stmt* (with or without subscript). For each of your routines specify the symbol string whose recognition invokes it.

7.12 Modify the semantic routines of Fig. 7.6 to permit *condition* to be a simple boolean variable as well as a relational expression.

7.13 What effect does backtracking by the parser have on the generation of intermediate code?

7.14 Describe, using examples, the actions taken during lexical analysis, syntactic analysis, and semantic interpretation which permit a compiler to disambiguate an identifier which is both (a) declared implicitly (by use rather than by explicit declaration) and (b) identical to a nonreserved keyword.

7.15 Explain how to construct the static chain which corresponds to a given display, and *vice versa*.

7.16 Whether a static chain or a display is used to access the environment, a new pointer must be created upon block entry. Explain, for each of the two representations, how the value of the pointer can be determined.

7.17 Describe both the compilation-time and the execution-time actions necessary to permit reference to a global variable declared in an enclosing block. Repeat for both a static chain and a display.

7.18 What compilation-time saving and what execution-time saving in array accessing result from the use of zero-origin indexing?

7.19 Consider the structure declaration

```
DECLARE 1  A(100) STATIC,
           2  B,
              3  C  FIXED BINARY,
              3  D,
                 4  E  CHARACTER (2),
                 4  F  BIT (4),
                 4  G  FIXED BINARY,
           2  H,
              3  J  BIT (12),
              3  K  FIXED BINARY;
```

in a subset of PL/I restricted to having no block structure and no duplicate identifiers anywhere in a program. Examples of references to the structure include A.B(50).C, H(11).J, F(99), and B. What specific information about the identifiers A through K must be held in the symbol table?

7.20 Describe the activation record management which must occur when the **goto** of the following program is executed. Assume the use of block-level storage allocation.

```
A:  procedure
    call B
    mark: ---
    B:  procedure
        call C
        mark: ---
    end B
    C:  procedure
        D:  block
            goto mark
        end D
    end C
end A
```

7.21 Design an extension of dynamic arrays which permits not only the bounds for each dimension but also the number of dimensions to be specified at execution time. Consider all relevant aspects of compilation and execution. Impose as few restrictions as possible on the programming language; justify any restrictions you do impose. What extra costs does your implementation incur over those of conventional dynamic arrays?

7.22 Rewrite A **xor** B using only **and** and **not** as operators.

7.23 Describe, making reference to the steps of a compiler, how you could modify each of the following to obtain a cross-compiler to run on the Univac 1110, translating from standard Fortran to CDC 6500 code:
a) only a Univac 1110 standard Fortran compiler;
b) only a CDC 6500 standard Fortran compiler;
c) both of the foregoing compilers [use both].

7.24 At least five optimizations are possible in compiling the PL/I fragment

```
DO I = 1 TO N;
    SUM = SUM + R(I,I);
    D = A*B + 2**10 * SIN(B*A);
END;
```

where all the identifiers (except SIN) refer to variables. Describe each optimization, state the extent to which it is machine-dependent, and explain at what stage of compilation you would perform it.

Chapter 8

PREPARATION FOR EXECUTION

8.1 FUNCTIONS

An object-code segment produced by a compiler or by a module assembler cannot be executed without modification. As many as five further functions must be performed first. Their logical sequence is the following. (1) If the segment is one of several which have been translated independently but are to be executed together, there will be symbols in one segment which refer to entities defined in another. Establishment of the proper correspondences and use of the correct attributes is called *resolution* of such intersegment symbolic references. (2) A symbol not resolved by comparison with the other segments may be a reference to the execution-time library of system-provided service routines and user-written subroutines. Means are required for managing the library. (3) Storage must be allocated for each segment's private needs, for any area accessed jointly, and for the required library routines. (4) Address fields must be relocated to match the allocation. (5) The segments must be loaded into the allocated storage. These five functions will now be examined, although in a slightly different order.

8.1.1 *Loading*

A translator which generates machine code in the locations from which it is to be executed, such as a load-and-go compiler or a load-and-go assembler, performs its own loading function. No separate loader is required. This organization requires the program to be translated each time it is used. Moreover, because there is no provision for modifying the program after translation, it is essentially limited to a single segment. Furthermore, storage space is required not only for the program but for the translator as well. Nevertheless, small programs which are frequently retranslated can be handled conveniently by such a translator.

Two situations exist in which the segment to be loaded is in absolute form ready for execution, but does not occupy the storage locations to which it is destined. One arises when the translator, usually an assembler, produces *absolute* machine code, in which all addresses are valid only if the segment is placed in specified locations. The other arises after a program has been copied to backing storage, from which it is later read in to resume execution. An *absolute loader* (or "binary loader") is used to load a machine-code segment. It need only place the code in the specified locations, perhaps checking the accuracy of the information transferred, and then branch to the starting location. Because this function is performed just prior to execution and does not involve translation, such a loader may quite properly be viewed as a control program rather than a translator.

8.1.2 *Relocation*

Most translators do not bind the locations which must be occupied by the code which they generate. Instead, they produce one or more relocatable segments, identifying in each which address fields are absolute and which relative. If multiple location counters are used, the origin to which each relative address field is relative must also be identified. The task of relocation is to add the applicable relocation constant (address of the segment origin) to each relative address in the segment. Different methods of performing relocation apply to machines with direct addressing and with base addressing. Although relocation can be performed prior to loading, this may bind the execution-time location before storage is allocated. Consequently, relocation is usually performed in conjunction with loading, by a program called a *relocating loader*, which is in part a translator. The actual adjustment of an address field often occurs after the field has been loaded, rather than before. It should be noted that the term "relocation" refers to adjustment of address fields and not to movement of a program segment. Movement of a segment requires relocation, but relocation does not require movement.

8.1.3 *Resolution of External References*

If a segment is to be executed in combination with others which have been translated separately, the translator prepares for each segment a list of symbols to be resolved. This list includes (1) internal references to externally defined symbols and (2) internally defined symbols which may be referenced externally. The two types of list entries may or may not be segregated. The resolution is usually effected by a program called a *linker*, which performs the following functions. It establishes the correspondences between symbol references and definitions, determines the relocatability attribute of symbols and address expressions, and substitutes for them addresses in the form required by the loader. It typically assumes that symbols still undefined are names of library routines. In many systems resolution is combined with loading (and usually relocation) in a *linking loader*. If intersegment references are limited to calls of other segments, whether library routines or not, resolution can be accomplished more simply than with a linker, by use of a *transfer vector* of collected branch instructions to the different segments.

8.1.4 *Library Management*

Strictly speaking, management of the library of routines available at execution time is not a function of translation, but performing it does affect several aspects of translation. The determination of which library routines are needed and of how much storage to allocate for them is an example. Although library routines used to be in absolute code, it is almost universal practice now to provide them in relocatable form. The size of the library can often be reduced by replacing similar portions of two or more routines with another routine, which is then called by the routines which it serves. In that event, execution-time calls will be generated not only to the routines named in the user's program but to yet other routines as well. If an index of calls made by library routines is available to the linker, it can determine the entire set of routines which will be needed, and link the references accordingly. If the library is on a linear medium such as paper or magnetic tape, it may be wise to have the copy of each calling routine precede copies of routines which it calls, even at the cost of space for duplicate copies. Then the necessary routines can be loaded in a single pass even if an index of calls is not constructed beforehand, provided that each routine names the others which it needs. If the library routines are on a rotating medium such as disk or drum, a dictionary of their placement should be maintained.

8.1.5 *Storage Allocation*

Although storage allocation within each segment is performed by the translator which generates the segment, there remains the problem of ensuring that all the pieces will fit at execution time. Space is required for each of the segments, for the largest of the common data areas used for intersegment communication, and for the library routines which may be called. The linker is the first program in a position to determine the total storage requirement, but it may lack information concerning space needed for library routines. If calls by one library routine to another are not discovered until the former is loaded, space information is not available until loading time. This provides one motive for deferring linking until loading. A more important motive for combining linking with loading is to reduce the total number of passes over the text. If any of the required library routines is to be generated at execution time rather than merely selected, even loading time is too early to specify the exact size, although it may be possible to determine an upper bound.

If more space is required than will be available, different segments or routines whose presence is not required simultaneously can share storage sequentially, each using a given portion of space in turn. This mode of storage use is called *overlaying*. If the writer of the program can predict in what sequence different program segments will be required, the segments can be replaced dynamically in a predetermined sequence. This *dynamic loading* is programmed in most systems by the user. Some linkers, however, can accept a specification of what dynamic loading is to be performed and generate the necessary execution-time calls to the loader. Although the loading is dynamic, the overlay structure is static, being unchanged from one execution of the program to the next. Sometimes, however, the selection of required segments cannot be determined prior to execution, because it is data-dependent. Such dynamic overlay structures are characteristic of transaction-oriented interactive systems, such as airline reservations or banking. The nature of the transaction dictates which processing programs are required, and they are loaded as appropriate and linked with the using programs. Because the translators are no longer available, the control program is called upon to perform this *dynamic linking*.

8.2　IMPLEMENTATIONS

8.2.1　*Absolute Loader*

The task of an absolute loader is virtually trivial. It reads a stream of bits from a specified source into specified storage locations and transfers control to a designated address. Loader input prepared by an absolute assembler is in the form of records, often card images, each containing the text (instructions, data, or both) to be loaded, the length of the text, and the starting address. The loader reads the record into a fixed location, examines the starting address and length, and copies the text as specified. The last text record is followed by a branch record, which contains the address to which the loader branches. The three main storage accesses required for the text (one for reading, two for copying) can be reduced to one by first reading only the length and starting address. The loader then reads the text directly into its final location.

An absolute loader provided for reloading programs which have been rolled out will surely be designed to effect the foregoing saving. The length and starting address of the entire program will have been recorded at the beginning of the program. If the program length exceeds the amount which can be fetched in a single read operation, the loader can fetch the program in pieces, incrementing the starting address and decrementing the remaining length as it proceeds.

8.2.2 *Relocating Loader*

A translator may generate object code intended to be executed when resident in storage locations whose addresses will be specified only after translation. Address references made by the object code to main storage locations which it will occupy after loading must be adjusted by the addition of a relocation constant before execution. Instruction and data fields which require this adjustment are termed *relative*; those which do not, *absolute*. Within an instruction, the operation code is absolute, as are register addresses. Operand fields may or may not be absolute. Immediate data and shift amounts are absolute; many address fields, although not all, are relative. An address specified numerically in the source program is absolute, but a symbol defined by its appearance in a label field of the same segment is relative. So is a literal, and so is the redefinable current line symbol *. Constants generated by the translator are absolute, except for address constants. The value of an address constant, typically written in source language as A(PLACE), is defined to be the execution-time storage address corresponding to the symbol named. Clearly such an address is relative.

The relocatability attribute of an address expression depends upon those of its components. If an address expression is limited to an algebraic sum of signed symbols (i.e. no products), such as PLACE+7 or HERE−LOOP +STAND, then its relocatability attribute is easily determined. Ignoring each absolute component and replacing each relative component by R reduces the address expression to the form nR, where n is a signed integer. If $n=1$, the expression is relative; if $n=0$, the expression is absolute. Thus if HERE and LOOP are relative and STAND is absolute, then we ignore STAND and replace HERE by R and −LOOP by −R. This yields zero and the address expression is found to be absolute.

If n has any other value than 0 or 1, the expression is ill-formed. This can be seen most readily from an example. The execution-time location A+B, where A and B are relative symbols, cannot be fixed even relative to the origin. Suppose A and B have location counter values 20 and 30, respectively. If the origin is 100, then the execution-time locations A and B are

120 and 130, and $A+B$ is 250, or 150 beyond the origin. But if the origin is 300, then the execution-time location $A+B$ is 650, or 350 beyond the origin. The address expression $A+B$ does not have a reproducible meaning. Similar problems arise if n is greater than 2, or is negative.

If the relocatability attribute of each symbol is known to the translator, as it is in the absence of internal references to externally defined symbols, then the translator can determine the relocatability attribute of every field in the object code which it generates. Until we discuss linkers, we shall assume that this condition holds.

We examine relocation for a direct-addressing computer first. The relocating loader, having no access to the source text, cannot determine from inspection of the generated text whether a field is absolute or relative. It cannot even distinguish instructions from data. The translator must therefore specify for each field whether it is relative. One way to specify these relocatability attributes, easily implemented in an assembler or in the assembly step of a compiler, is to emit with each line of text one *relocation bit* for each field. In Fig. 8.1(a), which shows object code generated for the sample assembler-language program of Fig. 2.2, the convention is that bit value unity indicates that the associated field is relative. The relocation constant to be added is the address of the origin of the segment, and is normally specified by the operating system.

The algorithm executed by the relocating loader is simple. It reads lines of object code one at a time. It copies the text of each line to addresses formed by adding the relocation constant to the indicated locations. For each relocation bit equal to unity it also adds the relocation constant to the corresponding text field. This second addition can be performed either before or after the text is copied. If the relocation constant is 40, the resulting content of storage is as shown in Fig. 8.1(b). The location counter values can be omitted from the object code if the lines are presented in serial order with no gaps, as they are in the figure. In that event the loader runs an actual location counter initialized to the origin location. If multiple location counters are provided, the object code must include with each relative address a designation of the location counter which applies, and the translator must either indicate the total amount of storage associated with each location counter or segregate the object code associated with each.

Interleaving relocation bits and length fields with the program text precludes reading the text directly into the storage locations it is to occupy. Moreover, it requires that the text be handled in small units, often of variable length. These disadvantages can be obviated by collecting all the relocation bits into a single contiguous *relocation map* which follows the text of the object code. Such a map is readily prepared by the assembler

	Source program				Object code		
Label	**Opcode**	**Opd1**	**Opd2**	**Locn**	**Len**	**Reloc**	**Text**
	COPY	ZERO	OLDER	00	3	011	13 33 35
	COPY	ONE	OLD	03	3	011	13 34 36
	READ	LIMIT		06	2	01	12 38
	WRITE	OLD		08	2	01	08 36
FRONT	LOAD	OLDER		10	2	01	03 35
	ADD	OLD		12	2	01	02 36
	STORE	NEW		14	2	01	07 37
	SUB	LIMIT		16	2	01	06 38
	BRPOS	FINAL		18	2	01	01 30
	WRITE	NEW		20	2	01	08 37
	COPY	OLD	OLDER	22	3	011	13 36 35
	COPY	NEW	OLD	25	3	011	13 37 36
	BR	FRONT		28	2	01	00 10
FINAL	WRITE	LIMIT		30	2	01	08 38
	STOP			32	1	0	11
ZERO	CONST	0		33	1	0	00
ONE	CONST	1		34	1	0	01
OLDER	SPACE						
OLD	SPACE						
NEW	SPACE						
LIMIT	SPACE						

(a) Before relocation

Locn	Machine code
40	13 73 75
43	13 74 76
46	12 78
48	08 76
50	03 75
52	02 76
54	07 77
56	06 78
58	01 70
60	08 77
62	13 76 75
65	13 77 76
68	00 50
70	08 78
72	11
73	00
74	01

(b) After relocation

Figure 8.1   Use of Relocation Bits

(or other translator), which produces a segment of relocatable text followed immediately by the associated relocation map. The segment and map are read as a unit into storage locations beginning at the segment's assigned origin S, resulting in the status depicted in Fig. 8.2(a). The assembler is required to furnish the lengths of the segment and of the map. Consequently the loader can determine the location M at which the map begins. The loader scans the map and adjusts the addresses which correspond to bits which signify relocation. The segment origin S for the first segment is specified by the operating system. For each succeeding segment it is defined by performing the assignment S ← M prior to reading. Figure 8.2(b) shows the status after the first segment has been relocated and the second one loaded.

A rather efficient compromise between line relocation and segment relocation is to divide the text into fixed-length chunks having precisely as many potentially relative fields as the machine word has bits. One chunk of relocatable text is loaded, together with one word of relocation bits. The relative addresses in the chunk are relocated before the next chunk is loaded. This approach captures much of the I/O efficiency of the map method, without requiring extra storage for the last segment map, and permits the use of fixed-length units throughout.

For a machine with explicit-base addressing, any program normally

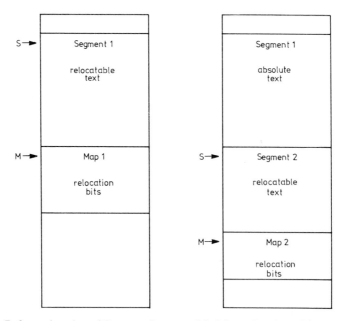

(a) Before relocation of Segment 1   (b) After relocation of Segment 1

Figure 8.2   Use of Relocation Map

incorporates instructions to load appropriate segment origin locations into base registers at execution time. Relocation is then performed even later during execution time by the machine's calculation of effective addresses for each instruction which references storage. Although this relocation applies to address fields of instructions, it is not performed upon address constants, which must be relocated in much the same manner as are all addresses in a direct-addressing machine. Because address constants typically constitute a very small portion of the text of a program, it is wasteful to supply relocation bits, all but a few of them zero, for all fields of the program text. Instead, the assembler appends a *relocation list* which specifies the adjustments to be made. For the program fragment

```
    0      PROG3      ---      ---
           ---        LOAD     POINTER
           ---        ---      ---
   38      LOCN       ---      ---
           ---        ---      ---
   71      POINTER    CONST    A(LOCN)
   72      TWO        CONST    2
```

(to which the location counter values have been appended), the object code assembled at address 71 for the address constant A(LOCN) is the number 38. The relocation list entry specifies the address (71) to be modified and the appropriate location counter (the one whose origin is associated with the symbol PROG3). The loader merely scans the relocation list after loading the text and makes the indicated adjustments. Address constants are normally not used when programming machines with implicit-base addressing.

The foregoing relocation methods all assume that the original program is free of external references. Relocation of addresses which incorporate external references must be postponed until after those references have been resolved.

8.2.3 *Transfer Vector*

If references to nonlocal data are made through a data area global to all segments (e.g. Fortran COMMON), then truly external references can be restricted to subroutine calls. The translator and loader together can resolve those remaining references by use of a simple mechanism. The translator (say, an assembler) prefixes the program text with a *transfer vector* of symbolic names of the subroutines. After loading the transfer vector and program text, the loader then loads each subroutine specified in the transfer vector, replacing its symbolic name in the transfer vector by the actual address of the subroutine. The assembled code then uses the modified transfer vector in calling the subroutines indirectly. If indirect addressing is available, a call of SUBR can be generated as a branch to the address stored at the transfer vector location associated with SUBR. If only direct addressing is provided, the loader can replace each name in the assembled transfer vector by a branch instruction to the actual subroutine address. In that situation a call of SUBR is generated as a direct branch to the associated transfer vector location, which will branch in turn to the desired subroutine.

Figure 8.3 illustrates the transfer vector mechanism for the direct-addressing machine defined in Chapter 2. The symbols SQRT and SORTFLD are externally defined subroutine names, which appear as branch addresses in (a). The assembler adjoins to the object code a transfer vector, shown at the top of (b), and generates branches to that transfer vector. The loader distinguishes the transfer vector elements from other text by means of a flag bit, or perhaps a special record to delimit the transfer vector. The result of replacing the transfer vector elements is shown in (c).

If the symbolic names used are longer than the space required to hold the address or complete branch instruction in the transfer vector, space can be wasted. This waste can be eliminated at the cost of extra processing by the assembler, which prepares a separate table of subroutine names and the associated locations within the transfer vector. The loader uses that table rather than the transfer vector itself to determine which subroutines to load and where to insert their addresses.

8.2.4 *Linker*

If external references are not limited to subroutine calls, then the definition of a symbol in one segment must be applied in translating each instance of its use in another segment. This resolution is performed by a *linker*, using information supplied to it by the assembler (or compiler). In translating a segment of source program, either the assembler assumes that symbols not defined within the segment are defined externally, or the programmer identifies such symbols explicitly. Symbols which are defined and are expected by the programmer to be referenced by other segments cannot be identified as such by the assembler. If they are not explicitly identified by the programmer, it will be necessary, whenever an externally defined symbol is encountered in some other segment, to search for its definition over all segments external to that other segment.

The detection of errors is easiest if both types of external references are signalled in the source-language program. Many different syntactic forms

		---		---	
		16 SORTFLD		16 BR	376
		18 SQRT		18 BR	200
---		---		---	
---		---		---	
BR	SQRT	52 BR	18	52 BR	18
---		---		---	
---		---		---	
BRNEG	SORTFLD	93 BRNEG	16	93 BRNEG	16
---		---		---	
---		---		---	
(a) Source text		(b) After assembly		(c) After loading	

Figure 8.3 Use of a Transfer Vector

occur, some of which use statement fields in a manner which is inconsistent with their use in other statements. For our illustrative assembler language we adopt two assembler instructions, INTUSE and INTDEF. The INTUSE instruction requires a label, which is a symbol internally used but externally defined. There is no operand. The INTDEF instruction, which is not labeled, takes one operand, which is a symbol which must appear as the label on another line. That symbol is internally defined and expected to be externally used. These instructions usually precede any other occurrences of the symbols which they contain.

The assembler prepares a *definition table* which lists each internally defined global symbol. There is one entry for each symbol, including the name of the program segment. Each entry includes the symbol, its address, and its relocatability mode. The assembler also prepares a *use table* which lists each internally used global symbol. There is one entry for each occurrence, not merely one for each symbol. Each entry includes the symbol itself, the location counter value (i.e. relative address) of the operand field in which it occurs, and the sign with which it occurs. The use table is preferably in address order. The first of two segments to be linked is shown in Fig. 8.4, both in source language and as translated independently. The relocatability mode M ("a" for absolute, "r" for relative) is shown after each word of object code. Although the definition and use tables are shown following the text, either or both can precede the text.

The translation of a symbol defined externally to the segment must necessarily be incomplete. The assembler assigns to it address zero and mode absolute. This permits uniform processing of address expressions as well as of lone symbols. The address corresponding to each global symbol can later be added or subtracted, as appropriate. Its relocatability mode is

```
PROG1     START   0
PROG2     INTUSE
TABLE     INTUSE
          INTDEF  TEST
          INTDEF  RESUMEPT
          INTDEF  HEAD
          ---
          ---
TEST      BRPOS   PROG2
RESUMEPT  LOAD    LIST
          ---
          ---
          LOAD    TABLE+2
HEAD      ---
          ---
          STOP
LIST      CONST   37
          END
```

Addr	Word	M	Word	M

10	01	a	00	a
12	03	a	30	r
14				

20	03	a	02	a
22				

29	11	a		
30	37	a		
31				

(a) Source program   (b) Object code

Symbol	Addr	Sign
PROG2	11	+
TABLE	21	+

Symbol	Addr	Mode
PROG1	00	r
TEST	10	r
RESUMEPT	12	r
HEAD	22	r

(c) Use table   (d) Definition table

Figure 8.4   First Segment Ready for Linking

also handled straightforwardly, in the manner explained after Fig. 8.8.
Thus PROG2 at address 11 is translated into address zero and mode absolute. Likewise, TABLE+2 at address 21 is translated into address 2
(zero for TABLE plus the stated 2) and mode absolute (for the sum of two
absolute quantities). The second segment, translated similarly, is given in
Fig. 8.5.

The design of the linker is simplified if it is assumed that the independently translated segments are eventually to be loaded into consecutive
areas of storage, hence subject to a single relocation constant. We shall
relax that restriction later. A two-pass algorithm collects the global symbol
definitions during the first pass and applies them during the second. As in
assembly, a symbol table is used, called the *global symbol table* (also "external symbol table" or "linkage symbol table"). During Pass 1 the linker
merges the definition tables of the several segments into one, taking ap-

```
PROG2     START   0
          INTDEF  TABLE
TEST      INTUSE
RESUMEPT  INTUSE
HEAD      INTUSE
          - - -
          - - -
          STORE   TABLE+HEAD-TEST
          - - -
          - - -
          BR      RESUMEPT
TABLE     SPACE
          SPACE
          SPACE
TWO       CONST   2
ADDRTEST  CONST   A(TEST)
          END
```

Addr	Word	M	Word	M
- - -
- - -
15	07	a	27	r
17
- - -
25	00	a	00	a
27	XX	a
28	XX	a
29	XX	a
30	02	a
31	00	a
32

(a) Source program   (b) Object code

Symbol	Addr	Sign
HEAD	16	+
TEST	16	-
RESUMEPT	26	+
TEST	31	+

Symbol	Addr	Mode
PROG2	00	r
TABLE	27	r

(c) Use table   (d) Definition table

Figure 8.5   Second Segment Ready for Linking

propriate error action if any symbol has more than one definition. For the first segment processed, the definition table entries are copied unchanged into the global symbol table. In processing the second segment, however, the length of the first segment is added to the address of each relative symbol entered from the second definition table. This ensures that its address is now relative to the origin of the first segment in the about-to-be-linked collection of segments. Either during this pass or during the second, the same adjustment must be made to relative addresses within the program and to location counter values of entries in the use table. In processing the third and subsequent segments, the linker adds the sum of the lengths of the two or more previously processed segments.

Figures 8.6–8.8 show the result of Pass 1 processing for the two segments previously presented, PROG1 having been processed first. It is assumed that the adjustment of addresses in the program text and use table, al-

```
PROG1      START   0
PROG2      INTUSE
TABLE      INTUSE
           INTDEF  TEST
           INTDEF  RESUMEPT
           INTDEF  HEAD
           ---
           ---
TEST       BRPOS   PROG2
RESUMEPT   LOAD    LIST
           ---
           ---
           LOAD    TABLE+2
HEAD       ---
           ---
           STOP
LIST       CONST   37
           END
```

Addr	Word	M	Word	M
---	---			
---	---			
10	01	a	00	a
12	03	a	30	r
14				
---	---			
20	03	a	02	a
22				
---	---			
29	11	a		
30	37	a		

(a) Source program   (b) Object code

Symbol	Addr	Sign
PROG2	11	+
TABLE	21	+

(c) Use table

Figure 8.6   First Segment after Pass 1 of Linker

though they could have been deferred to Pass 2, were performed during Pass 1.

During Pass 2 the linker updates address fields to reflect the juxtaposition of the segments, unless this was performed during Pass 1. Necessarily deferred to Pass 2 is the actual patching of external references. The object code is copied unchanged, except for the updating just described (if it was indeed deferred), until the field is reached whose address is given in the next entry of the use table for the segment being copied. The symbol in that entry is looked up in the global symbol table, and its address therefrom added to the object code field. For the programs of Figs. 8.6 and 8.7 this first occurs when word 11 is encountered. The symbol PROG2 is looked up in the global symbol table and found to have address 31. This value is added (as directed by the use table sign field) to the 00 in word 11 to yield the correct branch address. The relocation mode indicator of word 11 is also adjusted. The original address is absolute; the address added in is relative. The resulting sum is therefore relative. A similar adjustment

```
PROG2       START  0
            INTDEF TABLE
TEST        INTUSE
RESUMEPT    INTUSE
HEAD        INTUSE
            ---
            ---
            STORE  TABLE+HEAD-TEST
            ---
            ---
            BR     RESUMEPT
TABLE       SPACE
            SPACE
            SPACE
TWO         CONST  2
ADDRTEST    CONST  A(TEST)
            END
```

Addr	Word	M	Word	M

46	07	a	58	r
48				

56	00	a	00	a
58	XX	a		
59	XX	a		
60	XX	a		
61	02	a		
62	00	a		

(a) Source program   (b) Object code

Symbol	Addr	Sign
HEAD	47	+
TEST	47	–
RESUMEPT	57	+
TEST	62	+

(c) Use table

Figure 8.7 Second Segment after Pass 1 of Linker

Symbol	Addr	Mode
HEAD	22	r
PROG1	00	r
PROG2	31	r
RESUMEPT	12	r
TABLE	58	r
TEST	10	r

Figure 8.8 Global Symbol Table

occurs in processing word 21, which originally holds the absolute address 02 and is set to the relative address 60.

The processing of word 47 is somewhat more complicated. The original content is the relative address 58. Addition of the value 22 of HEAD yields 80, but HEAD is also relative, and the sum of two relative symbols is illegal. No matter. The linker continues, subtracting the relative address 10 of TEST to yield the legal relative address 70 for the address expression TABLE+HEAD−TEST. During the address adjustment, the linker must count the relative address components algebraically. If the final count is neither 0 nor 1, then an error has occurred. Intermediate values, however, may be other than 0 or 1. The branch address in word 57 and the address constant in word 62 are adjusted without difficulty, and the result of linking the two segments is shown in Fig. 8.9.

We imposed earlier a restriction that the linked program be relocated as

			Addr	Word	M	Word	M
PROG1	START	0					
PROG2	INTUSE						
TABLE	INTUSE						
	INTDEF	TEST					
	INTDEF	RESUMEPT					
	INTDEF	HEAD					
	− − −		− − −				
	− − −		− − −				
TEST	BRPOS	PROG2	10	01	a	31	r
RESUMEPT	LOAD	LIST	12	03	a	30	r
	− − −		14				
	− − −		− − −				
	LOAD	TABLE+2	20	03	a	60	r
HEAD	− − −		22				
	− − −		− − −				
	STOP		29	11	a		
LIST	CONST	37	30	37	a		
	END						
PROG2	START	0					
	INTDEF	TABLE					
TEST	INTUSE						
RESUMEPT	INTUSE						
HEAD	INTUSE						
	− − −		− − −				
	− − −		− − −				
	STORE	TABLE+HEAD−TEST	46	07	a	70	r
	− − −		48				
	− − −		− − −				
	BR	RESUMEPT	56	00	a	12	r
TABLE	SPACE		58	XX	a		
	SPACE		59	XX	a		
	SPACE		60	XX	a		
TWO	CONST	2	61	02	a		
ADDRTEST	CONST	A(TEST)	62	10	r		
	END						

(a) Source programs adjoined   (b) Object code

Figure 8.9 Program after Pass 2 of Linker

a single unit. A simple modification suffices to remove this restriction, and also permits the use of multiple location counters within a single segment. The relocation mode indicator of each word is not just a bit to indicate relative or absolute, but rather the number of the associated location counter. (Zero can be used if the field is absolute.) This information is included with entries in the global symbol table. The linker verifies during Pass 2 that each field is either absolute or else relative to exactly one location counter.

Although the examples of this section have assumed direct addressing, linking of programs for base-addressed machines is performed similarly. Address constants in different segments are then usually relative to different origins, which are identified in the global symbol table.

Just as assembly can be performed in what is nominally a single pass, so can linking. If there is enough storage to hold the linker and all the segments, the following scheme serves. Each segment is read in, preceded by its definition table and followed by its use table. The definition table of the first segment is copied into the initially empty global symbol table. The use table of the first segment includes references to subsequent segments only. Each symbol in that use table is also entered in the global symbol table, but marked as undefined. The remainder of each entry in the use table (address and sign) is placed on a chain linked with its symbol in the table. As each succeeding definition table is read, each symbol is compared with the global symbol table. If it is not in the table, it is entered as before with its definition and marked as defined. If it is already in the table, marked as undefined, its definition is entered in the table and is also used to patch the addresses on the associated chain, the space for which can then be released. If the symbol is already in the table, but marked as defined, a duplicate definition error has occurred.

As each succeeding use table entry is read, its symbol is checked against the table. If the symbol is not in the table, it is entered, marked as undefined, and a new reference chain started. If the symbol is indeed in the table, but undefined, an element is added to the existing chain. If the symbol has already been defined, its table definition is used to patch the specified word in the program, which has already been read in. Alternatively, a true one-pass linker issues to the loader a directive to effect the patch. This organization is not unlike that of the load-and-go assembler, which combines one full pass with a number of mini-passes.

8.2.5 *Linking Loader*

Although linking is conceptually distinct from relocation, the two functions are often implemented concurrently. This is particularly convenient, because the segments must be read for either linking or loading, and both functions require inspection of the relocation bits. Duplication of these efforts is obviated if linking can be deferred until loading time. A program which loads, links, and relocates segments is called a *linking loader*.

The over-all organization of a linking loader is similar to that of either the two-pass or the one-pass linker previously described. It is assumed, of course, that sufficient storage is provided to hold all the segments. The operating system makes a gross allocation of storage, which is known to the linking loader before the first segment is read. The relocation constant associated with each location counter can therefore be established before reading either the definition table or the text of any segment assembled with respect to that location counter. As the definition of each global relative symbol is read into the global symbol table, the appropriate relocation constant is added to its address. The relocation constant for each local relative address is added after the program text has been loaded into its allocated storage.

One important difference between a linker and a linking loader is that the former prepares relocatable code with interspersed relocation information, whereas the latter produces executable code with no insertions. In a two-pass linking loader it is therefore not until the second pass that the program code can be loaded into the locations from which it will be executed. For either the two-pass or the one-pass organization, this loading occurs as each program word is separated from its relocation information and packed next to the previously loaded and adjusted word.

During Pass 1, a two-pass linking loader allocates storage, determines the relocation constants, relocates global relative symbols, and builds the global symbol table. It can defer inspection of program texts and use tables. During Pass 2 it loads the text, relocating local relative symbols as it proceeds, and then adjusts and relocates fields with externally defined symbols. A one-pass linking loader performs all of these operations in a single pass, augmented by following chains of forward references.

The foregoing descriptions have ignored features such as products of global symbols, which are permitted in some assembler languages, and preparation for execution in the absence of enough storage. Mechanisms for handling the former are rather specialized, and will not be discussed here. The latter is the subject of the next two sections.

8.2.6 *Static Overlay Generator*

A program whose storage requirement exceeds its allocation can still be prepared for execution if not all of its segments need to be resident in main storage concurrently. If a reference is made to a segment which is not in main storage, execution must be delayed to allow that segment to be loaded. The resulting decrease in execution efficiency can often be held to a tolerable level by careful selection of the segments to be resident simultaneously. The translator has no practical way of identifying the groups of segments which should be resident simultaneously to prevent unacceptable loss of efficiency. Consequently, this information must be specified by the programmer. The specification customarily takes the form of a static *overlay structure* in the form of a tree, which may be multiply-rooted. Each node of the tree represents a segment. The tree has the property that two segments which are to be in main storage simultaneously lie either on the same path from a root to a leaf or on disjoint paths from a root to a leaf. An example is presented in Fig. 8.10. The unorthodox representation of that tree facilitates the visualization of storage use. Each node is drawn as a vertical line of length proportional to the size of the corresponding segment. The arcs to descendant nodes are drawn as horizontal lines from the bottom end of the parent node. Thus vertical position anywhere in the diagram is in direct correspondence with location in storage. Each segment is labeled by its number and by its storage requirement. Segments 1 and 5 are both root segments; of the others, only segment 3 is not a leaf. Segments 2 and 6 may not be co-resident because they lie on different paths (1,2 and 1,3,6) which are not disjoint. Segments 1, 3, 4, 5, and 8 may be co-resident because segments 1,3, and 4 lie together on one path, segments 5 and 8 lie together on another path, and the two paths are disjoint. The storage required for those five segments is 78K, the maximum needed for any set of segments which may be co-resident. It would require 132K, on the other hand, to store all nine segments simultaneously.

Segments with a common parent are never co-resident, and in fact are assigned the same origin just beyond the end of their parent's allocation. One such segment *overlays* another when it is loaded. A root segment, of course, is never overlaid.

The use of an overlay structure to save space requires the linker and relocating loader together (whether they are combined or not) to ensure that references external to a segment result in the correct execution-time accesses. In examining this requirement it is helpful to distinguish two classes of external references, those to a segment which is permitted to be co-resident (*inclusive* references in IBM parlance) and those to a segment which is prohibited from being co-resident (*exclusive* references). For example, an instruction in segment 1 which loads a word from segment 6 makes an inclusive reference; a call of segment 8 by segment 7 is an exclusive reference. An inclusive reference upward in a path presents no

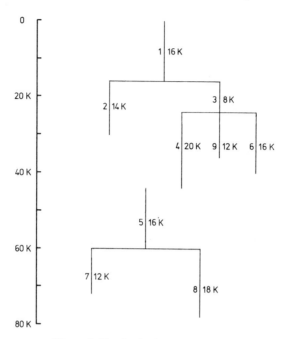

Figure 8.10   Static Overlay Structure

problem, because the referenced segment is necessarily in storage. This is true, for example, of a reference from segment 6 to segment 3. Other inclusive references, such as from segment 3 to segment 8, may require that the referenced segment first be loaded. This action can be effected at execution time only if a description of the tree structure is available and if the loader can be invoked as needed.

The linker must therefore generate a description of the static overlay structure. This description is often called a *segment table*. To ensure that the segment table will be available at any time during execution, it is placed in a root segment, thereby increasing the length of that segment. The segment table also indicates for each segment whether it is loaded or not. At execution time, a control program called the *overlay supervisor* interrogates the segment table for every external reference other than an upward inclusive reference. The overlay supervisor calls the loader if the referenced segment is not resident. It also updates the segment table entries of each overlaid segment and of each newly loaded segment.

The process of loading a segment is known as *dynamic loading*, because the decision to load is made dynamically at execution time. If a segment about to be overlaid has been modified since it was loaded, it is necessary first to copy that segment to backing storage, unless it is known that the segment will never subsequently be reloaded. This rollout of an overlaid segment is obviated if the segment is serially reusable and the overlaying occurs between successive uses, or if the segment is reenterable.

The linker must generate code for execution-time calls to the overlay supervisor. The moments at which these calls will be issued are, of course, not predictable. It is therefore hardly worth preparing and using an overlay structure if the overlay supervisor is not permanently resident in storage during execution of the overlaid program. This, too, somewhat reduces the space saving.

An exclusive external reference presents the further problem that the segment which makes the reference is overlaid before the segment to which reference is made becomes available. For this reason, some systems do not permit exclusive references. Those which do usually limit them to procedure calls and returns, because unrestricted communication between segments which overlay each other is intolerably inefficient. The linker generates a table of all symbols to which an exclusive reference is made. The overlay supervisor can interrogate this exclusive reference table to discover to which segment an exclusive reference is made, and then consult the segment table as before. For simplicity, the exclusive reference table can be incorporated in the root segment, to be available at any time. This may waste storage, however, particularly if the tree has several levels and many exclusive references are to nearby nodes. Although the total space required by the table cannot be reduced, the table itself can be overlaid. For a singly-rooted tree, the table entry for a symbol can be placed in a segment as low as the lowest common ancestor of the segment which contains the referent and those which refer to it. Thus the exclusive reference table may be distributed among as many as all the non-leaf nodes.

8.2.7 *Dynamic Linker*

The static linking of an overlay structure is possible only if the programmer is able and willing to specify at linkage time which sets of segments are to be co-resident at execution time. There exist situations, however, in which the programmer may prefer to, or need to, postpone the specification until execution time. An error routine, for example, may very well not be invoked in the course of a particular execution of the program. Although the programmer knows with which other segments the error routine is to be co-resident if invoked, he may prefer to allocate storage for it dynamically only if and when it is invoked. This precludes the binding, at linkage time, of references to the error routine. The programmer must choose between allocating a maximum amount of space which *might* be required and deferring the resolution of external references until execution time. In many transaction-oriented systems, the determination of which segments must be co-resident is highly data-dependent. There is often a large collection of processing routines, almost any small subset of which may be needed at a given moment, but hardly enough main storage to hold all. Dependence on a static overlay structure could cause intolerable service delays.

A solution is provided by performing dynamically not only the loading, but also the linking. The linker does not attempt to resolve external references beyond translating each into an ordered pair (s,d), where s identifies a segment and d is a displacement from the segment origin. A segment table is used, as before, to indicate for each segment whether it is in storage and, if so, where its origin is. If segment s is not in main storage when the reference is encountered at execution time, a control program causes the segment to be loaded. Dynamic linking is provided by adding the displacement to the origin to obtain a physical storage address. If no reference is made to a particular segment, no effort is wasted in linking it nor storage in holding it.

Some computers have segmentation hardware to perform the table lookup and addition as part of calculating the effective address. For these computers, all addresses can be provided as segment-displacement pairs, and dynamic linking becomes standard practice rather than a complex expedient.

Because program loading is effected just prior to execution, and because storage space is one of the resources managed by the operating system, the implementation of linking, loading, and relocation, particularly dynamic loading and linking, is closely tied to that of the control programs. This is a major example of the way in which translators and control programs work cooperatively to provide a programming system.

FOR FURTHER STUDY

Linking and loading are particularly well presented in the brief Section 8.4 of Brooks and Iverson [1969], the tutorial by Presser and White [1972], which is specific to the IBM 360, and in the following book chapters: Barron [1972, ch. 5], Graham [1976, ch. 6], Arms, Baker, and Pengelly [1976, ch. 13], and Ullman [1976, ch. 5].

EXERCISES

8.1 What is the advantage of considering an undefined external symbol to be the name of a library routine?

8.2 The library routines are usually relocatable. What savings would result from their being made nonrelocatable? What extra burdens and costs would such a restriction impose? Assume a two-pass module assembler, a linker, and a loader.

8.3 In a machine instruction which specifies a relative branch, is the address field an absolute or a relative symbol?

8.4 Explain how the transfer vector mechanism can be extended to other references than subroutine calls.

8.5 Why should the linker process a segment's internally defined external symbols before its internally used external symbols?

8.6 Show the changes in Figs. 8.4-8.8 under the assumption that PROGi uses location counter i.

8.7 The two assembler-language programs

```
A        START   0              B        START   0
         INTDEF  W              W        INTUSE
Z        INTUSE                          INTDEF  Z
         LOAD    Y                       LOAD    W
         STORE   Z                       STORE   X
W        CONST   15             X        SPACE
Y        CONST   13             Z        SPACE
         END                             END
```

have been independently assembled into the following object segments.

Text of A					Text of B				
Addr	**Word**	**M**	**Word**	**M**	**Addr**	**Word**	**M**	**Word**	**M**
00	03	a	05	r	00	03	a	00	a
02	07	a	00	a	02	07	a	04	r
04	15	a			04	XX	a		
05	13	a			05	XX	a		

Definition Table of A			Definition Table of B		
Symbol	**Addr**	**Mode**	**Symbol**	**Addr**	**Mode**
A	00	r	B	00	r
W	04	r	Z	05	r

Use Table of A			Use Table of B		
Symbol	**Addr**	**Sign**	**Symbol**	**Addr**	**Sign**
Z	03	+	W	01	+

The external references are to be resolved by a two-pass linker which does *not* assume execution-time contiguity of its input segments. After linking, a separate relocating loader will first load segment A with its origin at location 300 and then segment B with its origin at location 200. Assume that when A is loaded the origin of B is not yet known. Show any changed (or newly created) segments or tables after
a) linker Pass 1;
b) linker Pass 2;
c) loading of segment A;
d) loading of segment B.

8.8 [Donovan] Explain briefly, for the following program, the method by which each of the address constants listed is calculated by the assembler-linker-loader sequence. State the actions performed by each. Assume that the program is eventually loaded with its origin at location 1000. Where possible, specify numbers for actual locations. Repeat for both direct and explicit-base addressing.

```
           0      COMP240   ---
                            INTDEF BRAVO
                  OSCAR     INTUSE
                            ---
          20      ALFA      ---
                            ---
          50      BRAVO     ---
                            ---
          90      CHARLIE   ---
                            ---
         160      DELTA     SET    3
                            ---
   a)    201                CONST  A(OSCAR)
   b)    202                CONST  A(BRAVO)
   c)    203                CONST  A(OSCAR)-A(CHARLIE)
   d)    204                CONST  A(CHARLIE)-A(ALFA)+A(DELTA)
```

8.9 How can a one-pass linker ensure that each address expression is valid? Assume the use of multiple origins.

8.10 Explain the resolution of symbols defined (as in A EQU B) to be synonyms of externally defined symbols.

8.11 Consider a direct-addressing machine for which the translators collect relocatability information into a bit map, which accompanies the program text, definition table, and use table. Is it possible to construct a one-pass linking loader which accepts such modules? What about a two-pass implementation? Justify any negative answer. For any positive answer, describe the desired object code format and explain the steps in processing.

8.12 If the overlay structure has more than one root, where should the structure description be maintained?

8.13 Many airline reservation systems have been run on machines without hardware provision for segmentation. How do you think they handle the unpredictable call structure?

Rohl, J. S. [1975]. *An Introduction to Compiler Writing*. Macdonald, London.

Rosen, Saul [1964]. Programming Systems and Languages—a Historical Survey. *Proc. AFIPS Conf.* (SJCC) **25**: 1–15. Reprinted in Rosen [1967b].

Rosen, Saul [1967a]. Programming Systems and Languages—Some Recent Developments. Part 1B of Rosen [1967b].

Rosen, Saul (ed.). [1967b]. *Programming Systems and Languages*. McGraw-Hill, New York.

Rosen, Saul [1969]. Electronic Computers: A Historical Survey. *Comput. Surveys* **1**(1): 7–36, March.

Sevcik, Steven E. [1975]. An Analysis of Uses of Coroutines. M.S. Thesis, University of North Carolina at Chapel Hill. Available from University Microfilms International, Ann Arbor (MI).

Severance, Dennis G. [1974]. Identifier Search Mechanisms: A Survey and Generalized Model. *Comput. Surveys* **6**(3): 175–194, September.

Stone, Harold S. [1972]. *Introduction to Computer Organization and Data Structures*. McGraw-Hill, New York.

Ullman, Jeffrey D. [1976]. *Fundamental Concepts of Programming Systems*. Addison-Wesley, Reading (MA).

Waite, W. M. [1974]. Code Generation. Chapter 3.E of Bauer and Eickel [1974].

Wegner, Peter [1968]. *Programming Languages, Information Structures, and Machine Organization*. McGraw-Hill, New York.

Wirth, Niklaus [1977]. What Can We Do About the Unnecessary Diversity of Notation for Syntactic Definitions? *Comm. ACM* **20**(11): 822–823, November.

BIBLIOGRAPHY

Aho, A. V., and S. C. Johnson [1974]. LR Parsing. *Comput. Surveys* **6**(2): 99–124, June.

Aho, Alfred V., and Jeffrey D. Ullman [1977]. *Principles of Compiler Design*. Addison-Wesley, Reading (MA).

Allen, F. E. [1969]. Program Optimization. *Annual Review in Automatic Programming* **5**: 239–307.

Allen, Frances E., and John Cocke [1972]. A Catalogue of Optimizing Transformations. In *Design and Optimization of Compilers* (Randall Rustin, ed.). Prentice-Hall, Englewood Cliffs (NJ): 1–30.

Arms, W. Y., J. E. Baker, and R. M. Pengelly [1976]. *A Practical Approach to Computing*. Wiley, London.

Barron, D. W. [1972]. *Assemblers and Loaders*, 2nd ed. Macdonald, London.

Bauer, F. L., and J. Eickel (eds.) [1974]. *Compiler Construction—An Advanced Course*. Springer-Verlag, Berlin.

Bell, James R. [1973]. Threaded Code. *Comm. ACM* **16**(6): 370–372, June.

Berthaud, M., and M. Griffiths [1973]. Incremental Compilation and Conversational Interpretation. *Annual Review in Automatic Programming* **7**(2): 95–114.

Blaauw, G. A. [1966]. Door de Vingers Zien (inaugural lecture). Technische Hogeschool Twente, Enschede (The Netherlands), 3 March.

Blaauw, Gerrit A. [1970]. Hardware Requirements for the Fourth Generation. In *Fourth Generation Computers: User Requirements and Transition* (Fred Gruenberger, ed.). Prentice-Hall, Englewood Cliffs (NJ): 155–168.

Brooks Jr., Frederick P., and Kenneth E. Iverson [1969]. *Automatic Data Processing*, System/360 edition. Wiley, New York.

Brooks Jr., Frederick P. [1975]. *The Mythical Man-Month*. Addison-Wesley, Reading (MA).

Brown, P. J. [1974]. *Macro Processors and Techniques for Portable Software*. Wiley, London.

Campbell-Kelly, M. [1973]. *An Introduction to Macros*. Macdonald, London.

Cheatham Jr., T. E., and Kirk Sattley [1964]. Syntax-Directed Compiling. *Proc. AFIPS Conf.* (SJCC) **25**: 31–57. Reprinted in Rosen [1967b].

Cocke, John, and J. T. Schwartz [1970]. *Programming Languages and their Compilers*. Courant Institute of Mathematical Sciences, New York.

Cole, A. J. [1976]. *Macro Processors*. Cambridge University Press, Cambridge.

Conway, Melvin E. [1963]. Design of a Separable Transition-Diagram Compiler. *Comm. ACM* **6**(7): 396–408, July.

Conway, Richard W., and Thomas R. Wilcox [1973]. Design and Implementation of a Diagnostic Compiler for PL/I. *Comm. ACM* **16**(3): 169-179, March.

Donovan, John J. [1972]. *Systems Programming*. McGraw-Hill, New York.

Elson, M., and S. T. Rake [1970]. Code-Generation Technique for Large-Language Compilers. *IBM Sys. J.* **9**(3): 166–188. Reprinted in Pollack [1972].

Elson, Mark [1973]. *Concepts of Programming Languages*. Science Research Associates, Palo Alto (CA).

Feldman, Jerome, and David Gries [1968]. Translator Writing Systems. *Comm. ACM* **11**(2): 77-113, February.

Floyd, Robert W. [1963]. Syntactic Analysis and Operator Precedence. *Jour. ACM* **10**(3): 316–333, July. Reprinted in Pollack [1972].

Freeman, David N. [1964]. Error Correction in CORC, the Cornell Computing Language. *Proc. AFIPS Conf.* (FJCC) **26**: 15–34. Reprinted In Pollack [1972].

Freeman, D. N. [1966]. Macro Language Design for the System/360. *IBM Sys. J.* **5**(2): 62-77.

Freeman, Peter [1975]. *Software System Principles*. Science Research Associates, Palo Alto (CA).

Gear, C. William [1974]. *Computer Organization and Programming*, 2nd ed. McGraw-Hill, New York.

Glass, Robert L. [1969]. An Elementary Discussion of Compiler/Interpreter Writing. *Comput. Surveys* **1**(1): 55–77, March.

Graham, Robert M. [1975]. *Principles of Systems Programming*. Wiley, New York.

Gries, David [1971]. *Compiler Construction for Digital Computers*. Wiley, New York.

Griffiths, M. [1974a]. Run-Time Storage Management. Chapter 3.B of Bauer and Eickel [1974].

Griffiths, M. [1974b]. Introduction to Compiler-Compilers. Chapter 4.A of Bauer and Eickel [1974].

Hopgood, F. R. A. [1969]. *Compiling Techniques*. Macdonald, London.

Horowitz, Ellis, and Sartaj Sahni [1976]. *Fundamentals of Data Structures*. Computer Science Press, Potomac (MD).

Ingerman, P. Z. [1961]. Thunks. *Comm. ACM* **4**(1): 55-58, January. Reprinted in Pollack [1972].

Jazayeri, Mehdi, and Kenneth G. Walter [1975]. Alternating Semantic Evaluator. *Proc. ACM Conf.*: 230-234, October.

Knuth, Donald E. [1962]. A History of Writing Compilers. *Computers and Automation* **11**(12): 8-14, December. Reprinted in Pollack [1972].

Knuth, Donald E. [1964]. Backus Normal Form vs. Backus Naur Form. *Comm. ACM* **7**(12): 735-736, December.

Knuth, Donald E. [1965]. On the Translation of Languages from Left to Right. *Information and Control* **8**(6): 607–639, December.

Knuth, Donald E. [1973]. *The Art of Computer Programming*, vol. 1: *Fundamental Algorithms*, 2nd ed. Addison-Wesley, Reading (MA).

Lecarme, Olivier, and Gregor V. Bochmann [1974]. A (Truly) Usable and Portable Compiler Writing System. *Proc. IFIP Congress 74*: 218–221.

Lee, John A. N. [1974]. *The Anatomy of a Compiler*, 2nd ed. Van Nostrand Reinhold, New York.

Lorho, Bernard [1977]. Semantic Attributes Processing in the System DELTA. In *Methods of Algorithmic Language Implementation* (A. Ershov and C. H. A Koster, eds.). Springer-Verlag, Berlin: 21–40.

Lucas, P. [1961]. Die Strukturanalyse von Formelübersetzern. *Elektron. Rechen* **3**: 159-167.

Łukasiewicz, Jan [1929]. *Elementy logiki matematycznej*. Association of Math and Physics Students, Warsaw University. Translated as *Elements of Mat Logic*. Pergamon Press, Oxford [1963].

Marcotty, Michael, Henry F. Ledgard, and Gregor V. Bochmann [1976] of Formal Definitions. *Comput. Surveys* **8**(2): 191-276, June.

Maurer, W. D., and T. G. Lewis [1975]. Hash Table Methods. *C* **7**(1): 6-19, March.

McIlroy, M. Douglas [1960]. Macro Instruction Extensions of Cc *Comm. ACM* **3**(4): 214–220, April. Reprinted in Rosen [19 [1972].

McKeeman, W. M. [1965]. Peephole Optimization. *Comm* July. Reprinted in Pollack [1972].

McKeeman, William M., James J. Horning, and David V *piler Generator*. Prentice-Hall, Englewood Cliffs (NJ)

McKeeman, W. M. [1974a]. Compiler Construction. Eickel [1974].

McKeeman, W. M. [1974b]. Symbol Table Acces Eickel [1974].

Morgan, Howard L. [1970]. Spelling Correction i **13**(2): 90-94, February.

Pollack, Bary W. (ed.) [1972]. *Compiler Techr*

Pratt, Terence W. [1975]. *Programming Lc* Prentice-Hall, Englewood Cliffs (NJ).

Presser, Leon, and John R. White [1972] **4**(3): 149-167, September.

Rice, H. Gordon [1965]. Recursion r February.

INDEX

Numbers in bold face (e.g. **98**) indicate the first page of a multipage section in which the index term is a major topic.